THE RAISING OF INTELLIGENCE:

A Selected History of Attempts to Raise Retarded Intelligence

THE RAISING OF INTELLIGENCE:

A Selected History of Attempts to Raise Retarded Intelligence

Herman H. Spitz
Edward R. Johnstone Training and Research Center, Bordentown, NJ

With a chapter by
Ellis B. Page
Duke University

LEA LAWRENCE ERLBAUM ASSOCIATES, PUBLISHERS
1986 Hillsdale, New Jersey London

Lawrence Erlbaum Associates, Inc., Publishers
365 Broadway
Hillsdale, New Jersey 07642

Library of Congress Cataloging-in-Publication Data

Spitz, Herman H.
The raising of intelligence.

Bibliography: p.
Includes index.
1. Intellect—History. 2. Mentally handicapped—Intellectual levels. 3. Mentally handicapped—Education.
4. Nature and nuture. I. Title.
BF431.S637 1986 616.85'8806 86-11681
ISBN 0-89859-836-2

Printed in the United States of America
10 9 8 7 6 5 4 3 2

For *Ruth, Debra,* and *Kenneth*

Acknowledgment

I am grateful to Mrs. Patricia Conlow, who not only typed and retyped this manuscript, but did so graciously, unruffled by my many idiosyncracies.

Contents

Old Man. Alack, sir, he is mad.
Gloucester. 'Tis the times' plague when madmen lead the blind.

W. Shakespeare
King Lear—Act IV, Scene 1

1 Introduction

In 1962 a little-known chemist, Nikolai Fedyakin, working in a small technological institute in an isolated region of Russia, produced from ordinary water a fluid that had some extraordinary properties (my discussion of this incident is drawn from Franks's [1981] fascinating book, *Polywater*). While studying liquids sealed in very narrow glass capillaries, Fedyakin discovered that after a few days a small amount of liquid separated from the rest of the liquid, and over a period of about a month this secondary column of liquid grew to about 1.5 mm in length. This new liquid had a higher density than the presumably pure liquid from which it had spontaneously separated, and it had other remarkable properties as well.

After Fedyakin had published his finding we hear little more about him. A well-known Russian scientist, Boris V. Deryagin, took over Fedyakin's work and published a number of additional experiments describing this remarkable new anomalous water, or polywater (a polymerized form of water), which was said to be a new and more stable form of water; for even when removed from the capillary tube, polywater continued to exhibit its peculiar properties and somehow must have retained its unusual molecular structure. It did not boil at 100°C, solidification did not occur until −30°C, and the solid that did form was not ice. One possibility that was repeatedly raised was that impurities—from the glass capillary, for example—modified the composition of the water and consequently this was not a new form of water at all. But Deryagin and others were extremely careful and dismissed the idea that the results were due to impurities. From 1962 to 1966 Deryagin and his colleagues published 10 papers, refining their methods and using quartz capillary tubes to assure the water's purity.

When in 1966 Deryagin presented his findings to international societies, scientists outside the Soviet Union began to show greater interest, and additional mysterious results were reported. One scientist called the findings the most important physical-chemical discovery of the century, and many agreed. A letter published in the prestigious British journal *Nature* helped to spread the word, and by 1968 the mass media had been infected, first in Germany, then in Great Britain and the United States.

The structure of this new form of water was heatedly debated. Confirming experiments indicated that the spectra of anomalous water were different than those of ordinary water. The U.S. Office of Naval Research, sensing an important area of research (think of the military applications), contributed financial support, and many scientists shifted their line of research in order to study polywater, frequently with support from various federal granting agencies. In 1969, a publication in *Science,* the American equivalent of *Nature,* confirmed the existence of this newly found substance, and spectroscopic analysis gave no evidence for any contamination from the capillary tubes or by oils or greases. Heated debate and increased activity ensued, and the Western press hastened to claim American priority for this revolutionary discovery. A warning was published in *Nature* that polywater was extremely dangerous because once it is dispersed in the soil it will be too late; the more stable polywater will grow at the expense of ordinary water. In time, all water will be converted into polywater! This in spite of the fact that by 1969 a great deal of effort had managed to produce only a few millionths of a gram. Nevertheless, the popular press underscored the dangers, and entire scientific meetings were given over to the subject. Elaborate theories were introduced to explain the structure of polywater.

The publication list was substantial. From 1962 to 1974, in the United States alone there were 115 research publications and 112 popular articles, comments, and reviews, and there were 285 polywater-related publications in other countries. The peak years were 1969 to 1972, with a precipitous decline after that.

Inevitably, the truth won out. In late 1969, in an article in *Nature,* the suggestion was again raised that polywater was nothing more than water contaminated by soluble components of the glass or quartz capillaries despite the great care taken to keep the water pure. Because there were never more than a few micrograms of polywater available it was very difficult to analyze, but a 1970 paper in *Science* reported that polywater contained a number of inorganic substances, including 20- to 60% sodium, as well as potassium, chloride, sulfate, and traces of other elements. An international conference on polywater was called in 1970, for by now almost every issue of *Science* and *Nature* contained something about polywater. At the conference, Deryagin maintained that careless work accounted for the presence of contaminants, but many scientists who had defended the existence of polywater began to recant. In 1973, Deryagin finally agreed that the strange properties of anomalous water were due to impurities rather than to polymeric water molecules.

This curious episode encapsulates a number of interesting features of the scientific enterprise. For one thing, the logical impossibility of polywater was periodically pointed out by skeptics, but this did not deter workers from devoting a great deal of time to the subject. And why should it have? How often in the history of science has logic failed? Who wants to join the company of embarrassed scoffers of the past? What is logical about the earth being a round, rotating sphere revolving around the sun, or about humans evolving from another species, or about light being composed of many different colors, to mention just a few laughable theories?

On the other hand, truth will usually find its way if the scientific method is followed, and this too is illustrated by the polywater episode. There is in science a self-correcting mechanism consisting of constant probing and questioning and, where possible, the repetition of experiments. Invalidating the existence of polywater took no more than a decade because the battlefield was a confined one, the questions asked were precise and answerable, and the measuring instrument relatively refined. Furthermore, the object of study—the variable being manipulated—was quite specific. Consequently, a resolution was inevitable.

As we move away from these conditions the possibility of accurate, repeatable measurement quickly diminishes and it becomes immensely more difficult to verify or invalidate the many claims that are made. Consider the situation in the social sciences, and particularly in psychology. The object of study is hugely complex, the farthest thing from water in a test tube. Even within the field of psychology there is a range of preciseness. The measurement of some sensory processes by psychophysical methods is fairly accurate and has produced some lawful formulations. But as we go from very basic sensory measurements to more diffuse concepts such as learning and thinking, the precision and reliability of the measurement declines.

Placed in this context, it must be obvious that the scientific investigation of human intelligence is filled with hazards. The definition of intelligence itself is a source of debate. Many people are dissatisfied with intelligence tests, raising in particular the question of bias. These problems do not, and should not, deter us from studying intelligence, for—despite disagreements on its definition—no one can doubt that people differ in the degree to which they exhibit intelligent behavior. In fact there is a general consensus among experts, which is similar to the consensus among laypersons, about what types of behavior are characteristic of various kinds of intelligence (Sternberg, Conway, Ketron, & Bernstein, 1981).

Whatever intelligence is, and regardless of the degree to which intelligence tests measure it, the history of psychology is peppered with attempts to improve it. The bulk of these attempts have been made in the field of mental retardation, for mental retardation is by definition a syndrome characterized by low intelligence and poor adaptability. Mental retardation has been defined by the American Association on Mental Deficiency as "Significantly subaverage general intellectual functioning existing concurrently with deficits in adaptive behavior, and manifested during the developmental period" (Grossman, 1983, p. 1). On the Wechsler Intelligence Scales mild retardation is encompassed by IQs of 55 to 69, and on the Stanford–Binet Intelligence Scale by IQs of 52 to 67. Educators use a slightly different IQ range and terminology, in which individuals having IQs of from 50 to 75 are referred to as "educable mentally retarded" (Taylor, 1980). By one estimate, 90% of the individuals who have IQs below 70 are in the 50 to 70 IQ range (Dingman & Tarjan, 1960). It is usually with this mild and educable population, most of whom are from lower socioeconomic environments, that attempts to raise intelligence have been made, and debate about the origins of mild mental retardation has revived the venerable nature–nuture controversy.

What constitutes acceptable criteria that general intelligence has been raised? Standard individually administered intelligence tests are one useful criterion, but an intelligence test alone may be insufficient, particularly in those instances where the retarded children are being trained on test-related material, or even on specific items of the test (see Chapter 7). There are, in conjunction with intelligence tests, certain common sense criteria. Simply graduating from a regular high school that maintains reasonable standards would be ample proof, or even reading with understanding at a sixth grade level, or performing adequately on a job that requires some intellectual proficiency. However, it should be emphasized that isolated instances of dramatic improvement do not by themselves prove that a procedure has been found that, when applied to groups of retarded persons, will raise their intelligence and change their behavior. There have in fact been instances where individuals who had been diagnosed as mentally retarded have graduated from high school or even college, and successfully adapted to intellectually challenging jobs. There is enough variability in intellectual growth to account for some of these instances, and improper early diagnoses can account for many others. A classic misdiagnosis has been to label as retarded, children who were—unknown to anyone—hard of hearing, although this kind of misdiagnosis is not as frequent as it once was.

Furthermore, an IQ is not fixed. Variations in IQ upon retesting will invariably occur, simply from errors in measurement, among other things. Hill (1948), for example, found that over one-fourth of the students in a special education program varied by more than 7 IQ points over an average period of 3 years, 9 months, with the variations being equally distributed above and below the original score. Instances of marked changes in individual IQ scores are not unheard of. In comparing the test-retest IQs of large numbers of retarded individuals over an average of about 2 years, I found that the Wechsler IQs of two retarded children varied by 16 points, one up and one down. However, most of the changes in the retest scores on the same Scales were not more than 5 IQ points (Spitz, 1983). In that same study, the Wechsler Adult Intelligence Scale IQ scores of mildly retarded adolescents and young adults were appreciably higher than their scores on the Wechsler Children's Scales, although the reliability of the tests remained good; that is, even though the scores rose, most of the retarded individuals maintained their positions relative to each other. The score discrepancies apparently stemmed from differences in the standardization samples, and this points up the obvious fact that a person's IQ will vary not only because of changes in the individual but also because of imperfect reliability of the tests. Differences in the standardization samples and in the items of the different tests, as well as in the items of the same test that are included at different age levels, will affect the stability of the scores.

However, these instances of IQ variability do not provide scientific evidence that by application of a specific, well-defined technique the intelligence of a group of mentally retarded persons can be raised so that they can function at a nonretarded level. Although it is possible to train mentally retarded persons to improve their performance in many ways, development of specific skills should not be confused with raising the general level of intelligence. For persons with retarded intelligence to be trained so as to be in most respects indistinguishable from persons of average intelligence would require a rare metamorphosis, usually dependent on uncommon circumstances, such as recovery from extreme isolation during development, or recovery from a metabolic disorder. Unlike, say, the training of social skills, general intelligence—reflected in the pervasive manner in which we respond to everyday challenges, the speed with which we learn and the complexity and scope of material we can understand, the curiosity and interest we show in a range of subjects or in one engrossing problem, the intricacy of the problems we can solve, and so on—is particularly resistant to change in the lower range of intelligence. Despite all the efforts of the past, it has not yet been demonstrated that there is a replicable means of curing mental retardation.

This being so, why do the attempts continue? Why haven't they, as in the polywater episode, declined and eventually died out? There are a number of reasons. In the first place, it is a violation of logical principles to attempt to prove the null hypothesis. That is to say, it is very difficult to prove that intelligence can*not* be raised, because there is always the possibility that next week someone will prove that it can. This principle did not prevent the chemists from general agreement that trying to brew polywater was no longer worth their efforts, but in the field of human intelligence there is a never-ending stream of people ready to demonstrate new techniques that can raise the intelligence of mentally retarded persons, claims that the news media are quick to exploit. Furthermore, unlike the polywater experiments, the usual scientific safeguards are absent, and the area is replete with opinion, anecdote, personal bias, fraud, and self-deception. As we shall see, the strange history of attempts to raise intelligence is burdened with experiments in which conditions were poorly controlled or inadequately specified, where procedures could not be replicated, and where there was simply no possibility of isolating the variables that accounted for the results.

The desire for favorable results can influence our objectivity and, indeed, can be an agent of change (Rosenthal, 1966). I recall hearing the noted psychiatrist Nolan D.C. Lewis remark that when a new drug comes out, you should use it while it works (a similar comment is cited in Rosenthal, 1966, p. 134). His point of course was that enthusiasm for a drug will affect the behavior of both the doctor and the patient (the well-known placebo effect), but when enthusiasm fades, the beneficial effects of the drug will fade with it.

Numerous factors underlie the belief in unsubstantiated claims. A major factor is the failure to check original sources; second-hand descriptions are extremely unreliable. There is, too, the unfortunate fact that the laws of probability are not widely understood and a single correct prediction or intuition is remembered and preserved while hundreds of failures are forgotten. The dissemination of scientific findings is not immune from these selective effects. Research reports of negative findings are seldom submitted for publication, but when they are submitted they are usually rejected by reviewers and editors, who prefer to publish positive results in which differences between experimental and control groups are statistically significant. Unaware of the unpublished studies, it is likely that other scientists repeat basically the same experiments until by chance a statistically significant result is obtained. Once this positive result is published, unless it reports a finding of unusual interest the likelihood that the experiment will be repeated becomes very small and we are left with the illusion that the finding was statistically reliable (Sterling, 1959).

Human beings are prone to self-deception and are capable of the wildest imaginable fictions (see, for example, Randi, 1980). Scientists, being human, are not spared (Gardner, 1981). Gurus abound even in psychology, or perhaps especially in psychology. New ideas for raising intelligence are disseminated with messianic fervor, in rhythmic frequency over the years, so that we are rarely without our saviors. Disillusionment never lasts so long that new masters cannot rise from the ashes and be eagerly followed. The world is full of Candides, each with a favorite Dr. Pangloss.

There are, too, less savory forces at work. Despite the fact that most attempts to raise the intelligence of retarded individuals are being made by honest, sensitive psychologists, it is instructive to keep in mind the suggestions made by A.C. Hall (cited by Franks, 1981, p. 56) that among the reasons for the bandwagon effect in the polywater affair were pressures to publish and competition for federal funds. One should add also the drive in most scientists for prestige and notoriety, not only within their own field but also in the eyes of the general public. At the present time much effort and many resources are being expended on attempts not so much to raise intelligence as to prevent low intelligence from developing. This approach rests on the belief that low intelligence (excluding instances of known physiological origin) is largely a consequence of poor environment and that consequently if the environment is improved intelligence will be free to rise to its potential. Indeed, even if one believes that the broad heritability of individual differences in intelligence is as high as 70%, a substantial portion of the remaining variance can be accounted for by environmental effects, so that it should be possible, in theory, to induce changes at least to the extent that differences in children's intelligence are a reflection of differences in their environment. The philosophy of early intervention is, in short, that poor environments and limited opportunities restrict the full expression of the kind of intelligence valued in our culture. Although most intervention studies have been carried out with inner city children who are not actually in the mentally retarded IQ range (IQ less than 70), a number of influential studies have been aimed directly at preventing mental retardation.

Social and educational intervention studies can draw inspiration from successful instances of medical intervention. For example, phenylketonuria and galactosemia are metabolic disorders that produce mental retardation in, on the average, one of four children whose parents carry the particular recessive gene. However, if certain foods are avoided and dietary controls are instituted very early after birth, mental retardation can be prevented. This type of intervention is quite a different matter than the environmental intervention programs that are proliferating, a few of which are examined here.

Inevitably, a review of past attempts to raise intelligence must make contact with the debate—heated and persistent—over whether intelligence is primarily determined by our environment or by our genetic heritage. For example, one might think that it should be easier to raise intelligence if environment contributes more powerfully to intellectual variation than if genetic predisposition plays the major role. This does not necessarily follow, however, for the environment could produce an irreversible effect—although the evidence at this time suggests that this is not usually the case (Clarke & Clarke, 1976).

Recently, Kamin (1974) and Gould (1981), among others, have thoroughly described the poor science, foolishness, and outright fraud perpetrated by some proponents of the hereditarian viewpoint, but have neglected to mention the poor science, foolishness, and fraud produced by some proponents of environmentalism. Perhaps this book will help to balance the scales. Poor judgment, self-deception, and outright fraud prove nothing except that some scientists will eschew the moral, ethical, and procedural tenets of science to support a position they passionately believe in, or will do so for recognition, or even for material gain. Neither side in the nature-nurture debate is all good or all evil. The fact that fraud has been used to prove the inheritance of intelligence is not proof that the capacity for intelligent behavior is not primarily inherited, any more than fraudulent studies by environmentalists prove that the capacity for intelligent behavior is not primarily learned.

The purpose of this book is *not* to prove that the intelligence of groups of retarded persons cannot be raised; it is, as I noted, statistically inappropriate to attempt to prove the null hypothesis. The purpose is to present a selected, critical history of attempts to raise intelligence so that workers in this field will be alerted to the many pitfalls that await them, and will become aware of the possibility of fraud, unconscious bias, the effects of early enthusiasm, and just plain wishful thinking, on "scientific" findings. In a word, my hope is to encourage the adoption of an inquiring but skeptical attitude.

There is a heavy burden of proof on those who believe that retardation can be cured. So far-reaching and profound would be the effects of raising the intelligence of retarded individuals that our skepticism must be of equal magnitude, and the proof must be especially strong and incontravertible. We owe at least this much to the parents of retarded children, many of whom have lived through numerous false promises and hopes.

2 Early Attempts at Rehabilitation

PHILOSOPHICAL BACKGROUND

A major point of difference between the philosophical positions of René Descartes and John Locke, dating from the 17th century, has continued not only through the history of general psychology (Boring, 1950), but also through the history of one small section of psychology: the understanding of the nature of human intelligence. This dichotomy between the Cartesian and Lockian approaches is as fundamental as the two epistemologies they came to represent: empiricism (Locke) and rationalism (Descartes).

Empiricism was given its fullest early expression by Francis Bacon (1561-1626), who proclaimed that the primary source of knowledge is through the senses, and that no knowledge can exist without the evidence compiled by the senses that alone can provide the foundation for general propositions. This approach was a powerful spur for the inductive scientific method, and for the scientific advances that ensued.

Rationalism does not deny that the senses provide grist for the generation of knowledge, but insists that there is an innate directing principle that deals selectively with the sensory information. Rationalists point to the often illusory nature of sense data, and to the fact that, for example, mathematical formulas provide basic principles from which facts can be deduced.

These two philosophical schools represent different methods of examining the natural world and we can see how they also represent two essentially different approaches to the understanding of how *individuals* gain knowledge. In the study of human development, empiricists stress experience while rationalists emphasize the maturation of the mind's innate organizing principles. The differences generally are not in the complete denial of the opposing position, but rather in the primacy of the role played by experience versus innate processes. Locke's example of the brain at birth as a tabula rasa epitomizes empiricism; experience creates ideas. For the rationalist, on the other hand, there is nothing present in sensations that can produce ideas. Sensory data could not be rationally comprehended were the mind not constructed to act upon the data in certain ways. Experiences are structured by the prepared mind (see Robinson, 1976, for an excellent history and discussion of these issues).

In psychology, modified forms of Cartesian rationalism have been passed down by way of Leibniz, Kant, Hering, and the Gestalt psychologists, and at the present time are reflected in the approaches of ethologists such as Lorenz and Tinbergen, in the rise of sociobiology, and in the work of the linguist Noam Chomsky. Variants of the Baconian and Lockian empiricist doctrine have descended through Berkeley, Hume, Condillac, James Mill, John Stuart Mill, Helmholtz, Wundt, Thorndike, and Pavlov; in the associationism of most learning theorists in the United States; and in the behaviorist psychologies of Watson and Skinner. Skinnerian behaviorism represents as radical a form of empiricism as any previously expressed, although Condillac's empiricism was also extreme.

In the mid-18th century, Étienne Bonnot de Condillac introduced to France the empiricism of Locke, which he favored over the philosophy of innate ideas proposed by his compatriot, Descartes. He went even farther than did Locke, for Locke acknowledged an internal sense, which he called "reflection," as well as some innate (natural) connections of ideas, and even granted that the perception of shapes, sizes, positions, and distances are given to us intuitively by the senses, whereas Condillac argued that all knowledge is obtained from sensations without the need for reflection, and that emotion, memory, judgment, and imagination are simply transformed sensations.

THE PIONEERS

Perèire, Sicard, and Itard

It is likely that Condillac's first book, published in 1746, had aroused interest in the empiricist doctrine when, on June 11, 1749, Giacobbo Perèire demonstrated before the French Academy of Science that—using sign language, a manual alphabet, pantomine, and other methods he would not disclose—it was possible to teach deaf-mutes to read and to speak (Kanner, 1964; Lane, 1976). These accomplishments greatly impressed the audience, even though there is evidence that in the 16th and 17th centuries deaf-mutes had been taught to speak, and that finger spelling had been used (Wallin, 1955). Perèire's demonstration probably enhanced the Lockian position, showing as it did the power of education through the senses.

There can be no doubt whatever that the empiricist position greatly influenced Jean-Marc-Gaspard Itard, who, over a 5-year period starting early in 1801, attempted to educate the so-called Wild Boy of Aveyron (Itard, 1801, 1806/1962; Lane, 1976; Shattuck, 1980). Sighted first in 1797 in south-central France—a naked boy fleeing in the woods—this feral child was captured in 1798, only to escape shortly thereafter. Seen occasionally after that, he was captured again on July 25, 1799, escaping once more after 8 days, but this time he did not go far, periodically wandering into farmhouses where he was given potatoes, which he threw into the hearth coals for a few minutes before eating (a trick he apparently learned during a previous capture). On January 8, 1800, he entered the workshop of a tanner where he was captured for the last time and where his freedom ended.

The capture of an uncivilized young boy aroused the interest of, among others, the Abbé Pierre-Joseph Bonnaterre, professor of natural history at the Central School for Aveyron, and the Abbé Roche-Ambroise Sicard, the director of the National Institute for Deaf-Mutes in Paris, both of whom wanted to claim the boy for scientific examination before any civilizing influence had affected him. About 3 weeks after his capture, the boy was turned over to Bonnaterre, but 5 months later he was ordered to bring the child to Sicard in Paris, where they arrived 18 days later, having been delayed for 10 days en route when the boy became ill with smallpox.

Bonnaterre later published a very detailed description of the boy (see Lane, 1976, pp 33-48), whom he estimated to be 12 or 13 years old. He described him as 136 centimeters tall (4.5 feet), with a body covered with scars, including a horizontal scar about 41 millimeters long on his throat, apparently made by a sharp instrument and suggesting to Bonnaterre the possibility that someone had attempted to kill the child. He was mute, making only cries and inarticulate guttural sounds, and Bonnaterre conjectured that the neck wound might have interfered with his articulation. He payed no attention to shrill or loud noises but responded alertly to any noise related to food, such as the cracking of a walnut. In fact, he did not fixate on any object and showed little interest in anything but the finding, eating, and storing of food (which he always smelled before eating), except that he was always interested in looking for ways to escape. He was serene enough, particularly when caressed, but when he was provoked or frustrated he became very agitated, clenching his fists over his eyes and striking his head, letting out cries and biting and scratching the source of his rage. He disliked crowds and particularly children his own age. He rocked back and forth, had—before training—defecated wherever he happened to be except in bed, had been seen to walk on all fours (although rarely), and preferred to be naked even on the coldest days.

The boy was turned over to Sicard, who had been so successful in teaching deaf-mutes to communicate through sign language. Just previous to the boy's arrival in Paris, Sicard had helped found the Society of Observers of Man. Coincidentally, on the day of the boy's arrival in Paris, the Society had announced a 600-franc award for research to determine in infants the order in which the physical, intellectual, and social faculties develop, and how their development is favored or impeded by the influence of objects and persons in the infant's environment (Shattuck, 1980) (an announcement that should produce a feeling of déja vu in today's developmental psychologists).

Unfortunately Sicard, perhaps sensing the difficulty he would meet, did not immediately set to work educating the boy, who was growing obstreperous over a 3-month period of neglect by the adults and attacks by some of the other patients at the Institute. Consequently, in order to study the problem, the Society of Observers of Man appointed a five-member committee chaired by the famous Philippe Pinel, who had unchained the insane and who is known today as the father of psychiatry. The report he wrote at the end of their period of observation was very pessimistic. In one section he equated the boy's occasional shrill cries and peals of apparently unprovoked laughter with the behavior of the idiotic children and adults in his hospital for the insane (Shattuck, 1980), and he had no hope that Sicard would have any success with the boy, an opinion with which Sicard concurred.

Enter Itard, a young surgeon who had just been appointed resident physician of the Institute, and to whom fell the task of educating the wild boy (whom he later named Victor). Itard was a felicitous choice because he believed in the empiricist doctrine and consequently felt, despite the opinions of the experts, that the wild boy could be helped. For the 26-year-old Itard, here would be proof of the philosophy that the senses were the source of all knowledge, for through the senses Victor would learn to talk. If deaf-mutes could be taught to speak, surely Victor could learn to speak, and if the senses were the source of all knowledge then surely Victor could be socialized and educated to become a contributing member of human society. The following quotation from Itard (1801, 1806/1962) records the debt he owed to the Lockian viewpoint.

> We are indebted to the works of Locke and Condillac for a just estimation of the powerful influence that the isolated and simultaneous action of our senses exerts upon the formation and development of our ideas. The abuse that has been made of this discovery destroys neither its truth nor the practical applications that can be made of it to a system of medical education. These were the principles I followed, when, after completing the main

> projects which I had first proposed and which are made known in my first work, I devoted all my attention to the exercise and individual development of young Victor's sense organs. (p. 55)

Itard believed that intellectual dullness is "much more the result than we realize of the defective management of education, whose principal fault is that it is essentially the same for all children and never adapted to the innumerable variations in the intellectual makeup of the individual." He noted that the retarded "for the most part are no different from other men save in their reduced sensory capacities, which can certainly be developed." In the full flush of Victor's early progress he declared that using in his education Victor's own "habits, moods, needs, passions, social intercourse, and the particular workings of [his] basic desires and innate tendencies . . . will finally return to society one who seemed destined to live so far from its embrace" (the above three quotations are given in Lane, 1976, pp. 77-78).

If Itard owed a debt to Locke and Condillac for his inspiration, he owed an equal debt to Perèire, Sicard, and others who had taught deaf-mutes to communicate. However, Itard tried to teach Victor to speak rather than use sign language, a strange choice because sign language was taught at the Institute where Itard worked. The founder of the Institute, Sicard's predecessor the Abbé de l'Eppée, inspired by Perèire, had expanded on signs used spontaneously by his own deaf-mute pupils. With time, and with new signs created by the many deaf-mutes together in the Institute busily signing to each other, Sicard eventually developed a rich sign language (Lane, 1976).

Itard never learned to sign and persisted in teaching oral speech even after he had failed to teach Victor to talk. Only in his later years did he come around to the view that sign language was the preferred manner of speech for the deaf. Had he believed this when he was educating Victor the results might have been more favorable, but we must remember that although Victor was mute he was not deaf, and it was natural therefore to assume that he could learn to speak. Furthermore, Itard had to believe that thought would be facilitated when expressed in written or spoken language compared with sign language, for he subscribed to Condillac's theory that ideas must be linked to signs (symbols). Consequently ideas cannot be linked to each other unless the signs are linked to each other, a linkage that is forged more easily in standard than in sign language. In any case, we now know that ideas can exist without language (Furth, 1966), so that this application of Condillac's theory could not possibly be correct.

Placed in the care of Madame Guérin, whose husband apparently worked on the premises of the Institute, Victor lived alone in a room above the Guérins apartment at the Institute (according to Shattuck, 1980, who claims that Lane's, 1976, description of Victor's living arrangements is inaccurate). He ate his meals with the Guérins, and Itard describes how Madame Guérin took him on daily outings and notes that Victor's friendship and affection for Madame Guérin was naturally greater and more constant than it was for him, who had taken the role of teacher to a reluctant pupil. We must appreciate the fact that Madame Guérin does not always receive the credit due her for Victor's improved social behavior, as is frequently the case with attendants and cottage workers in daily contact with institutionalized children.

Itard set as one of his initial goals the development of Victor's senses so that his pupil would react not only to food but to a variety of environmental stimuli, including people. Over the first few months, by various means including baths and massages, he and Madame Guérin succeeded in developing in the boy a sensitivity to his own body and even a strong sense of cleanliness, as well as developing his sense of taste and touch. Itard then tried to teach Victor to speak by creating a situation in which the only way that Victor could satisfy a physical need would be to imitate a particular sound. (Itard found no damage to the vocal organs from whatever had caused the long scar on Victor's throat.) He did succeed in getting Victor to say the word "milk" (*lait*) when he poured some milk into Victor's glass, but Itard's joy soon dissolved when it became obvious that Victor was not naming the milk but was merely using the word as an exclamation of pleasure. Victor also articulated a few other sounds and words, in particular a distorted pronunciation of the exclamation, "Oh God!" (*Oh Dieu!*), which he picked up from Madame Guérin and which he frequently used when he was happy. Unable to speak, Victor nevertheless frequently got what he wanted by using pantomime.

Because Itard was also unsuccessful in teaching Victor to read, he discarded Sicard's association method and devised a number of novel approaches to help Victor discriminate shapes and colors. Victor learned to match the letters of the alphabet and, to Itard's great satisfaction, learned to arrange the four letters L, A, I, and T in the correct order and associated them with a cup of milk. But he did not, unfortunately, use this symbol to ask for milk.

In less than a year Itard and Madame Guérin turned Victor from an inattentive, uncivilized child into one who, though mute, could not at first glance be distinguished from ordinary children, and who, according to Itard, demonstrated attention, discernment (discrimination), judgment, and understanding, accomplishments that led Itard to claim support for the philosophical theories of Locke and Condillac.

What occurred over the next 4½ years was described by Itard in his 1806 report to the Minister of Interior. He set about "awakening" each of the senses, starting with the sense of hearing, which he thought contributed most particularly to the development of intelligence, then going to the sense of sight and the sense of touch. For example, using an opaque vase in which Victor's arm fit snugly through the neck, Itard placed some hot chestnuts and cold, hollow ones. In Victor's other hand he placed either a hot or cold chestnut, and Victor unerringly retrieved a correct match. He could not do so well, however, in choosing between an acorn and a chestnut, so Itard once again backed up and used highly dissimilar objects (e.g., stone and chestnut, ring and key), gradually using less distinctive objects until the chestnut-acorn distinction was readily made (just as he had previously taught Victor to distinguish between letters that were very similar, such as B and R, I and J, C and G).

Itard then returned to the development of Victor's intellectual functions, by which he meant language instruction, using the method of associating words with objects that Sicard used with the deaf. Before long Victor could retrieve an object after seeing only its name. However, Itard added an interesting embellishment to Sicard's method by introducing increasing delays between seeing the name and retrieving the object, by using the name of an object that was some distance away, in Victor's room. Soon he was showing Victor the names of a number of objects (up to four) simultaneously, all of which were in Victor's room, and all of which Victor was capable of memorizing and bringing back to his proud teacher. Most encouraging of all, perhaps, was the fact that Victor used written words to request various objects, something he had failed to do when he had first learned to associate "lait" with milk.

But Itard's elation at Victor's success was followed by a depressing discovery: For Victor, each word was tied to a single, specific object, not a class of objects, so that when he was shown the word for stick, or bellows, or brush, he ignored these objects that were all within view and looked only for the specific stick, bellows, or brush with which the word had first been associated. As Itard points out, this overspecificity is the opposite of the overgeneralization of young children who, when starting to talk, call all men "daddy."

Setbacks are the lot of such pioneers, and overcoming them is a measure of their patience and innovative spirit. Itard set about teaching Victor the parts of a whole by, for example, tearing out some pages from a book, teaching the written word "page," then putting the pages back in the book and having Victor point to the word "book." Similarly, he taught the parts of the body as distinct from the concept of the whole person. In this manner Victor learned that an object had a general name that was separate from the names of its parts.

To generalize the concept, Itard introduced the adjectives "big" and "little," and combined them with a large and small book, advancing "painfully and by endless detours" to additional descriptive adjectives, and finally to verbs (Itard, 1801, 1806/1962, p. 82).

In the course of instruction one incident was especially encouraging. Once before, Itard had used a chalk holder for a very small piece of chalk, but a few days later, when a chalk holder was needed and none was around, Victor took an old larding needle (used in roasting), which lay discarded in his cupboard, and converted it into a chalkholder by replacing the slide with a few turns of thread. This creative use of an object was indeed inspirational and by itself suggests that Victor was not more than mildly retarded, and was certainly not a "low-grade imbecile," as he was later described in a popular text (Wallin, 1955, p. 7), as well as by many others (e.g., Doll, 1962, p. 25). (At one time the terms *idiot, imbecile,* and *moron* referred, respectively, to what we now call profound, severe to moderate, and mild retardation [Terman, 1916/1975, p. 79].) If Victor knew how the larding needle was actually used, his novel use of it would be even more remarkable, for it would have required him to break into a confirmed set, which he apparently was unable to do in another instance. Observing that Victor tried to use a razor to cut bread, Itard made certain that Victor saw him shave with the razor, and from then on Victor never considered using the razor as a knife. But then, perhaps Victor was afraid to, and Itard relates still another instance, when Victor tried to use a glass picture frame with a picture in it as a plate, which Itard considered bizarre.

Victor's inability to learn to speak gnawed continually at Itard. He tried once again to teach Victor to talk by the use of imitation, and with exquisite patience made Victor exercise in turn the muscles of the eyes, forehead, mouth, and jaw, and then the lips and tongue, but again he failed. For Itard, speech was the ultimate act of imitation and the principal agent of education, and consequently God must have made the imitative faculty powerfully present at an early age. Only in early childhood is this imitative faculty dedicated to the learning of speech, thereafter abandoning the "vocal instrument" in order to move on to other functions. In this conception, Itard anticipated the idea of a critical age for learning language, and he attributed Victor's inability to learn to speak primarily to his being beyond the age when the imitative faculty can be applied to speech. He assigned a somewhat lesser role in Victor's muteness to Victor's inability to make fine discriminations in hearing.

In the emotional sphere, Itard noted—as he concluded his report—that Victor had become socialized to the extent that he displayed gratitude and affection, sadness at his failures and shortcomings, pleasure at success and in helping others, and anger when an injustice was done to him. Yet, according to Itard, Victor remained essentially selfish and lacking in pity. Most devastating of all was his inability to deal with his sexual urges. He was ambivalent with women, first seeking their caresses then pushing them away, uncertain about how to behave. Victor's education was interrupted by periods of hysteria that occurred with increasing frequency and in which "he sighs, sheds tears, utters shrill cries, tears his clothes, and sometimes goes as far as to scratch or bite his governess," then repenting and asking to kiss the hand he had just bitten (Itard, 1801, 1806/1962, p. 98). In these states he worked himself into such a fever that he occasionally hemorrhaged, and blood flowed from his nose and ears. Itard feared that if he revealed to Victor the source of his restlessness Victor might have tried to satisfy these needs "as publicly as his other wants and which would have led him to acts of revolting indecency" (p. 99).

At this point, after more than 5 years of effort, Itard gave up his experiment and Victor went to live with the now widowed Madame Guérin, who was given a continuation of her annual salary of 150 francs to care for the boy. In 1810, three administrators of the Institute, along with Sicard, noted in a letter to the Minister of the Interior that Victor's presence at the Institute was creating problems with the other students, and they also pointed out that Madame Guérin's daughters frequently visited what had become an all-male institution. Consequently, Madame Guérin was provided with 500 francs (the amount that had been given annually to Itard for working with the boy), in addition to her 150-franc salary, to take Victor to live elsewhere, and she and Victor lived for the next 17 years in a nearby house (Shattuck, 1980, pp. 155–156). There is no information about his life during these years, although a visitor who saw him around 1820, some 8 years before he died, described him as fearful and half-wild (Lane, 1976, p. 167).

Itard went on to unsuccessfully search for the causes and cure of congenital deafness, and to successfully develop and apply some of the techniques he had used with Victor to train finer auditory discrimination (physiological training, in his terms) in children and adolescents who were not completely deaf, and to teach deaf and hearing-impaired patients to speak. His writings included the influential and important book, *Treatise on Diseases of the Ear and Hearing,* and his reputation earned him a successful private practice. In his later years, in ill health and wracked by pain, he received only a few friends, including a favorite pupil, Edouard Séguin (see Lane, 1976, pp. 186–204, 257–258). Itard died in 1838.

Many of the methods used by Itard have since been used by teachers, as well as by experimental psychologists, many of whom have no idea that they were originally used at the beginning of the 19th century. But more to the point, the dedication of this consummate teacher has rarely been matched, and it ill suits us to claim that with modern methods Itard would have been more successful in educating Victor. Each new generation of teachers feels that somehow their dedication, and the techniques they use, are superior to those of their predecessors. When carefully examined, however, the various techniques used by workers who claim to raise retarded intelligence turn out to be little different than teaching and training techniques used for centuries, so it is always surprising when someone claims that his or her methods have suddenly become so extraordinarily effective.

The implications of Itard's natural experiment for the nature–nurture debate are clouded by questions concerning the age at which Victor was isolated and whether or not he had been retarded before he was abandoned. But no one could argue with Itard's statement that if a baby boy and girl were isolated at the same time as "two of the least intelligent species of animal, I do not doubt that the latter would show themselves much superior to the former in providing for their own needs and in attending both to their own preservation and that of their young" (Itard, 1801, 1806/1962, p. 49) (although, I might add, if the human children managed to survive and propagate they might care for their young quite adequately). In general, the lower the species on the phylogenetic scale the more independent are the young at birth. Itard's inference is that in humans the role of learning is crucial, consonant with the empiricist doctrine.

Human infants are helpless at birth because any further development of their large brains would impede their passage through the female pelvic birth canal. The fact that compared to other animals it takes humans a relatively long time to mature, and that normal maturation requires the triggering and modifying influence of certain kinds of basic environmental stimulation at certain periods of development, does not logically lead to the conclusion that environmental stimuli are the *source* of such human capacities as language, for example, or the ability to categorize. It means only that without the environment's initiating and modifying influences the innate program for development will not be fulfilled. A flower will not grow or blossom without water, but water does not create flowers.

Itard's attempt to supply support for the empiricist doctrine by showing that training the senses would eventually lead to intelligent behavior has been repeated with happier outcomes, under somewhat different circumstances, such as in the subsequent development of the blind and deaf Helen Keller or Laura Dewey Bridgman (who had, in addition, very little sense of taste or smell), and of children isolated in closets and dark rooms (Clarke & Clarke, 1976; Lamson, 1881/1975). But this success does not prove that the brain at birth is a blank slate; it demonstrates only that the releasing influence of environmental input can be implemented beyond any fixed critical period and can frequently awaken at later ages the dormant power of the brain. It also raises questions about so-called "psychosocial" or "sociocultural" mental retardation, for if children isolated sensorily can with training through one sense organ (touch) exhibit the kind of intelligence displayed by a Helen Keller, why cannot children whose retardation is attributed to cultural or environmental deprivation but who nevertheless have had all their senses intact and interacting with other human beings from the time of their birth—why cannot they also be trained to the level of Helen Keller's obvious intellectual capacities?

Perhaps, after all, Victor was from birth or an early age a mildly retarded child who, because he was difficult to teach and control—and perhaps even, for whatever reason, could not learn to speak—was abandoned to die in the woods. Surely his experience in the wild, no matter for how long, hampered his educability. Under Itard's tutelage Victor learned to make a number of relatively simple associations. That he advanced as far as he did is a tribute to his extraordinary teacher; that he progressed no further suggests that isolation from human contact in late childhood (he would not likely have survived in the wild as a very young child) was not the primary cause of his intellectually deficient behavior. Perhaps it was a combination of mild retardation and isolation that prevented Victor from learning to speak, either factor alone being insufficient to prevent the expression of such an ingrained human trait.

A word here about the distinction, or lack of distinction, between intelligence (a descriptive word) and education (a process). Other things being equal, children's potential for benefiting from education is very generally related to their intelligence. But because other things are not equal in any society, educational potential never corresponds completely with amount of education, and countless individuals with limited educations are more intelligent than their more educated peers. For Itard the empiricist, following Condillac's philosophy, educated people are intelligent *because* they were educated, not educated because they were intelligent. Intelligence is the sum total of experience, especially educational experience.[1] Consequently, Itard was not simply trying to educate Victor, as we now understand the term; he was attempting to raise Victor's intelligence. For Itard, the two words were essentially synonymous.

Itard's teachings were inspirational for the young Séguin and probably influenced the work of Johann Jakob Guggenbühl, whose interesting career we examine briefly before turning to the work of Séguin.

Guggenbühl and the Cure of Cretinism

In the history of the care and treatment of the mentally retarded—up to and including our own time—there have been many workers who have been filled with ideals and have sacrificed much in order to dedicate themselves to curing mental retardation, an accomplishment that would place their names on the long list of innovators to whom the world is

[1]Yet he also stated that education had to be tailored to a child's intellect, an apparent contradiction unless he assumed that individual differences were created by experiences prior to school entry.

forever indebted. When after varying periods of effort their grandiose hopes go unrealized, some of them—with less fortitude and honesty than were shown by Itard—attempt to delude the world by unrealistic claims. Johann Jakob Guggenbühl (1816–1863) exemplifies this syndrome just at a time when a more enlightened approach to the care of the retarded was emerging (Barr, 1904; Kanner, 1959).

Guggenbühl was moved by the suffering of individuals who had *cretinism,* a term sometimes used indiscriminately for many different types of severe retardation in Switzerland, where true cretinism was relatively common. Guggenbühl, however, distinguished it from "idiotism," where outward physical stigmata are slight or not present at all (Brown, 1847). Uplifted by the sight of an "old cretin . . . stammering a half-forgotten prayer before an image of the Virgin" (Brown, 1847, p. 113), and puzzled by the fact that so much had been written describing cretinism and so little on its cure, Guggenbühl decided to devote his life to curing this debilitating disorder. In 1839 he accepted a post as a physician at Hofwyl, a pedagogical institute that eventually became a teachers' training center, so that he could gain experience in the field of education from one of its finest practitioners, Phillip Emanuel von Fellenberg. He was convinced, furthermore, that some sort of residential setting would provide the best treatment environment and, because cretinism was unknown in higher elevations, he built a number of cottages and two large buildings in the Abendberg mountains near Interlaken, 4,000 feet above sea level. His patients, cared for by the Evangelical Sisters of Mercy, were provided with nutritious meals, baths, massages, and exercises, plus a variety of medications, including supplementary nutrients and elements. Note especially that the water in the Alps flows through calcareous rocks, and that he was supplementing his patients' diets with iodine which he felt, according to an observer, "must be used with caution." "Iodine, with steel, has often a beneficial effect," according to this same observer (RT, 1853/1976, p. 122). Other foods, including vegetable juice, and in the summer fresh aromatic plants grown in their gardens, were included in the diets.

Although it was recognized at that time that cretinism was often closely related to goiter (Brown, 1847), Guggenbühl could not know that it is a metabolic disease that can be familial or acquired, and that it is caused by a deficiency of thyroid hormone during fetal or early life, a result of a defective or deficient thyroid, prolonged iodine deficiency, or inborn errors of iodine metabolism. It is endemic in many areas of the world where there is a deficiency of iodine in the soil and water, as is the case in the valleys of Switzerland but not in the higher elevations. It is now treated by giving desiccated thyroid or a synthetic thyroid hormone. Where iodine deficiency is the cause, it can be relieved in most instances by supplying the necessary iodine in the diet (which we do now by producing iodized salt).

The younger the age when treatment is begun the better the prognosis, although treatment can dramatically improve an afflicted child while nevertheless leaving a residual mild retardation.

The regimen at the Abendberg also included training of the senses, speech, and memory. A description written in 1842 by Dr. William Twining and quoted by the unknown author, RT (1853/1976), indicates that Guggenbühl relied on many of the methods used by Itard and others with deaf-mutes, while adding some interesting refinements, such as placing phosphorous letters on the walls of darkened rooms and using "electromagnetism" to evoke a response in cases where the patient was extremely insensitive (Brown, 1847). The report by RT (1853/1976) is filled with case histories showing the improvement of a number of children not only at the Abendberg but also at the Park House, Highgate, in England, an institution modeled after the Abendberg, but where—at least according to the descriptions—there were few children with cretinism, and where improvements appeared to have resulted from careful training and improved nutrition. Most of the cases end with a sentence to the effect that the child was "continuing to improve" or was "making satisfactory progress."

The reports and observations convincingly demonstrated that their retarded patients received far better treatment in residential settings than they could possibly have received at home in often uncaring families and frequently wretched conditions.[2] At that time, as Brown (1847) pointed out in the first sentence of his discussion of the Abendberg, the improved treatment of the insane had set the stage for the improved treatment of the retarded. Add to that the great advances in training deaf-mutes and one can see why this period was so filled with hope.

The Abendberg's fame spread. Guggenbühl traveled extensively and solicited endorsements that he quoted in his writings and disseminated by every means possible. Up to the Abendberg came people of distinction, many of whom made monetary contributions and reported to the world the marvelous advances being made. Similar facilities were constructed in many other countries, and hope was expressed that soon cretinism would be cured in all of Europe. Guggenbühl was hailed as a font of wisdom, dedication, and purity, and he presented himself as an instrument of God, chosen to perform one of His miracles.

The expanding enthusiasm, which drowned out the few voices of criticism, was doomed to burst, the first major demonstration of a phenomenon that was periodically repeated in subsequent years. It starts with reports of successful treatment or training in a project dominated by the force of a single driving, relentless, ambitious individual. Many important and respected

[2]Today the deinstitutionalization movement takes the opposite position, for reasons we touch on later in this volume.

persons testify to the validity of the results, and the skeptical voices of critics are unheard or disregarded. Guggenbühl could not have known the source of the improvement of his patients who had cretinism (the exhilarating mountain air was one of the prime candidates), but he must have observed that most of his patients—though no doubt responding initially, and sometimes dramatically, to the improved care and diet—were not reaching the level he had hoped they would reach. He then did what others since his time have done: He frequently and for long periods of time absented himself from the source of his fame, traveling widely, proselytizing, and selling the magnificance of his work, while all the time the work itself crumbled into disrepair.

In 1858 the British minister to Berne paid a surprise visit to some English patients at the Abendberg and found them, and the institution, in a state of disgusting disarray (Guggenbühl was away at the time). The absence of one patient, killed in a fall from a precipice, went unnoticed for some time. Another patient died and by the time a carpenter was summoned to make a coffin, the body had decomposed. A government investigation resulted in a list of charges, including the fact that at most only one-third of the patients were cretins; normal children were presented to audiences as cured cretins; not a single cretin had been cured; the director was away for 4 to 6 months a year without providing a substitute physician; heating, clothing, and food were inadequate; no account books were kept, nor records of patients' progress; and so on. Shortly thereafter the Abendberg was closed, and when his former supporters began to turn on him, Guggenbühl accused them of lack of faith, spending his last years defending himself and his life's work (Kanner, 1959).

Guggenbühl died in 1863, leaving—futilely as it turned out—600,000 Swiss francs to continue his institution (a measure of the large amount of money he had made from the Abendberg). He left as an unwritten legacy the concept of residential facilities for mentally retarded persons throughout the world.

Guggenbühl's clinical experiment was confounded by a problem common even today, the problem of isolating from a spectrum of treatment variables the particular variable(s) responsible for any improvement that might occur. It is conceivable that some of his patients were helped by some of his procedures, perhaps by the addition of iodine or other nutrients to their diets, but it is impossible to know for certain. Most of them could not be cured by any such regimen, and apparently Guggenbühl, unwilling to accept failure, resorted to various subterfuges in order to claim success.

As we have seen, early in the 19th century the methods used to teach deaf-mutes were borrowed for training the mentally retarded (the "deaf and dumb," after all, had previously been grouped with the mentally retarded).

Certainly releasing the trapped intellectual resources of deaf-mutes was a triumph of patience and innovative pedagogy, but most deaf-mutes have at least average intellectual potential which can be reached through unimpeded senses. Nethertheless, because of this success the emphasis in training retarded persons also centered on "educating the senses," which, by way of Itard, became an essential part of the methods used by Séguin and Montessori.

Edouard Séguin and the Magic Trinity

In the introduction to his book, *Idiocy: And its Treatment by the Physiological Method,* Edouard Séguin wrote that Guggenbühl in Switzerland, and Saegert in Berlin, opened schools for idiots "without having any knowledge of our practice, or of our four successive pamphlets on the treatment of idiots, already published and exhausted" (1866/1907, p. 12). Because he saw himself as Itard's successor, it must have surprised him that his methods were not known and emulated by the early founders of residential facilities. This was a temporary slight, however, for Séguin's work became the cornerstone for educating the mentally retarded.

Born in France in 1812, Séguin studied medicine and surgery under Itard, who had been a fellow medical student of Séguin's father. Séguin was influenced by Itard and used many of the great teacher's methods. Yet, though he acknowledged his debt, Séguin specifically stated that his methods were different from Itard's (Pichot, 1948). For one thing Itard, adhering to Condillac's philosophy of sensations, had failed to train the intellect or the "social and moral" feelings and this, according to Séguin (1856/1976), was a principal deficiency in Itard's approach (a charge that was quite unfair). He also pointed out that Itard did not believe that the mentally retarded were curable, and therefore had attempted to train Victor only because he thought that Victor's muteness was the result not of low intellect but of isolation from other humans.

"Can idiots be educated, treated, improved, cured?" asked Séguin (1866/1907, p. 7), and he answered "To put the question was to solve it." Séguin, you see, did believe that idiots can be cured, and, furthermore, that he was the one who would show the way because he was guided by a theory that provided him with the "only superiority over my predecessors" (Séguin, 1856/1976, p. 156). This guiding principle, which allowed him to go beyond Itard and Esquirol and other "alienists" (healers) who had preceded him, was the philosophical and religious system called Saint-Simonism.

Claude Henri de Rouvroy Saint-Simon, whose views made little impact during his lifetime, advocated scientific socialism, mutual love, and the dedication of society to uplifting the poorest class. After he died in 1825, his work was extended by others into the doctrine of Saint-Simonism. In

1830, these socialist reformers demanded community ownership, the abolishment of the right of inheritance (rewards should be based on merit), and the enfranchisement of women. In their view, two forces have vied for control throughout history: the critical (negative) forces of war, egotism, and anarchy, against the organic (constructive), religious spirit of obedience, devotion, and association. Man is the will of God, expressed in the trinity of the independent life of activity, the dependent life of passivity, and the life of relations or interchange of activity and passivity, freedom and obedience, loving and being loved.

Physiological education, the phrase Séguin used to describe his methods, follows "the great natural law of action and repose, which is life itself." During education each function (presumably the cerebral, muscular, and sensorial functions that Séguin mentions elsewhere) must in its turn be active or at rest, "the improvement of one reacting upon the improvement of all others; contrast being not only an instrument of relaxation, but of comprehension also" (Séguin, 1866/1907, p. 26). The reader can see how Séguin adapted Saint-Simonism for his philosophy of educating the retarded, although how this was to be implemented is perhaps not so obvious.

The concept of a trinity pervades Séguin's ideas. As a basis of the "laws of philosophical medicine" there is first of all (to paraphrase Séguin) the religious belief in the trinity, reflected in all human beings—made in the image of God—including idiots, who are, however, infirm in modes of its expression. They are infirm in (a) mobility and sensibility, (b) perception and reasoning, and (c) affections and will (1856/1976, p. 156). Education develops the physical, intellectual, and moral capacities (1866/1907, p. 26), and requires the development of the organs of thought, movement, and sensation. Humans feel, understand, and will, and can only reach their potential when they are taught the maximum of sensibility, intellect, and morality (Boyd, 1914, p. 95). Training of the trinity of functions must be hierarchical: first the bodily functions of movement and feeling, then the intellectual functions of understanding, and finally the highest functions of will and morality, although when any one of the functions is being trained the others also must come into play.

How Séguin bridged the gap from the religious aspects of the trinity to the triad of functions that require training is difficult to fathom. Séguin, as did many of the writers of his day, wrote in flowery prose, which sometimes led to embellishments and distortions. At one point, for example, he wrote that Itard gave the name "Victor" to the wild boy "doubtless as a sign of the victory which education should achieve in him over brute nature" (1856/1976, p. 154). But Itard explained in his report (1801, 1806/1962, p. 29) that the wild boy quickly turned his head whenever someone said "Oh" in a sentence, and that he only gave this alert response to the vowel O and to no other vowel. Consequently Itard chose the name Victor because (in French) it ended with the sound of O, so that Victor would be very responsive to his name, a strategy that proved to be correct.

Séguin had read Itard's report, about which he says "we quit with regret his few unrivalled pages" (1866/1907, p. 23), so it is difficult to understand how he could have garbled so striking an incident.

Throughout Séguin's writings one feels the religious fervor and intense driving force of an optimistic, dedicated, totally devoted and driven man who believed in the inherent potential and perfectability, through proper education, of all human beings. As a young man of 25, and against the prevailing opinion of his time, he had the chance to prove the educability of retarded individuals when Itard, too old and infirm to attempt to educate a mute, apparently retarded child referred to him for language instruction, agreed that the child should be turned over to Séguin. In constant consultation with Itard, and meeting once a week with Esquirol (one of the pioneers of psychiatry)—who was pessimistic about the possibility of educating retarded children—Séguin worked with the boy for 18 months, achieving admirable success. In 1839 he reported his pupil's progress, and Esquirol attested to the fact that Séguin, using the late Dr. Itard's methods, had taught the student "to make use of his senses, to remember, to compare, to speak, to write, to count, etc." (Lane, 1976, p. 264).

Séguin opened his own "school for idiots" in 1839. Two years later he was invited to work with idiot children at La Salpêtrière, and a year after that a commission was so delighted with his results that they appointed him director of a school for idiots at the Bicêtre. Three commission reports over the period of 1842 to 1844 praised Séguin's work, and one of them concluded that he had to a large extent overcome the extreme difficulties involved in educating idiots. However, because of administrative problems, he left the Bicêtre to devote himself to his private pupils. His second major book (Séguin, 1846) was very well received, and prompted Pope Pius IX to express his gratitude to Séguin for services to humanity (Barr, 1904; Kanner, 1964). Visitors came from many nations to observe his work, leading to the development of a number of schools throughout the continent and in England. Based on an earlier visit to Séguin by George Sumner, Samuel G. Howe persuaded the Massachusetts legislature to appropriate $2,500 annually for 3 years, starting in 1848, for an experimental school for idiotic children, to be established in association with the Perkins Institute for the Blind, where Howe was the Director and where the deaf, mute, and blind Laura Bridgman was educated. At almost the same time, Hervey B. Wilbur, who also was influenced by Sumner's report of Séguin's successes, opened a private school in Massachusetts, and later went on to develop and direct schools in New York State.

The politically active Séguin supported the French revolution of 1848 but disapproved of the subsequent developments and thought it best to leave for the United States. He opened a private medical practice in Cleveland, directed briefly the Pennsylvania Training School for Idiots, moved to Mount Vernon, New York, and finally, in 1861, to New York City, where he established a private practice. There were relatively long periods of time when he pursued other interests, including voyages to Europe with his ailing wife.

By 1876 there were in the United States 11 schools for the retarded (Wilbur, 1888/1976), for many of which Séguin was a valued consultant. On June 6th, 1876, during the Centennial Exposition in Philadelphia, six superintendents met at the Pennsylvania Training School (now the Elwyn Institute) near Philadelphia to discuss the formation of an organization to further their work. The next day, joined by a seventh superintendent, they adopted a constitution that created The Association of Medical Officers of American Institutions for Idiots and Feeble-Minded Persons,[3] elected Séguin as its first president, and on that day and the following day elected nine additional members, including a number of Superintendents' wives (Kerlin, 1877). Before he died in 1880, Séguin founded—with his second wife—the Séguin Physiological School for Feeble-Minded Children in New York City.

It is not possible, nor fair, to summarize Séguin's methods in a short space, and in any case a close scrutiny of training methods is not the primary purpose of this book. In Séguin's third major book (Séguin, 1866/1907) the interested reader will find a full account of his approach to educating the mentally retarded. Suffice it to say that despite his disclaimer that his methods were different from Itard's, he did use and expand upon many of Itard's techniques (see especially Lane, 1976), particularly when "educating" the senses. On the other hand, in order to develop motor control and physical adroitness—the first step in training his trinity of functions—he had to develop novel training methods (Itard had no need for such training with the agile Victor), and he did so with commendable ingenuity.

Following motor training, the senses were trained, and although he maintained that all the senses must collaborate, the sense of touch was considered foremost. Referring to Perèire's use of tactile sensations to teach deaf-mutes to speak, Séguin wrote that "all the senses are modifications of the tact, all touch of some sort" (1866/1907, p. 19). To paraphrase Séguin, the conclusion one reaches from the training of deaf-mutes is that each of the senses can be given physiological training, one sense can be substituted for another sense, our most abstract ideas are generalizations of what we perceived through our senses, educating perceptions is food for

[3]Referred to hereafter in this book as the Association, or the Association of Medical Officers. In 1906 it became the American Association for the Study of the Feeble-Minded, and in 1933 the American Association on Mental Deficiency (Milligan, 1961).

the mind, and finally, "sensations are intellectual functions performed through external apparatus as much as reasoning, imagination, etc., through more internal organs" (p. 20).

This list of pronouncements reveals Séguin's ultimate debt to Locke and Condillac's sensory philosophy, and also clearly illustrates that methods for educating retarded persons were drawn from the methods used to teach deaf-mute (and blind) individuals to communicate. Condillac, in fact, believed that we *learn* to see objects, and do so by generalizing from the sense of touch. Lane (1976, p. 137) quotes Condillac as follows: "It is from touch that the eyes, which by themselves would only have sensations of light and color, learn to estimate sizes, forms, and distances; and they are trained so quickly that they seem to see without having learned." This solution to the mystery of how we are able to see objects merely transformed the problem from vision to touch; that is, the question of how the fingers construct shapes that are recognized by the mind is no less a problem than how vision performs the same feat, but Condillac's solution is wrong in any case. The ability to visually perceive objects is inborn and does not require touch, as is proven beyond doubt by the visual facility of unfortunate infants born without limbs. In studies with infants and adults, when vision and touch are in conflict it is vision that dominates, not the other way around (Bower, Broughton, & Moore, 1970; Rock, Mack, Adams, & Hill, 1965; Singer & Day, 1969).

Séguin's debt to empiricism is further revealed by his conception of the senses as doors to the intellect. Because the sense organs of retarded children are available to us they must be trained first so that, through them, we can reach the organ of thought. To support this view, Séguin (1870) cited the case of the Wild Boy of Aveyron as well as of Kaspar Hauser—a young man who was discovered when he was about 17, and who apparently had been isolated in a dark room most of his life, yet made fairly good progress educationally and socially after he was discovered and until he was murdered by an unknown assailant 5 years later (e.g., Shattuck, 1980, pp. 195–197). Séguin then gave three rather absurd interpretations of how the use or neglect of sensory education affected entire cultures, and concluded that *"the physiological education of the senses is the royal road to the education of the intellect: experience, not memory, the mother of ideas"* (Séguin, 1870, p. 26, his italics).

Following sensory training, intelligence was trained. Séguin believed that mental training improved intelligence, much as physical training develops muscles. In 1877, just 3 years before he died, he wrote that "cases of enlargement of the cranium, consequent on the training of the brain, are too familiar to delay the conclusions of our main ideas . . . (that) the form of the cranium continues to influence that of the brain, as the form of the brain does that of the cranium" (p. 17). Séguin's physiological method implied that the senses, and through them, intelligence, can be trained, and that progress would be reflected in a change in the shape of the cranium.[4]

Although, as noted, a detailed description of Séguin's teaching methods is not given here, a short description of some typical classroom activities may convey the flavor of what took place (Boyd, 1914; Lane, 1976; Séguin, 1866/1970). Individual training was prescribed for students initially, but the aim of individual sensory education was to have students reach a level at which they could join groups, where imitation could play an important role. Group singing and dancing, for example, were considered important, particularly because music was an essential element in training. Students were also taught practical knowledge, such as the days of the week, the months, and the seasons. They were taught academic subjects at a very basic level. Vocational training, such as farming, shoemaking, and carpentry, was part of the curriculum because, according to Séguin, training fails if the children cannot perform some useful function in society. In training the intellect, not just names of objects but ideas about objects—and particularly an understanding of relationships between objects—must be appreciated. In moral training (the apex of the trinity) students were taught, among other things, to obey commands, and Séguin made use of a strategy used frequently now in behavior modification: tickets given for good behavior earned a student the use of the garden (see Rosen, Clark, & Kivitz, 1976, p. 108, who also point out that Séguin's students included blind, paralytic, and epileptic children). The aim of moral treatment also included the development of positive volition that expressed itself in sociability, affection, thinking, and useful activity. Because the work ethic was strongly implanted in Séguin's personal philosophy—if people consume, they must produce—an important goal for his students was to learn to work productively, at least to the limits of their abilities.

At a time when relatively few attempts had been made to educate mentally retarded children, Séguin's accomplishments were extraordinary, but now—thanks largely to his pioneering efforts—such training is commonplace. It is obviously possible to control, train, and educate all but the most profoundly retarded, up to a point. What has not proven possible, then or now, is to change mentally retarded persons so that they are no longer intellectually deficient. Kuhlmann (1940) perhaps put it best when he noted that the acquisition of skill and information was being confused with the acquisition of intelligence. Séguin's (1866/1907, p. 54) statement that "idiots have been improved, educated, and even cured," at first suggests

[4]The idea that function determines structure is reflected in the Lamarckian hypothesis that structural changes are passed down hereditarily and account for evolutionary changes. Lamarck was greatly influenced by Locke and Condillac (Oppenheim, 1979), so we see once again the widespread influence of the empiricist position.

that in his later years he had become more cautious in his claims, but only a few pages later (p. 57) he would blithely write that "most idiots . . . may be relieved in a more or less complete measure of their disabilities by the physiological method of education."

Despite Séguin's statements that training of the senses is a means of opening a path to the intellect, he elsewhere writes as though the senses are themselves intelligent organs. For example, he states that "the *initiative* of a certain order of capacities . . . resides in the periphery and sensibility," and therefore, "instead of referring all the *initiums* to the *basilic* brain, or co-locating it in the triumvirate brain, spinal cord, and sympathetic, we must recognize the power of millions of peripheric brains to give the impulse as well as to receive it." And finally, "If the idiot whose case is represented to you has improved under the care of his good teacher; if hundreds of others improve in the public institutions . . . the sovereignty of the brain is at an end, and the new physiological doctrine of decentralization contains in germ a new doctrine and new methods of education" (the quotations in this paragraph are from Séguin, 1879/1976, p. 167, his italics).

Séguin's emphasis on motor and sensory training for his students was surely desirable, but there is no good theoretical rationale for believing that such training will have any appreciable effect on intelligence. Séguin himself pointed out that many nonhuman species have much better sensory capacities than humans, and he stressed that sensations had to be associated with each other in order for the mind to produce ideas (Séguin, 1866/1907, pp. 139–141). There are in fact numerous natural experiments which demonstrate that motor and sensory ability are unrelated to intelligence. For example, many intellectually brilliant individuals are afflicted with cerebral palsy and have very limited control of their motor systems, and some individuals deprived of vision or hearing, or both, give ample evidence that they are highly intelligent.

Nevertheless, the optimistic viewpoint that sensory training of mentally retarded children will improve their intelligence is one of the many fallacies that are a legacy of the empiricist philosophy. It arose from the illogical analogy that if deaf-mute and blind individuals can exhibit intelligent behavior after their minds are reached via other sensory pathways, then surely alternate sensory and even multisensory training will reach the minds of retarded individuals. Unfortunately, although sensory education may be the "royal road to the education of the intellect," there remains the problem, once having breached the sensory gates, of how to educate an intellect whose potential is extremely limited.

The Montessori Method

Most of the early pioneers in the care and teaching of mentally retarded children were physicians, and Maria Montessori was no exception. Born in 1870 in Chiavalle, Italy, she was determined to pursue a medical career, and when she graduated from the Medical School of the University of Rome in 1894 she was the first woman ever to receive a medical degree from an Italian University. That she was able to reach this milestone in the face of extreme prejudice tells us a great deal about the intensity of her will and resolve. She had the kind of inner strength and almost mystical sense of mission that always seems to drive those who—in spite of the apathy and even hostility of other professionals—undertake to prove the power of an idea or method by demonstrating that they are able to raise the performance level of retarded children well beyond anyone's expectations.

As an "assistant doctor" in the Psychiatric Clinic at the University of Rome, studying diseases of children in asylums for the insane, she became interested in the retarded children who were housed there. She turned to Séguin's (1846) book for guidance because she, unlike her colleagues, felt that mental deficiency was primarily a pedagogical rather than a medical problem (Montessori, 1912/1965). A course of lectures to the teachers of Rome on the education of feeble-minded children led to the directorship of the State Orthophrenic School for deficient children who were unable to benefit from regular classes, and this in turn led to the founding of the Medical Pedagogic Institute, which served not only retarded public school children but also retarded children from the insane asylums.

She traveled to London and Paris to observe methods of teaching retarded children, but found instead a desire for new methods and fresh ideas because "far too often Séguin's claims that with his methods the education of idiots was actually possible, had proven only a delusion" (Montessori, 1912/1965, p. 36). Nevertheless, when she returned home to her retarded pupils she dedicated herself for 2 years, from 1898 to 1900, "from eight in the morning to seven in the evening without interruption" (p. 32), to the education of her retarded charges. She made a large variety of instructional devices that were to be the foundation of her method; but instructional devices were not by themselves sufficient. Others had failed, she wrote, because they acted as if they were educating babies, approaching their retarded pupils with games and "foolish stories." She, on the other hand, showed how to reach the adult in the soul of the child; her voice awakened the children and "encouraged them to use the didactic material, and through it, to educate themselves" (1912/1965, p. 37). As Séguin had written, it is the spirit of the teacher that is the secret of success.

Whatever the secret, in those 2 years Montessori achieved some remarkable results. She succeeded in teaching a number of the mentally deficient children who had been transferred from the asylums (but apparently none of those whom she had received from the public schools) both to read and write so well that they passed the examination for normal children (1912/1965, p. 38). Exhausted from her efforts—"a peculiar form of exhaustion prostrated me. It was as if I gave to them some vital force within me" (p. 38)—she nevertheless reasoned that these mentally retarded children could never have reached the level of normal children if the normal children had been given a "proper" education.

At this point, feeling the need for meditation, Dr. Montessori withdrew from active teaching and—not one to rest in the usual sense—translated into Italian the writings of Itard and Séguin so that she could "weigh the sense of each word, and to read, in truth, the *spirit* of the author" (p. 41). Having just finished copying the 600-page French volume (Séguin, 1846), she translated, with the help of a friend, Séguin's 1866 English language book in which he recommended that the physiological method be applied to normal children. For some time she had believed this to be the logical next step and she had a chance to take it when she was invited in 1906 to organize classes for 3- to 7-year-old preschool children who lived in the model tenements recently constructed in Rome. Each tenement was to have its own schoolroom, with children from 3 to 7 in the same room. The development of this *Case dei Bambini* (Children's House) initiated the Montessori educational program for preschool children (and, later, elementary school children) that, in spite of much opposition, had a profound impact on education throughout the world.

As Séguin did in referring to Itard, Montessori denied that her work in the Children's House had been an application "pure and simple" of Séguin's methods, but she acknowledged that she had been greatly influenced by both Séguin and Itard. For 10 years prior to the establishment of the Children's House she had, through "reverent meditation absorbed the work of these noble and consecrated men." Thus, she goes on, "my ten years of work may in a sense be considered as a summing up of the forty years of work done by Itard and Séguin," and consequently "fifty years of active work preceded and prepared [me] for this apparently brief trial of only two years" (Montessori, 1912/1965, pp. 45–46).

As with her mentor, Montessori's reputation was built initially on her success with mentally deficient children, but unlike Séguin she turned thereafter almost entirely to the education of young normal children. There are many aspects of her techniques that are of general interest, but only a limited number are pertinent for this volume. Primary, of course, is her adoption of Séguin's physiological method, with its emphasis on motor and sensory training followed by language and academic subjects, all to be taught using specially constructed "didactic material," in line with the empiricist doctrine that the way to educate the brain is to first educate the senses.

Nevertheless, in a curious and contradictory way her educational philosophy was quite at odds with what she claimed were its historical roots. For her, the impetus for learning and developing must come from within the child, each of whom has an inborn, vital force that must be liberated. The means of liberation are the spirit of the teacher in her position as a role model, and the use of didactic devices in a classroom atmosphere of freedom without anarchy.

She adapted some of the didactic material, which are pictured and described in many of her books (e.g., Montessori, 1914/1964), from Itard and especially Séguin, but developed many others herself. Many of these were designed to train increasingly finer discriminations, as Itard and Séguin had recommended. Although the teacher introduced each apparatus to her pupils by first demonstrating it, Montessori pointed out that an important feature of this equipment was that it forced the children to undertake their own training and gave them an opportunity to correct their errors without the teacher's intervention.

For Montessori, the period from ages 2 to 7 years is a time when the senses develop, and consequently sensory training for preschoolers lays the groundwork for later development. The use of her didactic material educates the senses to discriminate fine dimensional differences and the children thereby train themselves to observe, to make comparison, to form judgments, and to reason (1914/1964, pp. 32–33).

Her belief in the power of sensory education is made clear in the preface to one of her books, where she wrote that "Helen Keller is a marvellous example of the phenomenon common to all human beings: the possibility of the liberation of the imprisoned spirit of man by the education of the senses. . . . If only one of the senses sufficed to make of Helen Keller a woman of exceptional culture and a writer, who better than she proves the potency of that method of education which builds on the senses?" (Montessori, 1914/1964, Preface).

This, it seems to me, captures the essence of the sensory fallacy. It was not the training of the single sense, touch, that made the blind and deaf Helen Keller such a remarkable woman. Controlled and resourceful communication through that sense brought her into increased contact with the outside world. When she grasped the idea that every object had a name that could be signed through the sense of touch, a structured, lawful world opened up to her. The sense of touch became a pathway that allowed her mind to contact the world of impressions and, with the help of her teacher, her highly intelligent mind was liberated to develop its great potential. It is not the case that "if one only of the senses" can produce a Helen Keller then a method of education that trains the senses can produce many Helen

Kellers. It all depends on the potential capacity of each brain, the senses being merely its tool and its means of communication. There is simply no evidence that training very fine discriminations of touch, vision, or hearing has any effect whatever on the development of intellect.

The extraordinary results Montessori obtained with some of her mentally deficient pupils have not, to my knowledge, been repeated in subsequent Montessori classrooms. Furthermore, her original accomplishments have been exaggerated. Whereas she wrote (Montessori, 1912/1965, p. 38) that she "succeeded in teaching a number of the idiots from the asylums" to pass the examination (with no mention being made of the children placed in her class from the public schools), this event is described in 1970 as: "Montessori's 'defectives' improved so radically that they were able to pass the state test given to admit normal children into the primary school!" (Gitter, 1970, p. 16), the implication being that all her students passed the test.

The disillusion that Montessori found in workers who had tried to educate retarded children using Séguin's method was soon transferred to *her* methods. For example, Stanley Porteus (1973) described the excitement that had been generated in 1913 by Montessori's success with retarded children. "The idea quickly spread," he wrote, "that subjects definitely feebleminded were responding so well that they had narrowed the gap between them and normal individuals. . . . It looked like a major educational breakthrough" (p. 1). Consequently, as was happening elsewhere, a city school in Melbourne, Australia, was converted into a Montessori center for retarded children, but failure of the pupils to progress led Porteus to conclude that it was useless to try to teach retarded children isolated skills when they had no idea what the end product would look like. In one of the Montessori tasks—finger tracing around the outline of objects—the students had difficulty because, according to Porteus, they were unable to anticipate changes in direction of movement and consequently they cut across or rounded the corners. With this in mind, Porteus subsequently developed his Maze Test to measure this capacity for foresight and planning, which he considered to be deficient in retarded individuals.

By the 1920s, under a barrage of criticism, the popularity of the Montessori method for younger normal children went into a period of decline. Though not the primary cause of this decline, it was nevertheless clear that it had not fulfilled its early promise to dramatically raise the academic performance of children with low intelligence, although there are those who argue that it is a particularly useful method for training retarded children (e.g., Gitter), or that it can be modified for use with retarded children (Mink, 1964). Goodman (1974) carefully reviewed the use of Montessori's method with handicapped children and concluded that where appropriate assessment procedures have been used the Montessori system proves to be no better than any other system in raising performance. In a very carefully controlled study, Miller and her colleagues (Miller & Bizzell, 1983; Miller & Dyer, 1975) measured the relative effectiveness of four preschool programs, one of them a Montessori program, on disadvantaged, primarily black children. Although there were differential effects depending on the particular program, a surprising result was the steady decline in IQ following the initial impact of the prekindergarten program. The one exception to this decline was a group of 13 boys from the Montessori preschool. Their mean IQ at the end of the eighth grade was about the same as it had been when they were 4 years old. Carefully controlled assessment procedures provide no evidence that the Montessori method produces any remarkable or lasting improvement in the intelligence of nonretarded children, and certainly not in retarded children. Once again we observe the real-life scenes of a play in which a forceful individual produces a remarkable effect on the performance of retarded individuals, raising hopes that at long last retarded persons can be imbued with some catalyst that will allow them to behave in a far more intelligent manner. But no such effect can be produced by others, disillusionment sets in and the play closes, only to open again at a later date with new actors and a new director but with the same old denouement.

Maria Montessori has left her mark. She did away with rigid seating arrangements and dull drill, introduced ungraded classrooms where children advance at their own pace, and gave her young pupils a large measure of freedom in the classroom within the limits of not offending others or behaving in an ill-bred manner. Many of her ideas have been incorporated by traditional education, and Montessori schools and societies can be found throughout the world. In fact, the Montessori movement is now showing something of a renaissance. In its stress on sensory education, and despite her allusion to the freeing of innate vital forces, Montessori's basic educational philosophy is essentially Lockian, in contrast to the rationalist doctrine of inborn capacities and specific domains of behavior released by maturation and the triggering and molding influence of environmental events. It is, therefore, compatible with current compensatory and early education movements aimed at retarded children and preschool children from impoverished homes, the very groups with whom Montessori originally developed her methods.

In her later years she personally brought her system to Spain, England, India, and the Netherlands before she died in 1952 after a long and productive life.

3 Disillusion and Overreaction

Whereas the pedagogical philosophies of Itard and Séguin were extended by Montessori to the education of nonretarded children, the primary legacy of their work was in the demonstration that mentally deficient children could be educated and trained. The formation in 1876 of the Association of Medical Officers of American Institutions for Idiots and Feeble-Minded Persons signaled the start of concerted efforts in the United States to increase the number of residential institutions where retarded persons could be properly educated. The early writings and lectures of Séguin and Howe, among others, had generated the unrealistic expectation in many people that retarded residents who were educated by the new scientific methods—in particular by Séguin's methods of physiological education—would emerge much improved, perhaps even indistinguishable from their normal peers. The 13 training schools established in the United States by 1877 (Wilbur, 1888/1976) were initially conceived as extensions of regular schools, and consequently it was assumed that their retarded residents would be educated and then released (Doll, 1962; Nowrey, 1945).

In 1877 the Association published the first issue of its *Proceedings.*[1] A perusal of its contents up to the 1913 issue in which Goddard made his frank statement on the immutability of retarded intelligence provides an instructive illustration of early enthusiasm turning sour. But even in 1877 there had been ample evidence that the institutions were having difficulty

[1]In 1896 its title was changed to the *Journal of Psycho-Asthenics,* which in 1918 was incorporated into the *American Association for the Study of the Feeble-Minded,* and in 1940 became the *American Journal of Mental Deficiency.*

meeting their goals, especially because they failed to comply with Howe's admonition not to admit untrainable retarded children (Kuhlmann, 1940). Indeed, throughout this period there were many respected and dedicated professionals who stated categorically that retarded children could not be turned into normal children, that only a small percentage could become self-supporting, and that too much was being promised.

The recognition that there are many different kinds and varying degrees of mental deficiency emerged more clearly during these years, and with it a better understanding that not all mentally deficient residents could benefit equally from institutional training. Some could become self-sufficient; some could be taught trades; some could become useful in the institution's farm, laundry, or kitchen; and some would always require care and custody (e.g., Carson, 1891, Salisbury, 1892). William Fish (1892, p. 204) quoted an 1888 committee report that 10- to 20% of those in institutions improve enough to "enter life as bread-winners," another 30- to 40% improve enough to be returned to their families, and about half remain in custodial care. But the dominant sentiment had shifted to permanent institutionalization because even after training, "Once feeble-minded always feeble-minded, only in a less degree" (Rogers, 1891, p. 32. See also Fernald, 1893).

The changed purpose of the institutions is evident in Fish's presidential address to the Association, in which he pointed out that "less than three thousand of the seventy-six thousand idiots and imbeciles were being cared for in public and private institutions," and he asked: "How much of misfortune and suffering do these figures represent? How many saddened homes? How many worn and weary mothers? How many fathers struggling to keep their families from want, weighed down by this burden of misfortune?" (Fish, 1889, p. 15). Obviously he felt that an important function of institutions was to relieve families of the burden of retarded children. Institutions that originally had been designed to train their charges and return them to the community became instead their permanent homes.

The metamorphosis of institutions in the United States from centers of education to colonies for lifetime custody has been attributed to society's perception of the mentally retarded as deviants who must be segregated (White & Wolfensberger, 1969). According to this view, it was an unfortunate fact that new institutions were directed by superintendents who discarded the philosophies of their dedicated predecessors. But why were those noble philosophies discarded? There must have been complex reasons, among them the changing nature of the residents—the fact that State institutions could not be selective and were admitting many more residents, most of whom had very low intelligence and many of whom had been neglected at home, were badly behaved, and had medical problems related to their mental deficiency (Sloan, 1963). A very large percentage of the residents were epileptic.

When, under these conditions, the hopes generated by Séguin, Howe, and Wilbur could not be fulfilled, disillusionment was bound to prevail and philosophies were sure to change. Of course new treatments were periodically introduced. For example, craniectomy for microcephaly, and brain surgery for lesions or injury, were tried and heralded, then shown to be useless (Rogers, 1898). Although most persons involved in direct care of the residents were realistic about the extent of improvement that could be achieved, the press—then as now—occasionally printed wildly optimistic statements. The following section of an editorial by Wilmarth (1898a) could serve as a prototypical denial.

> Society at large craves sensation, and the romance is always more popular than the essay. While such literature is always entertaining and sometimes instructive, it is occasionally deplorable when it deals with subjects of scientific interest, as it strongly impresses our minds with its subject while its inaccuracy makes it worse than valueless.
>
> Not long since a New York physician published a thrilling account of studies on the action of the cells of the human brain, and actually illustrated his article with a picture of the microscope arranged for the study of these tiny cells through a hole, cut for the purpose, in the skull. Any person who realizes the delicate adjustment of a high power microscope must see how the natural movements of the living brain would make such a study absolutely impossible. Equally rash and unfounded are the statements regarding the restoration of idiots as a class to the intelligence of normal people. Attention is forcibly called to this in the last annual report from Elwyn, Pennsylvania, quoting from an article widely published and probably read by many thousand people, and written by an inexperienced man who wrote in a very interesting and readable manner some amazing absurdities. While the improvement of the feeble-minded under training is very marked and often borders on the marvellous, still, the following statement, which is quoted from the article in question, is really grotesque:
>
> "Through its gate is constantly tramping inwards an army of staring soulless eyes, of flat or conical heads, of watery, open mouths; clumsy, listless, stupid soldiers."
>
> "After a longer or shorter series of years, this same army marches forth again into the world, little inferior, and, perchance, equal to its average citizens."
>
> What shall we do in this matter? We can no more follow and eradicate the effect of such exaggerations, written for a salary with an utter carelessness as to accuracy, by irresponsible people, than we can exterminate the weeds from our fields by picking up the seeds. A portion of the harm done may be possibly neutralized by placing the exact truth before the people, in legitimate publications, whenever practicable, and leaving the issue with time. (pp. 121–122)

Unfortunately, time has not had the palliative effect that Wilmarth hoped for.

In the professional community, as the 19th century drew to a close, the pendulum was swinging past disillusion to negative overreaction.[2] At that same meeting in which Fish made his plea for universal institutionalization for all retarded individuals, Kerlin (1889) raised the issue of "moral imbecility." Why he presented this paper to a society dedicated to the care and study of feeble-minded persons is difficult to understand, and indeed he later noted that the paper seemed to "fall flat" and was criticized by some members of the audience (Kerlin, 1892a). But although in this paper he nowhere stated that retarded persons are necessarily moral imbeciles, he had planted an idea that was to have unhappy consequences; and in another report (quoted in Salisbury, 1892) he very emphatically associated criminality with imbecility. If retardation, criminality, and degeneracy are associated with each other, then containment and sterilization are more easily justified. Dugdale's (1877/1976) famous study of the "Juke" family, in which he attempted to separate the influences of heredity and environment by following the lineage of six sisters (plus the father of two husbands of two of the sisters), was cited as evidence that from a single feeble-minded woman there "descended many generations of paupers and criminals, while the worst of vices characterized a large majority of her descendants" (Bicknell, 1896, p. 62).[3]

Pleas for the prevention of retardation by permanent custody and/or sterilization entered increasingly into the presented papers and discussions, although Kerlin (1892b) considered sterilization only a future possibility in view of the opposition to it. Following Bicknell (1896), Wilmarth (1898b) pointed out that if the retardation is due to trauma or acute disease it cannot be transmitted, but if "a family trait exists, . . . society has an absolute right to expect that they shall not be allowed to reproduce their kind" (p. 123), and consequently he recommended permanent care and custody of imbeciles, with continued education so that they may become useful and happy. Many of the residents spent much of their time working in the institutions' farms, shops, kitchens, and dormitories, and caring for those who were more severely retarded.

In a chapter titled "Asexualization" in his classic text on mental deficiency, Barr (1904) described an 1895 Connecticut law that forbade "epileptic, imbecile, or feeble-minded" women under 45, or men of any age, from marrying or cohabiting. According to Barr, this law and others like it did not go far enough, for they did not reach the "waifs and strays, the vicious and lawless, and above all the unrecognized, unsuspected defectives in all ranks of society." Furthermore, "the only protection is that which the surgeon gives" (p. 190). He then went on to report approvingly the

[2]More than 70 years later Sloan (1963) found it necessary to remind us of this danger: "Let not our enthusiasm carry us too far, because the inevitable result is like a pendulum. Disillusionment can set us farther back than where we are" (p. 13).

[3]Actually the Dugdale study provided no good evidence for the hereditary transmission of mental deficiency, although it provided plenty of evidence for the transmission of syphilis by infection.

asexualization of 58 boys in a Kansas institution, 26 epileptics in a Massachusetts hospital, and 116 women who had "myoma, dysmenorrhea, hysteria and hystero-epilepsy" (p. 197). His own experience in operating on three boys and three girls "resulted in improvement mental, moral and physical—especially marked in the boys" (p. 197).

At the same time that these (probably illegal and certainly immoral) deeds were enacted, a more felicitous movement was stirring in the United States. Special classes in the regular school system already had been established in Europe, the first one having opened in Germany in 1859 (Scheerenberger, 1983; Shuttleworth, 1899). Indeed, a special class had been tried in Cleveland in 1875 in the high expectation that with proper teaching the retarded students would become normal, only to close in disappointment at the end of the year with "the poor teacher [suffering] a mental collapse which necessitated a sojourn at our State Hospital" (Steinbach, 1918, p. 104). Twenty-five years later, spurred by more realistic expectations, day schools and special classes were opening in a number of cities in the United States (Esten, 1900; Fort, 1900). Stress was placed on educating the senses, and Channing (1900) made an interesting and prophetic recommendation. "The sooner we can begin to train the special senses," he wrote, "the better it will be, for it is through them that we must expect to reach the highest centers" (p. 41), and he suggested that such training should begin before the child reaches 4 years of age. The idea was planted that early education would benefit mentally deficient children, and though it grew slowly, it now dominates the field.

At the turn of the century, then, there were at least two opposing lines of thought, one recommending institutionalization and the other stressing nonresidential special classes. Despite the notoriety given to the institutional movement it actually was not very successful, though it seems to have occupied an inordinate amount of discussion time. At any given time in the United States there have been no more than approximately five percent of all retarded persons in residential institutions, despite the continual growth of state and private facilities (Baumeister, 1970; Robinson & Robinson, 1976, p. 434; Scheerenberger, 1978; Tarjan, Wright, Eyman, & Keeran, 1973); and since 1967 there has been a sharp decrease in the number of retarded persons in public facilities (Lakin, Krantz, Bruininks, Clumpner, & Hill, 1982). Institutions have come increasingly to be populated by that relatively small segment of retarded persons who are very low in intelligence and who, having multiple problems, require almost constant attention as well as great patience and dedication (Sabagh & Windle, 1960; Scheerenberger, 1978; Tarjan, Dingman, & Miller, 1960).[4] A proportion of

[4]Certainly the deterioration of care in a number of State facilities is a betrayal of trust that requires public outcry, along with public outlay, but when residential facilities are properly run it is not for us self-righteously to dictate the course to be taken by families already burdened with guilt, or to deprive them of an opportunity to make an informed choice.

mildly retarded children are institutionalized because they are orphans or for other reasons are wards of the state, or because they have severe behavior problems and/or come from very inadequate or destructive home environments.

From 1900 through 1906 the contents of the *Journal of Psycho-Asthenics* featured papers on etiology, diagnosis, classification, treatment, and education, particularly education in special classes. Occasional experimental studies were reported, but the issues of permanent custody, sterilization, and moral imbecility continued to stir the most debate.

One particularly illuminating item, a translation of a paper by Kellar (1905), expressed bemusement at the American practice of grouping moral defectives, including those who have no intellectual deficiency, under the rubric of "feeble-mindedness." He pointed out that unless Europeans realized that this was the general practice in America, they could not understand the achievements of the "feeble-minded" reported by Americans, nor the legitimacy of the treatment and management "so zealously discussed at the annual meetings of the chiefs of the institutions" (p. 128). In Europe and Scandinavia, surprise "amounting almost to indignation" greeted the American request for information on asexualization. They simply did not respond. Kellar was "inclined to believe that when the American feeble-minded institution defines 'feeble-mindedness' the same as the old world does and turns away the morally, but not intellectually, defective the whole question of asexualization will drop" (p. 129).

There were others, including members of the Association of Medical Officers, who were concerned with the trend. Murdoch (1906) gave this assessment, in which one can feel the powerful effect that group concensus played in restraining his dissenting opinion.

> I, personally, feel that the pendulum is swung too far towards the custodial care of feeble-minded children. The original work among the feeble-minded was education, with the idea of sending them out into the world. Lately we are talking a great deal of permanent custody of feeble-minded children. I think we have gone just a little bit too far in that direction and the tendency will be to go more on those border-line cases and give a few more of those children a chance, and if, as Dr. Fernald said, after one trial, or possibly two trials, they are not capable of adjusting themselves in society, we will find it out. (p. 215)

At that same meeting, Keating (1906) was more forthright.

> I remember meeting Dr. Fernald in New York, in 1898. He was a strong advocate at that time, if I remember correctly, of the permanent care of the feeble-minded. I was rather surprised, but agreeably so, to find he had changed his views considerably. When I first started this work, ten years ago, I had very strong views on the matter but I have also modified them. I am

> opposed to any children being committed to an institution except those who have been convicted of some criminal act. In Maryland none of the children are committed. (p. 216)

These two quotations were from particularly fascinating discussions during the Association's thirteenth annual meeting (published in the June 1906 issue of the *Journal of Psycho-Asthenics*), discussions that epitomized the concerns of the participants. When Miss Gundry commented that there are differences between persons who are simply backward and those who are feeble-minded and consequently should be in institutions, she was challenged on how many of these backward children she thought could be cared for in public schools. Questions were raised concerning the moral and legal implications of permanent care, and doubts were expressed about moral imbeciles being classified as feeble-minded. Fernald did not want to be misunderstood (referring, no doubt, to Keating's reference to him), and proclaimed before all that he believed that life-long care is necessary for the great majority of feeble-minded persons; but nevertheless, he went on, a small percentage of border-line cases, some of whom are "so-called" moral imbeciles, must have an opportunity for legal revision of what amounted to life sentences that were in any case unconstitutional. But in the end, the president of the Association, G. Mogridge, summed up the discussion by saying that although there were differences in viewpoints, there would be general agreement that only a small percentage of children in institutions should not be there. "The class that we want to keep are what we call the high-grade imbeciles, the fairly capable imbeciles, who are, however, imbeciles and always will be such and if there is reproduction, the issue will be imbecile, so that I do not think that we differ very much" (p. 220); hardly the conclusion that an unbiased observer would have reached.

The concerns of the Association members, as expressed in their papers and discussions, changed little over the next few years, although there was some increase in the application of the methods of experimental psychology to the study of mental retardation. The issues of heredity and moral imbecility continued to build, and it is ironic that Goddard, who in a few years was to bring these issues to a head with his Kallikak study, here proclaimed that "imbecility may be hereditary, but the moral part is a question of environment" (Goddard, 1909a, p. 38). Even more prescient was his allusion, in another context, to the fact that "our experience with these Binet tests is on the whole encouraging. They do indicate the grade of the child with surprising accuracy" (Goddard, 1909b, p. 52). The intelligence test, developed in France in 1905 by Alfred Binet and Théodore Simon, had reached the United States and was to play a major role in the question of the immutability of retarded intelligence.

4 Intelligence Tests and the Heritability and Immutability of Mental Retardation

The development of intelligence tests and of the concepts of intelligence quotient (IQ) and mental age (MA) are too well known to require detailed exposition here (e.g., Goodenough 1949a). The impact on the field of mental retardation was enormous. In 1924, Fernald commented that "The theory and practice of mental testing and the discovery of the *concept of mental age* did more to explain feeble-mindedness, to simplify its diagnosis and to furnish accurate data for training and education, than all the previous study and research from the time of Séguin" (p. 209). It was in the field of mental retardation that intelligence testing flourished in its early years before being applied to individuals of higher intellectual levels.

Goddard and Kuhlmann were instrumental in calling the Binet–Simon intelligence scale to the attention of American psychologists.[1] In 1906 Goddard had become the first director of the laboratory for the psychological study of mentally defective children at the Training School in Vineland, New Jersey, and 2 years later was still searching for some way to study the retarded residents. In 1908, in the hope of assimilating some new ideas, he made a 2-month trip to Europe where the educator, Ovide Decroly, called his attention to an article by Binet in *L'Année Psychologique.* Very shortly after his return, Goddard (1908) published a brief description of the first Binet-Simon test, but it was a subsequent article by Binet and Simon, describing their revision of the 1905 test, that eventually turned Goddard

[1]I am using *test* and *scale* interchangeably but *scale* is the more accurate term for an assessment measure made up of a number of items so that individuals can be ordered and compared. The original Binet–Simon was composed of 30 items, ranging from easy to difficult.

into a disciple. For the first time the tests were grouped according to the age at which they were commonly passed; the age level at which no more than one test was failed became the child's "mental age."[2] In recalling that period, Goddard wrote that he laid the article aside with the mental comment that there was nothing in it because it was "impossible to measure intelligence in any such way" (Goddard, 1943, p. 155). However, he later reread the article and published it in English.[3] Using this revised scale he tested 378 residents at the Vineland School and related their mental ages to three levels of retardation (idiot, imbecile, and moron) and to the levels of work they could perform. Additionally, his five assistants tested about 2,000 nonretarded children in the Vineland public schools (Goddard, 1910a, 1910b, 1911). Kuhlmann (1911, 1912a, 1912b, 1914a) published an extended translation and an early revision, and analyzed the scores of 1,006 retarded children and 1,000 public school children. Developed and initially used for the assessment of mentally deficient children, intelligence testing spread rapidly to the assessment of average and superior children, spurred particularly by the work of Lewis Terman at Stanford University.[4]

The attraction was obvious. Here at last was a single standardized assessment instrument that gave a good indication of a child's mental level when compared with other children, as indexed by performance on a variety of mentally challenging tasks. At each age, children's scores distributed themselves around the mean so as to produce an acceptable approximation of a normal, bell-shaped curve. The test predicted scholastic achievement with some accuracy; that is, within a reasonable margin of error. The Binet-Simon scales were flawed, as Kuhlmann (1912c) pointed out in a detailed review, and over the years numerous revisions, restandardizations, and mathematical manipulations have been made in order to improve the instrument (e.g., Fisher & Zeaman, 1970; McNemar, 1942; Pinneau, 1961; Roberts & Mellone, 1952; Terman & Merrill, 1973). In addition to the revisions and adaptations of the Binet-Simon scale, there

[2]William Stern (1912/1914, pp. 36–42) in Germany and Kuhlmann (1913) in the United States suggested that the ratio of mental age to chronological age would be a useful measure of retardation or acceleration, and this ratio began to be used even before it was incorporated by Lewis Terman in his 1916 revision of the Binet-Simon scale where, when multiplied by 100, the ratio was referred to as the intelligence quotient.

[3]The translations were primarily by Elizabeth Kite, Goddard's assistant. Originally published in 1910, this and other relevant translated papers by Binet and Simon were collected and published by The Training School at Vineland, and have since been reprinted (see Binet & Simon, 1916/1975). For insightful studies not directly related to the intelligence scale, see Binet and Simon (1916).

[4]For an international bibliography of the early papers related to the Binet-Simon scale, see Kohs (1914), who provided an annotated list of 254 references.

was a proliferation of both individual and group intelligence tests (Anastasi, 1976).

Binet believed in inherited differences, but also that faculties could be enhanced by training, up to a point. "Progress [in learning] is ruled by a law of remarkable fixity; the ordinarily great progress at the beginning diminishes . . . [until] the moment arrives when it becomes practically equal to zero." This limit "varies according to the persons and the functions under consideration" (cited by Wolf, 1973, p. 207). "An imbecile even of twenty years cannot read, and can never learn to read" (Binet & Simon, 1908, 1909/1916, p. 133).

Yet Binet's position was vague enough to allow a wide range of interpretations. To enhance the intelligence of retarded children, Binet advocated "mental orthopedics," a series of exercises aimed at getting children to improve their ability to listen, remember, judge, and develop a stronger will and desire to succeed (Wolf, 1973, p. 207). Believing that intelligence, like the structure of his test, was composed of a number of faculties, including attention, discrimination, observation, memory, reasoning, abstraction, and so on, it followed for Binet that in training children to improve their attention and memory by recalling an increasing number of briefly exposed objects, or their will power by standing completely still when told to "freeze," and so on, he was actually making them more intelligent. His statement (see Wolf, p. 207) that a strong will is a key to all education is a curious one considering that he and Simon had mercilessly attacked Séguin for "the extraordinary idea that idiocy depends on a weakness of the will" (Binet & Simon, 1905/1916/1975, p. 24).

There were (and are) unjustified claims from some defenders of the tests. Individual IQs were reified, particularly by those who did not understand test construction and the amount of error that accompanies any test score. Occasional large score fluctuations are not unusual. The person who administers the test must be trained, and sensitive to any behavior by the testee that might invalidate the results. Moreover, test scores cannot be valid when the test-takers are far less familiar than was the standardization sample with the language or, in some instances, with the material being used. The IQ is based on inference: It is assumed that brighter children will be more curious and alert, and will learn more quickly, and consequently that during their life they will pick up more information than will duller children. It is also assumed that they will adapt better and perform more efficiently when faced with novel mental challenges. But when opportunities for the satisfaction of intellectual drives have been restricted, or where there have been unusual depriving circumstances, the validity of a test result is suspect. It is this possibility that has sustained the belief that many persons scoring in the retarded range on intelligence tests are victims of unequal opportunity and actually have inherent mental capacities well above the retarded range. Furthermore, there are those who point out that we have no satisfactory theory or definition of intelligence, and that consequently these scales are misnamed (e.g., Block & Dworkin, 1976).

Despite their flaws (or some would say because of them), standardized individual intelligence tests became the *bete noire* of those who claimed to have special techniques for curing mental deficiency. No longer was it good enough simply to give anecdotal impressions that retarded intelligence had been appreciably raised, for now there was an objective instrument that provided some safeguard from biased subjective judgments. Interestingly, when Binet published his 1911 revision—one of his last papers before his untimely death—he included an experiment demonstrating the inadequacy of teachers' judgments of intelligence (in Binet & Simon, 1916/1975).

It is certainly true that if there are special methods that help retarded individuals to adjust better, to learn certain skills and to hold a job, the question of intellectual change is of little relevance and consequently intelligence scales are superfluous. But for those interested in the nature and malleability of retarded intelligence, these scales have proved essential and will remain so until they are replaced by better measures. A return to subjective judgment would only be a step backward.

INTELLIGENCE TESTS

We must digress here to examine some aspects of intelligence testing that are crucial to any discussion of intellectual change. If intelligence scales are to be used as an important gauge of whether or not intelligence has been raised, then we must know something about their stability, or test-retest reliability, over a period of years. The best measure of stability of the IQ is the correlation coefficient, which tells us how consistently individuals maintain their relative position on the normal curve. A high correlation, however, doesn't necessarily mean that the actual score will remain the same, or nearly the same; it tells us only that individuals will maintain their positions *relative* to other individuals in the same sample. For the tendency of a score to remain *absolutely* the same we will use the term *constancy.* It is possible in some rare instance for a test to be very stable (high test-retest correlation, or relative stability) but mask large changes in absolute IQ, as when a group of infants with hypothyroidism is treated and all their IQs rise, but without changing the relative positions of the individuals comprising the sample (Fishler, Graliker, & Koch, 1965); or when correlations between two different tests are high even though one test produces higher IQs than the other because of differences in standardization samples (Flynn, 1984; Spitz, 1983). These examples illustrate the desirability of obtaining measures of IQ constancy (absolute scores) as well as of IQ stability (correlation coefficients).

Both the stability and constancy of IQs are influenced by a test's standard error of measurement. Because tests are not perfectly reliable (not perfectly consistent within themselves), a certain amount of change in IQ score for any individual taking the test a second time is to be expected. Furthermore, the error of measurement is about twice as high for individual IQs in the average range (90–109 IQ) as for IQ scores below 70 (Terman & Merrill, 1937). This means that persons scoring below 70 IQ are less likely to show large retest variability than are persons in the average range because, as we shall see, reliability of an intelligence test is inversely related to level of intelligence, and the reliability of a test, along with the test's standard deviation, determines its standard error of measurement.[5]

The importance of understanding the error of measurement is illustrated in the following example. Assume that the standard error of measurement of an intelligence scale is 5 points for a sample of children within the IQ range of 60 to 69. If a child's IQ is 65 on the scale we can estimate with 68% confidence that this child's "true" score lies between 60 and 70, and with 95% confidence that the "true" score lies between 55 and 75. Note that if 100 individuals are retested, it can be expected that some will vary in IQ by quite substantial amounts. Indeed, this is almost always the case. The amount of change itself approximates a normal curve, with most members of retarded groups changing in IQ by no more than 5 or 6 IQ points, and gradually fewer members of the groups showing large decreases or large increases in IQ when retested. This fact is such an important one that the evidence for it is presented later in this section.

There are a number of other variables that contribute to the inconstancy of the IQ, some of which are inherent in the tests and have nothing to do with changes in the individual. For example, on Form L of the 1937 Stanford–Binet the standard deviations (SDs) of the normative samples were not the same at every age level (Terman & Merrill, 1937). At 12 years of age the SD was 20 compared to an SD of 12.5 at 6 years of age. This means that an individual who scored 1 SD below the mean at age 6, and also when retested at age 12, would nevertheless decrease in IQ from about 88 to about 80. Although these and other defects in the Binet have been corrected (in the 1960 revision the standard score, or deviation IQ, replaced the ratio IQ, and the mental growth level was raised from 16 to 18 years), they must be kept in mind when evaluating past studies of the stability and constancy of retarded IQs.

---

[5]The formula for the standard error of measurement is $SD\sqrt{1-r}$, where SD is the standard deviation of the test scores of a group, and r is the reliability coefficient for that group or a similar group.

One other statistical concept should be mentioned: "regression toward the mean," which is related to the imperfect reliability of the tests. When a member of a particular group—a school district, say, or a particular age group—has an initial test score that is much higher (or much lower) than the mean of the group, his or her retest score is very likely to be closer to the mean score of the group; that is, it will "regress" toward the mean, because fortuitous factors that produced the extreme score on the first test are unlikely to recur on the second (e.g., Clarke, Clarke, & Brown, 1959; Furby, 1973). Of course this also means that a person close to the mean on first testing could "egress" from the mean on second testing. But note that mental, like physical, growth fluctuates more in the early years and tends to stabilize at later ages, so that extreme deviations are more likely to occur on early than on later testing. This concept turns up in many discussions of studies claiming to raise intelligence.

Before we look at the literature on the IQ stability of retarded groups, a word should be said about the copious evidence on nonretarded groups (e.g., Bayley, 1970; Bloom, 1964). The findings are so consistent that they have become established principles. The first principle is that infant tests (actually, developmental scales) up to about 2 years of age are inadequate predictors of intelligence scores at later ages. One of the reasons frequently given for this is that infant tests measure primarily motor and sensory abilities that have little to do with the verbal, memory, and conceptual abilities that are measured in childhood and adulthood. (For descriptions and discussions of infant tests, see Lewis, 1976.) There have been repeated attempts to rectify this situation and some hope has been raised that measures of infant attention, novelty preference, and visual recognition memory will improve the predictive power of infant tests (Fagan, 1984a, 1984b; Fagan & McGrath, 1981; Fantz & Nevis, 1967; Lewis & Brooks-Gunn, 1981). Such measures might also lead to fewer misdiagnoses of cognitive impairment that can result when mentally competent but physically handicapped infants are measured by sensorimotor tests (Kearsley, 1981).

A second principle of intelligence test stability is that, with age of initial testing taken into account, the longer the retest interval the lower the test-retest correlation. A third principle is that the stability of the IQ increases with increasing maturity (but not into old age). And finally, the lower the intelligence the higher the retest correlation in all of the above circumstances. It is this last principle that is of interest here. Once the Binet Scale was recognized as a useful tool for the diagnosis and study of mental deficiency, the flood of stability studies began and it has not yet abated, in large part because retarded individuals both within and outside of institutions are so frequently tested that no special effort need be made to collect the IQ data. But retest data on average and above average groups have also been collected.

Some idea of the longitudinal test–retest correlations for nonretarded groups can be gleaned from a number of studies and reviews (Bayley, 1949; Bloom, 1964; Bradway, Thompson, & Cravens, 1958; Honzik, 1976; McCall, Hogarty, & Hurlburt, 1972; Sontag, Baker, & Nelson, 1958), from which I have compiled the range of test–retest correlations given in Table 1. All ages and correlations are approximate, and sex differences have been ignored. A number of different infant tests were used, with the Binet Scales predominating in childhood and adulthood. Although there were occasional deviations from these ranges of correlations, they encompass most of the data.

Table 1 shows why it has been concluded that infant tests do not adequately predict adult intelligence scales, but many of these correlations were obtained from groups made up of individuals in a limited range of IQ at the average or above average level. When groups include a more representative selection of subjects from the intelligence curve, the test–retest correlations are somewhat higher. For example, McRae (1955) compared five ratings (from superior to mentally deficient) based on tests given prior to 3 years of age and again at 9 years of age, and obtained a test–retest correlation of .65. The retest correlation with initial tests given before the age of 1 was a reliable .56. Similarly, Werner, Honzik, and Smith (1968) reported a retest correlation of .49 for 639 children initially tested at about 20 months and retested at about 10 years. For 39 children who had scored below 80 IQ at 20 months, the correlation rose to .71. Similar findings have been reported by Knobloch and Pasamanick (1963, 1967).

TABLE 1.
General range of test-retest correlations of nonretarded groups

Age at First Test	*Age at Retest*	*Correlation*
1 to 3 mo	1.5 yr	00
4 to 6 mo	3 yr	00 to .10s
1 yr	5 to 18 yr	.10s to .30s
1 to 1.5 yr	5 to 7 yr	.30s
1 yr	3 yr	.40s
2 yr	8 to 10 yr	.20s to .50s
3 to 4 yr	12 to 30 yr	.40s to .60s
5 to 8 yr	12 to 18 yr	.50s to .80s
11 to 15 yr	18 to 30 yr	.70s to .90s

In general, then, not only are higher correlations found when samples have a more representative range of intelligence, but the test–retest correlations of retarded groups are appreciably higher than are those of nonretarded groups. Results of a survey of 14 publications that provided correlations and in which the Binet Scale was used—along with, where appropriate, infant scales—are presented in Table 2.[6] For the early years, the groups were composed of noninstitutionalized infants and children, while all but two of the groups contributing to the three oldest ranges were composed of institutionalized individuals.

Comparison with the data from nonretarded groups shows that during the early years the correlations for retarded groups are much higher than the correlations for nonretarded groups, and this difference persists until the later years when ceiling effects impose a restriction on the emergence of differences between the two groups. Although infant tests are not adequate measures of later IQ in restricted nonretarded samples, they are fairly good predictors for retarded samples.

A number of Binet retest studies did not supply correlations but did supply data on absolute changes in IQ. Table 3 gives the data from 11 studies that supplied some or all of the relevant information for groups of low intelligence. In every instance the majority of subjects changed no more than 5 IQ points on the second testing. A small percentage of subjects changed more than 10 IQ points, and as the test–retest interval increased

TABLE 2.
General range of test–retest correlations of retarded groups

Age at First Test	*Age at Retest*	*Correlation*
6 mo	5 to 6 yr	.50s
1 yr	5 to 6 yr	.50s to .70s
1 to 2 yr	6 to 10 yr	.60s to .70s
1 yr	3 to 4 yr	.60s to .80s
7 to 9 yr	9 to 16 yr	.60s
11 to 14 yr	14 to 18 yr	.70s to .90s
15 to 34 yr	Over 40 yr	.80s to .90s

[6]Studies from which Table 2 data were drawn are: Allen, 1942; Birch, 1955; Drillien, 1961; Erikson, 1968; Fisher, 1962; Fishler, Graliker, & Koch, 1965; Knobloch & Pasamanick, 1967; Rushton & Stockwin, 1963; Share, Koch, Webb, & Graliker, 1964; Silverstein, 1982; Spaulding, 1946; Walker & Gross, 1970; Werner, Honzik, & Smith, 1968. For a brief review of test–retest correlations using the Wechsler Scales, see Spitz (1983).

(going from the upper to the lower section of the Table), the percentage of subjects changing more than 10 IQ points also increased. The Engel (1937) study is out of line with the others, and is extraordinary in that almost all the subjects who changed more than 10 IQ points showed a drop in IQ, despite the fact that the sample was not drawn from a residential facility.

Additional studies providing somewhat different data could fit nicely into Table 3. Chipman (1929), for 1,751 retarded residents over a range of years, found that 79% changed less than 5 IQ points; 72% of Stott's (1960) nonresidential group changed less than 10 points over retest intervals of 1 to more than 3 years; 98% of Earhart and Warren's (1964) residential students changed by less than 15 points over a period of 37 to 39 years, 81% changed by less than 12 points and all but one remained in the 20 to 59 IQ range; and Walker and Gross (1970) reported that after about 3 years, 55% of their 29 nonresidential subjects changed by less than 5 points, 86% by less than 10 points, and none by more than 14 points.

The IQ fluctuations of retarded groups are dependent in varying degrees

TABLE 3.
Binet IQ Changes of Retarded Groups for Varying Retest Intervals

	% of Groups Changing by Various Amounts							
Study	*< 6*	*6–10*	*11–15*	*> 15*	*> 10*	*Average Interval (yr)*	*Average CA Range (yr)*	*Institutionalized*
Kuhlmann, 1921	93	6	1	0	1	1	7 to 20	Yes
Minogue, 1926	72	19	5	4	9	1	life span	Yes
Scarr, 1953	82	17	1	0	1	1	6 to 14	Some
Collmann & Newlyn, 1959	89	11	0	0	0	1	6 to 14	Most
Silverstein, 1982	—	—	—	—	8	1	10 to 14	No
Berry, 1923 (50–69 IQs only)	60	33	6	1	7	1 to 3	6 to 14	No
Elwood, 1952	63	26	10	1	11	2	5 to 8	No
Poull, 1921	64	23	11	2	13	.5 to 3	4 to 28	Yes
Spaulding, 1946	51	32	11	6	17	4	14 to 18	Yes
Engel, 1937	—	—	—	—	29*	5	10 to 16	No
Hoakley, 1932	59	26	10	5	15	.5 to 12	4 to 28	Yes

*Of 79 subjects who changed more than 10 IQ points, all but 5 decreased.

on the ages of the subjects, degree of retardation, diagnostic category, institutional status, duration of retest interval, and the tests that are used. There is evidence suggesting that, based on the Binet Scale, mentally deficient groups decline in IQ until early to mid-adolescence, after which the more mildly retarded show an increase in IQ (Chipman, 1929; Collmann & Newlyn, 1958; Engel, 1937; Fisher & Zeaman, 1970; Hoakley, 1932; Rheingold & Perce, 1939; Rushton & Stockwin, 1963; Scarr, 1953; Woodall, 1931). For the more mildly retarded individuals this increase continues into their late 30s, a longer mental growth period than for nonretarded individuals. Fisher and Zeaman (1970) derived a correction factor for these fluctuations that can be used in place of the IQ to provide a more nearly constant score for retarded individuals from childhood across the entire life span.

There have been occasional reports of extreme changes. Arthur (1933) mentioned one young subject whose IQ went from 63 to 111, and she suggests that this can happen when young children have delayed speech. Roberts (1945) mentions two individuals each of whom gained 26 points (one in 10 months!) and he suggests that instances of large IQ gains can result when some persons entering an institution are in the midst of crisis and care little about the intelligence test. When retested later, however, they realize that good performance will influence decisions about their release and consequently they attend to the test. Large losses in IQ also occur, of course, particularly when there is progressive neurological deterioration.

There are a number of reasons, then, why some individual IQs shift dramatically: (a) Children grow mentally at different rates, just as they grow physically at different rates; a child in a lag period on first testing and in a spurt period on second testing would show a rise in IQ; (b) Trauma, disease, and malnutrition can cause progressive mental deterioration, just as therapeutic intervention can raise mental functioning; (c) An individual taking a test may be ill, poorly motivated, rebellious, or emotionally upset (presumably the trained tester will be alert to these possibilities); (d) When the same test is repeated after a short interval there are some practice effects, and merely taking tests a number of times can improve performance—however, changes are unlikely to be very large; (e) There may be extreme changes in an individual's life, such as a change from an environment in which there is practically no stimulation to one in which there is adequate or superior stimulation. Children raised in extreme isolation, such as in darkened rooms or closets, and subsequently removed to healthier environments exemplify this condition. Infants who lie untouched in their cribs for long hours over weeks and months also will not develop normally, but when transferred to a more natural environment they will usually show improved intellectual performance. There are varying degrees and forms of impoverishment and maternal deprivation occurring at varying ages and for different lengths of time, and the extent to which these variables affect the degree and permanency of mental retardation are matters of intense study (e.g., Ainsworth, 1966; Clarke & Clarke, 1976). (The question of whether infants and young children who receive ample stimulation will test in the retarded range when it is not the "right kind" of stimulation is discussed in a later section.) (f) Finally, there are all the imperfections of the measuring instruments, some of which have already been discussed. These include the test's standard error of measurement, the fact that there are different items and different standardization samples at different ages and on different tests, and so on. One glaring example has been mentioned: the Wechsler Adult Intelligence Scale IQs of retarded individuals are, on the average, 12 to 14 points higher than their IQs on the Wechsler Children's Intelligence Scales; they are also higher than their IQs on the Stanford-Binet Scales, particularly at older age levels (Fisher, 1962; Flynn, 1985, Spitz, 1983).

As noted in (c), attitude can affect test scores. A mean IQ of 82 obtained by eight children on Form A of the Peabody Picture Vocabulary Test was raised to 97 on Form B merely by giving candy rewards for each correct response (although the gain was due entirely to six of the eight children), whereas children who had average or above average IQs on Form A were unaffected by the same procedure (Clingman & Fowler, 1976). But the results of many studies have not resolved the issues concerning the effect of reinforcement on IQ scores. Apparently the effect is complexly related to a number of variables, including the subjects' age, race, IQ level, and socio-economic status, as well as the test used, the reward given, and the reinforcement schedule followed. The effect may even occur primarily on the Verbal rather than the Performance Scale of the Wechsler (Johnson, Bradley-Johnson, McCarthy, & Jamie, 1984). In one series of studies Breuning and his coworkers reported that, when reinforced, children with a mean IQ of around 80 gained as much as 18 IQ points relative to a control group (reviewed in Matson & Breuning, 1983, pp. 100–102). However, low IQ children showed no reinforcement effect if they were receiving certain therapeutic drugs. These findings raise intriguing questions not only about the variables associated with children's desire to perform well on intelligence tests, but also about the negative effects some therapeutic drugs may have on some children's intellectual performance.

In summary, then, a number of important points must be considered when evaluating claims that intelligence can be taught and mental deficiency cured. When any group of retarded individuals is retested after a period of years, *some* members of the group will gain (and some will lose) as much as 10 to 15 points, and, if the group is large enough and composed of mildly and moderately retarded persons, one or two will gain (and one or two will lose) as much as 20 or more IQ points. This will occur even when there is no claim for a unique training method. Consequently, when supporters of some special treatment program claim that they can raise retarded intelligence, and support their claim by descriptions of selected individuals whose IQs have sharply increased, the knowledgeable observer will find this evidence unconvincing. The only acceptable evidence that some method has raised retarded IQ is a demonstration that the mean IQ of a group of retarded persons rises reliably higher than that of an appropriately constituted and treated control group, and the tester should be unaware of the membership of the persons being tested. Continued assessment will determine the durability of the effect. Anecdotal and single subject evidence are unacceptable, for we know that even though the test-retest mean IQs of groups of retarded persons tend to remain constant over time, there are always upward and downward shifts in the IQs of individual members of the group.

Of course this also shows the high probability that some individuals, initially labeled as retarded on the basis of an IQ test, will score in the low average or average range on some future test. The probability of an appreciable change in a group's mean IQ is very much smaller than the probability of an appreciable change in the IQs of some individual members of the group. While this should temper undue finality in predicting the immutability of retardation for any single individual, it does not call for undue optimism, because it is impossible as yet to predict with certainty which individuals will be the ones to change.

HERITABILITY AND IMMUTABILITY OF MENTAL RETARDATION

Shortly after the introduction of the Binet, growing interest in intelligence tests coalesced with the continued interest in moral imbecility, eugenics, and the immutability and heritability of retarded intelligence. The stability of the IQ reinforced the pessimism that permeated the Association. In a paper presented to the Association's 1912 meeting, Fernald (1913a) stated unequivocally that "The fact that feeble-mindedness is the result of pathological conditions of the brain . . . makes it obvious that the resulting defect is incurable and permanent" (p. 88). In this address alone he reiterated his belief in the hereditary nature of mental deficiency—including the fact that although "Acquired characteristics are not likely to be transmitted, . . . alcoholism, syphilis, tuberculosis and other environmental factors may initiate germinal variation which may become hereditary" (p. 89)—noted that "feeble-mindedness is the mother of crime, pauperism and degeneracy" (p. 92), and recommended segregation and surgical sterilization. When, at that same meeting, Goddard (1913) announced that on the basis of repeated testing on the Binet Scale it was evident that the vast majority of feeble-minded children were not changing or improving, Fernald (1913b) gloomily agreed. "What Dr. Goddard has just told us," he said, "is the most significant, in a way, and the most discouraging statement that we have ever known. I am afraid it is true" (p. 127). Kuhlmann (1913), on the other hand, was more conservative, pointing out that a child's MA gave only a high probability of future MA and was not an infallible predictor.

Of course time often changes our view of things. It is extraordinary to read the statements of Fernald and Goddard many years later. In his 1924 presidential address, Fernald (1924) talked about the "legend of the feeble-minded" which "conveyed the impression that [they] were almost all of the highly hereditary class; . . . invariably immoral, . . . nearly all were antisocial, vicious and criminal; . . . idle and shiftless" (p. 211), a legend that flourished because "the only known large group of defectives of that period . . . *had* got into trouble and *were* in institutions, . . . *were* largely of the hereditary class and *had* behaved badly and *were* shiftless and lazy" (p. 212, his italics). Well-behaved retarded persons from good homes had been ignored. Yet he did not challenge the immutability of retardation, and in fact pointed out that it was modern diagnostic methods that had uncovered the far larger percentage of defectives living and adjusting at home and in the community. As he concluded his paper, he remarked that its optimistic tone was "a natural reaction from the period of pessimism through which we have passed." Most retarded persons, "seven-eighths of the iceberg," were not degenerates and consequently the iceberg "seems less gloomy and terrifying and even has certain graceful outlines" (p. 219).

Goddard (1928) in later years was swayed by the fact that at the upper level of mental retardation some adults who had MAs between 8 and 12 years (the "moron" level) adjusted perfectly well in the world while others did not, and he concluded that this was because of differences in personality that could be changed by education and training. Consequently, even though intelligence remained unchanged, in this sense morons *could be cured* and most of them need not be segregated in institutions nor denied marriage and parenthood. Only those with MAs of 7 years and below required permanent segregation and custodial care, and should be labeled mentally deficient or feeble-minded.[7]

Though Goddard changed his mind about the relationship between retardation and delinquency, he was firm in the belief that mental deficiency was to a large extent a genetic disorder, a trait that was transmitted

[7]It is interesting that the years between about 7 to 8 and 11 to 12 correspond to Piaget's concrete operations stage, while the years thereafter correspond to his formal operations stage. In Piagetian terminology, Goddard was suggesting that retarded adults in the preoperational stages require care and custody.

in an hereditary manner. In 1912 and 1914 he published two books, the first a small monograph describing the history of the Kallikak family (a fictitious name), the second a lengthy treatise charting the pedigrees of 327 residents at the Vineland Training School. The Kallikak family was, for him, only a single, though especially interesting, example of hereditary retardation, while a greater variety of cases was given in his 1914 book, which he prized more highly as a scientific contribution.

But it was the Kallikak study that captured the greater interest. In tracing the ancestry of Deborah Kallikak—who had entered the Training School at Vineland in 1898 at 8 years of age and was 20 when the study began—Goddard and his assistants were surprised at the "appalling amount of defectiveness [that] was everywhere found" (1912/1973, p. 16). At the same time they were perplexed that the field workers increasingly encountered good families bearing the Kallikak name. Concluding that there must be two branches from a single stock, they eventually tied together the scattered evidence. They knew that Deborah's great-great-grandfather was Martin Kallikak, and it turned out that Martin's father, Martin Kallikak, Sr., had impregnated a "feeble-minded" girl while he was a soldier during the revolution. The child from this union, Martin Kallikak, Jr., had 480 descendants of whom, according to Goddard, 143 were feeble-minded, 46 were normal, and the rest unknown or doubtful. These descendants married into other families, resulting in the charting of 1,146 individuals, of whom 262 were feeble-minded, 196 normal, and the rest undetermined.

After leaving the revolutionary army, Martin Sr. married a "respectable girl of good family," producing a lineage of 496 descendants, all of whom, according to Goddard, were of normal intelligence, although three were "somewhat degenerate." The descendants of this "good" line married into the best families, whose members were doctors, lawyers, judges, educators, and so on.[8]

Goddard (1912/1973) presented the pedigree charts of both lines of descent and concluded that the large number of feeble-minded descendants of Martin Jr., when compared with the absence of feeble-mindedness in the descendants of his half-brothers and half-sisters, proved conclusively that heredity and not environment was the root of the problem. He did mention, however, that a few children who were descendants of the bad side had been adopted by good families and were not feeble-minded (pp. 61–62). But in these cases he raised the possibility of misdiagnosis, and

[8]The name Kallikak was derived by joining the Greek words for beauty or good (*kallos*) and for bad (*kakos*). Deborah Kallikak died in 1978. For a brief description of her life, first in the private and then in the state institution in Vineland, see Doll (1983). Gould (1981) points out that in Goddard's book three photographs of members of the "bad" line had been touched up "to give eyes and mouths their diabolical appearance" (p. 171). Who did the retouching is unknown.

pointed out that in still other instances similarly adopted children were nevertheless feeble-minded.

Goddard's books, initially well received, were attacked in 1925 by Myerson, who expressed in biting sarcasm his envy of the remarkable ability of Goddard and his field workers to diagnose feeble-mindedness merely by observation and hearsay, and even more remarkably to diagnose the intelligence of Martin Kallikak, Jr.'s paramour and their long-dead descendants. Strange too, he wrote, how exceptionally free of taint the good line of descendants was. Scheinfeld (1939) later pointed out that no single dominant gene could produce such complex degeneracy (or even feeble-mindedness) as displayed by the bad Kallikak line, and therefore recessive genes from both parents had to be involved. Consequently, Martin Kallikak, Sr. had to be a carrier and some of these "bad" genes would have been passed to the good line of descent.

Replying to his critics, Goddard (1942) noted some of their factual errors and defended his group's field method of diagnosing feeble-mindedness. Furthermore, he wrote, "the Binet tests were extensively used . . . in both studies" (p. 575). He agreed that Martin Sr. must have been a "simplex" (instances in which the only allele of a pair is located on the X chromosome of the male), but dismissed this as an argument because a trait may remain recessive for generations so long as possessors do not mate with "duplexes."

At about the same time that Goddard was publishing his results, another even larger study was under way. In 1910, under the direction of A.C. Rogers, superintendent of the State School and Colony at Faribault, Minnesota, and Charles B. Davenport, director of the Eugenics Records Office at Cold Spring Harbor, New York, a project was begun whose monumental goal was to study the families of all the patients in the institution. Supported by a special appropriation from the Minnesota legislature, two trained workers from the Eugenics Records Office started in 1911 to collect information on the Faribault institutions's residents and their families, including their grandparents, parents, siblings, spouses, aunts, uncles, first cousins, and sometimes children, nieces, and nephews. Whenever possible, the newly developed intelligence test was administered by Maud Merrill and Frederick Kuhlmann, among others. Unfortunately, shortly after Rogers died in 1917, the project ended and the data were left unpublished.

The project was reopened in 1949 by Elizabeth and Sheldon Reed, of the University of Minnesota, who obtained the data on 549 residents at Faribault and their families that had originally been collected during that 1911 to 1918 period. Reed and Reed decided to include in their study only the probands (original patients) who had no history of epilepsy prior to institutionalization, and whose IQ was no higher than 69. This left 289 probands. They then began the long search for all known descendants of the grandparents of those 289 residents, a search that ended more than a dozen years later with information on over 80,000 persons.

The results should be of interest to anyone who is curious about the etiology of mental retardation. Included in their book (Reed & Reed, 1965) are pedigree charts for the descendants of the grandparents of 289 probands, 84 of whom are classified in the primarily genetic category, 55 as probably genetic, 27 as primarily environmental, and 123 as of unknown causes.[9] Based on their data, the authors are convinced that in a very large number of cases mental retardation is hereditary. One of their major conclusions is that the presence of retardation in one or more relatives is the greatest predisposing factor for the appearance of mental retardation in the person concerned. Consequently, they suggest that voluntary sterilization of retarded individuals would decrease by 50% the number of retarded persons in each generation.

Determining the role of heredity in transmitting mental deficiency continues to be an important goal of geneticists. It has recently been suggested, with some corroborating evidence, that because mental retardation is more frequent in males than in females, some percentage of nonspecific retardation is transmitted as an X-linked recessive (Lehrke, 1974), an hypothesis related to one proposed in 1931 by Rosanoff.[10]

Since 1956, when human chromosomes were first clearly observed and counted, the number of chromosomal abnormalities found to produce mental retardation has increased at a phenomenal rate. In 1958, the extra chromosome in Down's syndrome was discovered. In 1969, the fragile X syndrome was first described, and with subsequent improvements in the laboratory techniques used to search for a fragile X chromosome, it soon became evident that this syndrome rivals Down's syndrome as a genetic cause of mental retardation (Hagerman & McBogg, 1983). Identification of the fragile X syndrome was a most significant development

[9]Genetic retardation is not necessarily hereditary; Down's syndrome, for example, is a genetically determined disorder (an extra chromosome) that is not hereditary. A familial trait is also not necessarily hereditary; syphilis, for example, may run in families but it is not transmitted via the genes. The question of whether or not the vast majority of retarded individuals—those in the 50 to 70 IQ range—fall at the lower end of the normal intelligence curve because of polygenic inheritance is still being debated (Gottesman, 1971). For a short review of the genetic etiology of some forms of mental retardation and the probability of having one or more retarded offspring, see Lubs and Maes (1977).

[10]Of course over the years there have been many studies attempting to link heredity and mental deficiency, a number of which have been cited by Scheerenberger (1983). Note that Scheerenberger quotes Punnett's (1917) calculations that by preventing retarded persons from mating it would take 8,000 years to eradicate mental deficiency, but he fails to cite Fisher's (1924) commentary on the inaccuracy of Punnett's derivation, in particular Punnett's incorrect assumption of random mating.

because affected individuals usually do not have obvious physical pathologies prior to puberty. The Mendelian law for X-linked disorders such as the fragile X syndrome is that the mother is the carrier and, on the average, there is a 50% risk that her son will be affected and that her daughter will be a carrier. In the fragile X syndrome, carriers can also be affected, however.

The search for hereditary transmission of limited intelligence and of disorders limiting intelligence always stirs up the empiricist-rationalist, nature-nurture controversy. The response of empiricists has been that the majority of retarded persons in the 50 to 70 IQ range—that level of retardation often referred to in recent years as "cultural-familial" retardation—are mentally defective not because of the transmission of defective genes, or genes for low intelligence, but rather because they have been raised in such poor environments that intelligent behavior cannot develop.

Myerson (1930) foresaw this argument. He went even further in suggesting the possibility that environmental injury to the germ-plasm could manifest itself for one or more generations, and furthermore that there might be certain environmental conditions that would prevent the manifestation of hereditary diseases. In his 1930 paper he proposed the following experiment.

> There is room for a great experiment which would repay society more than any number of studies of so-called feebleminded families. . . . Children of known defective groups, both parents being feebleminded, might be removed very early in life from the environment created for them by their parents. . . . If placed under the best environmental circumstances, it would not take more than ten years to discover whether or not they were destined to be feebleminded, and whether or not there was an upward rise in their intelligence as contrasted with that of their parents. (p. 224)

This "great experiment," or at least variants of it, has been carried out, not once but many times. In fact, in no other single area of psychology has so much money and effort been expended, and the voluminous literature it continues to generate must intimidate even the heartiest reviewer. Only a selected portion is reviewed here.

5 Early Intervention and Compensatory Education

THE IOWA STUDIES

In 1939 a psychologist, Harold Skeels, and the superintendent of the Glenwood, Iowa, Institution for Feebleminded Children, Harold Dye, presented to the Association a paper that, along with a number of other papers from the University of Iowa Child Welfare Research Station, challenged the concept of intelligence as a fixed, unmodifiable entity, and gave impetus to a movement that has continued to gain momentum (Skeels & Dye, 1939). The serendipitous event that impelled the study was their observation of two children, both under 17 months of age, and with IQs of 46 and 35, who had been transferred from an orphanage to an institution for the feebleminded, where they were placed in a ward with older retarded girls and women. When Skeels visited the ward 6 months later he was greatly surprised at the children's development. Retested on the Kuhlmann-Binet, they obtained IQs of 77 and 87, and at about 42 months had IQs of 95 and 93. Skeels and Dye attributed this improvement to the stimulation provided by the attendants and the residents of the ward, who grew attached to their young visitors and played with them constantly. When they were no longer classified as retarded, the two children were returned to the orphanage, where they maintained their average IQs.

Skeels and Dye then transferred 11 retarded children from the orphanage to the Glenwood Institution. These children, plus the 2 original transfers, become the experimental group. It consisted of 13 children (3 of them boys), ranging in age at the time of transfer from 7 to 30 months (mean = 19.4 mo), and in IQ from 35 to 89 (mean = 64; I have rounded off the IQs, and occasionally the ages). These young children were apportioned to four different wards, where they received the special attention of the staff and the retarded residents. Most of them were "adopted" by one adult who became particularly attached to the child.

There was no control group for this experiment, but when it was completed, 12 children (8 of them boys) who had remained in the orphanage were selected to act as a comparison group. At initial testing, this group ranged in age from 12 to 22 months (mean = 16.6 months), and in IQ from 50 to 103 (mean = 87). Note that the mean IQ of this group was reliably higher than the mean IQ of the experimental group, making it inadequate even as a "contrast" group. Even more curious is the fact that these subjects were part of the control group of a previous experiment (Skeels, Updegraff, Wellman, & Williams, 1938), and consequently the authors already knew that they had declined an average of 26 IQ points over an average of 31 months!

Nevertheless, the results for the experimental group were dramatic. After an average of only 9.5 months in institutional wards, the mean IQ rose to 90, and it remained close to that score (92) when the experiment ended.

On the surface, the results appear to be clear cut. Most children in the uninspiring atmosphere of the orphanage, who had been of average or close to average intelligence when first tested, declined in intelligence to the retarded level over the ensuing 2 years. On the other hand, other children from the same orphanage, initially of borderline or retarded intelligence, increased to average intelligence when placed in a more stimulating and attentive atmosphere. As usual, the results of this and related studies were trumpeted and glamorized in the popular press, and have been glowingly cited in education and psychology texts to the present day (see the critical comments of Goodenough, 1939; McNemar, 1940; and most recently Longstreth, 1981). We would be remiss if we did not carefully scrutinize this initial study before examining the studies that followed.

First it should be pointed out that there was no set time limit for the experiment. Children were transferred from time to time to the Glenwood Institution and were returned to the orphanage when they were considered no longer retarded. Six of the 13 were returned after an average of only 10 months. These six had a mean IQ of 73 prior to initial transfer, and of 98 at the time they were returned to the orphanage, a gain of 25 points after less than a year.

Two other children, with pre-transfer IQs of 77 and 57, had IQs of 96 and 94 after only 6 and 7 months stay in the wards of the institution, but nevertheless remained in the institution another 9 and 16.5 months, respectively (during which the latter child lost 17 of the 37 IQ points she had gained over the first 7 months). Of the remaining five children, two had pre-transfer IQs of 72 and 75, which rose, respectively, to 88 and 78 after 6 and 16 months, and which were 79 and 82 when they were returned to the orphanage another 16 and 18.5 months later.

From these figures it is clear that for most of the children the major increase in IQ was very rapid, occurring by 6 to 10 months after transfer. Indeed, there was no reliable correlation between duration of stay in the wards and size of IQ gain. Whatever force produced the rise in scores, it acted very quickly. We return to this point later.

The three remaining children, who had the lowest IQs when the experiment started, included the two original children, with IQs of 46 and 35, and a child with an IQ of 36. These three made by far the largest gains: from 46 to 77 only 6.5 months after transfer, and to 95 18 months later; from 35 to 87 after only 6 months, and to 93 after an additional 18 months; and from 36 to 70 after 15 months, and to 81 after 37 months in the wards of the Glenwood Institution.

Skeels and Dye provided some relevant background information on these three children. We are not told how long the two original children had been in the orphanage, but they were first tested at 13 and 16 months of age, so presumably they entered the orphanage at about those ages. Neither gave evidence of physiological or organic defects. Both were illegitimate. The mother of one was retarded (IQ = 56) and a legal guardian had been appointed. The mother of the second was a resident of a state hospital, diagnosed as psychosis with mental deficiency. The children were described by Skeels (1966, p. 5) as "pitiful little creatures [who were] emaciated, undersized, . . . and spent their days rocking and whining." Neglected by their mothers and ignored by their relatives, they were malnourished and frail. They were transferred to the institution when they were 15 and 18 months old. The third child, the oldest of both groups, was "committed to the orphanage at twenty-eight months of age and came from a home where extreme neglect was typical" (p. 119). These three children would appear to qualify for the category, mentioned in the previous chapter, in which a robust rise in IQ follows the change from an environment that is unusually depriving to one in which there is adequate stimulation.

But what about the other 10 children? Over an average period of 9.4 months their mean IQ rose an average of 22 points. Some of them, too, may have been from unusually deprived backgrounds prior to their placement in the orphanage, but we have no way of knowing. Three were premature. One had congenital syphilis but was treated, apparently successfully, following birth. Information about the others is not given, except that "the children of both experimental and contrast group came from homes of low social, economic, occupational, and intellectual levels" (p. 121).

Critics of this study repeatedly raise two related points to account for a major portion of the results. The first is the well-known unreliability of infant intelligence tests, and the second is the specter of regression effects, a statistical concept discussed in the previous chapter. Errors of measurement are of course larger, and regression effects more potent, when intelligence tests are given to children younger than 3 or 4 years old. In the Skeels and Dye study the mean IQ of the contrast group was reliably higher than it was in the experimental group, even without the three lowest experimental children. Because the 25 children were drawn from the same population, one would expect that retesting—even almost immediately—would bring the extreme scores closer to the total mean score of that particular sample; that is, would raise the scores of the lowest scoring children and lower the scores of the highest scoring children. Furthermore, the largest drop and the largest rise in IQ in the respective groups should occur on the first retesting. All these conditions were fulfilled by the Skeels and Dye data.

Additionally, from the data provided by Skeels and Dye, correlations of pre-transfer IQs with size of increase (or decrease) in final IQs are −.72 for the experimental group and −.76 for the contrast group. In general, then, in the experimental group the lower the initial IQ, the greater the IQ gain, while in the contrast group the higher the initial IQ, the greater the IQ loss, results that are consistent with regression effects.

One of the selection criteria for the 12 contrast children was that they had not been adopted by 4 years of age, despite the orphanage's policy to place children as soon as possible (Skeels, Updegraff, Wellman, & Williams, 1938). Consequently, questions of selection bias have been raised. Whereas the experimental children had been considered unsuitable for adoption because they were mentally retarded, there must have been some other reason why no one had adopted the contrast children, 9 of whom were considered of normal mental development and 10 of whom had IQs ranging from 81 to 103.

According to the authors, five of the contrast children were not placed because of poor family history. Two had congenital syphilis, one of whom was apparently treated successfully. One was premature, delivered by breach extraction, and presented early symptoms of intracranial hemorrhage, with subsequent convulsions that were later controlled. Two were not placed because of improper commitments, another because of "health problems," and only one because of mental retardation (Skeels, 1966). Whatever the physical and other problems suffered by most of these children, they were severe enough to prevent adoption, and no one really knows what effect they had on subsequent mental development (see Skeels, 1966, pp. 47–48).

Not only was the initial mean IQ of the contrast group much higher than that of the experimental group, it was also more than 20 points higher than the mean IQ of their natural mothers, which was not the case for the experimental children, whose scores were comparable to those of their mothers (where these data were available). Add to this the fact that the correlations between first and second testing for the contrast group was a nonsignificant .23, while the correlation between second and third testing was a reliable .76, and one must seriously entertain the very real probability that the initial scores obtained when the children were an average of only 16 months of age were simply unreliable (Longstreth, 1981).

In the contrast group, the duration of the period from initial to final retest ranged from 21 to 43 months, but the correlation of the length of time between tests and the size of the IQ decline was essentially zero ($r = -.06$). In other words, there was no relationship between length of time in the orphanage (over the duration of the experimental period) and decline in IQ, and consequently the orphanage environment could not by itself have been directly related to the size of IQ decline.

It also should be pointed out that the persons who tested the members of the two groups were aware of each individual's group membership, and unconscious examiner bias may have influenced the test results (Goodenough, 1939). Of course Skeels and Dye had not planned a tightly controlled experiment; they simply took advantage of a situation that was presented to them and that might not arise again. It was praiseworthy that they did so, but the fact that this uncontrolled study was subject to numerous artifacts must always be kept in mind.

Consider how quickly the change in environment affected the experimental children. The six who were retested after the least amount of time in the wards gained an average of 30 IQ points (with a range of 16 to 52 points) over a period of 6 to 7 months. This bears repeating. Six children placed in wards with older retarded females for an average of about 6 months went from a mean IQ of 63 to a mean IQ of 93, a rise in IQ that was based on initial tests given when five of the six were less than 17 months of age. Presumably the retarded residents of the wards were too old, or for other reasons could not themselves benefit from the fast acting therapy they were dispensing.

Skeels followed the fortunes of the children in the two groups. After 2.5 years the mean IQ of the experimental group rose another 4 points, with some wide fluctuations (Skeels, 1942). Four children gained 10, 13, 13, and 16 points, and one child lost 17 points. Eleven of these experimental children had been adopted.

The contrast group gained an additional 6 IQ points, also with wide variability. Four children gained 17, 22, 24, and 26 IQ points, and two children lost 11 and 19 points. Two children had been transferred to the Glenwood State School when they were 41 months old, and at the end of 34 months one had lost 4 points while the other had gained 24 points, was returned to the orphanage, and then sent to an institution for the mentally retarded, where she died at age 15. Six others had been transferred to an institution for epileptic and feebleminded persons. Three others had remained in the orphanage and attended public school, and one of these children, who had spent a year in preschool, gained 22 points (it was discovered that he had a hearing loss and he was transferred to a residential school for the deaf). The final child was placed with his grandparents.

Skeels suggested that the wide IQ fluctuations and variability were related to particular environmental changes. Whatever the reason, the standard deviations (variability) of the IQs of the experimental group were 16.4 and 16.7 on initial testing and follow-up, respectively, while for the contrast group these standard deviations were 13.9 and 16.5. Obviously the environmental experiences did not have a leveling effect on the members of either group.

Another follow-up was started about 20 years later (Skeels, 1966). Using great determination and persistence, the field investigators located all 24 living members of the original study. No intelligence tests were given. All 13 members of the experimental group were doing well. Eight of the 10 women were married and had previously worked as a nurse, a teacher, beauty operator, clerical worker, and so on. The two women who had never been adopted worked as a domestic and a nurse's aide.

Members of the contrast group, on the other hand, were not doing well. The three remaining women were unmarried; one was in an institution for the mentally retarded (she had had congenital syphilis as an infant), one was discharged from a similar institution at age 26 and was a dishwasher, and the third (who had been a breech delivery with second stage of labor slightly complicated) was a part-time cafeteria worker. Of the eight contrast men, six never married and one had been divorced. Three were institutional residents, two were dishwashers, one was an institutional gardener's assistant, and one was a drifter. The one successful contrast subject (the one in whom a hearing loss had been discovered) was a compositor and typesetter who was married and had four children. The mean education level for this group was 3.95, compared to a mean of 11.68 for the experimental group.

As previously noted, this study had a powerful impact on subsequent theory and practice in the area of mental retardation research. But there have been critics, Goodenough (1939) and Longstreth (1981) in particular. Jensen (1969) attributed the results to recovery from extreme sensory and motor restriction. Clarke and Clarke (1976, Chapter 12) argued that the relatively brief experience in the institutional wards was probably of little long-term relevance except as it initiated differences between the groups, "thus providing the belief that the experimental children would not grow up to be mentally retarded" (p. 218). They attributed the success of the experimental group to their placement in good homes, and the failure of the contrast group to their continuation in unstimulating environments.

Conclusions 4 and 5, given by Skeels in his 1942 paper, sum up his estimate of the comprehensive significance of this study.

4. A change from marked mental retardation to normal intelligence in children of preschool age is possible in the absence of organic disease or clinical deficiency by providing a more adequate psychological prescription.
5. Conversely, children of normal intelligence may become mentally retarded to such a degree as to require permanent institutionalization under the continued adverse influence of a non-stimulating environment. (pp. 349–350)

One can agree with conclusion 5 if it is assumed that "non-stimulating environment" refers to conditions that are extremely adverse. An infant placed in such an environment very early in life cannot develop normally, and only a dramatic improvement in the environment will allow the child's native ability to express itself. Numerous instances of this phenomenon have been documented (e.g., Clarke & Clarke, 1976).

But conclusion 4 is a general statement that is not necessarily the counterpart of conclusion 5. It is an unqualified statement that in the absence of organic damage or disease, mental retardation can be cured. It states that functional retardation is a result of poor environment and consequently will be alleviated by an improved environment, in this case a relatively short stay in the wards of an institution for retarded persons.

It is astonishing that these conclusions were drawn, and continue to be drawn, on the basis of data from 25 children, especially considering the numerous flaws in the experimental design and execution of this study, and the peculiar composition of the contrast group. A careful consideration of the data, and indeed of much related data, suggests the important but well-known and even obvious fact that extreme deprivation (mental, physical, and nutritional) of an infant will produce retarded behavior, and that in these instances an improved environment will "cure" the mental deficiency. Generalizations beyond this fact are unwarranted because of the unreliability of the tests given to children as young as those in the Skeels and Dye study. But the major fallacy has been in the extrapolation of the effects of extreme deprivation to mental deficiency generally, and particularly to instances in which there has been no unusual or extreme deprivation. It is this logical fallacy that has led to hundreds of studies, and to false hopes and additional disappointments for those who believed that mental deficiency could be cured by placing retarded persons, or infants at risk for mental retardation, in more stimulating environments.

How frequently do children suffer from unusual and extreme deprivation, and how are these conditions to be defined? How do varying degrees of deprivation interact with the child's innate potential? These and a number of other questions remain to be answered, yet it does seem that the kind of appalling neglect that leaves an infant listless and apathetic cannot be responsible for even one percent of the incidence of mental retardation. This appears to be recognized by environmentalists who now claim that development can be retarded not only by extreme lack of stimulation but also by the wrong kind: by mothers not talking enough to infants, not saying the right things, not providing the right toys, not providing books to children, and so on. The Skeels and Dye study as well as other studies from the Iowa group have been generalized in this way, and these generalizations have been translated into an avalanche of studies and claims that overwhelm and impress by the sheer weight of their number. But no one should accept these claims without intensive examination of the studies, one by one, in minute detail. A scrutiny of a few of the studies will be surprisingly rewarding.

The study from which Skeels and Dye drew their contrast group was a preschool project reported by Skeels, Updegraff, Wellman, and Williams (1938) in which a group of orphanage children who spent several hours a day in a preschool were compared with a control group of orphanage children who were not in the preschool program. At the start of the 3-year project the groups were approximately matched on CA, IQ, sex, nutritional status, and duration in the orphanage.

The changing composition of the groups makes it difficult to extract the data on which the final statistics were based. For example, the 23 children who were added to the preschool group 5 or more months after the project started had a mean IQ of 91, compared to the mean IQ of 83 for 21 children added to the control group (McNemar, 1940). Although at one time or another there were a total of 59 children in the preschool program, only 35 were enrolled in the preschool program for .5 to 2.5 years, and according to the authors these 35 children represented the primary experimental group. Nevertheless, after excluding 10 children who attended preschool less than 6 weeks, and 1 who was not tested at the correct period, the initial mean IQ of 48 experimental children was given (86.6), along with their mean CA (3.5 years.)

The total control group numbered 53 children, but the initial mean IQ (82.1) and mean CA (3.5 years) were given for 48 of them, excluding 4 who were in residence less than 6 weeks and 1 who was not tested at the proper time.

The authors partitioned their results into IQ levels and into three lengths of duration in residence: 1–199 days, 200–399 days, and 400 or more days. The resulting IQ changes for 46 experimental and 44 control children were presented in tables, but the number of *cases* totaled more than 200 in each group because each child could contribute to different interval comparisons. For example, if a child was a long-term resident and was tested and retested four times, his or her IQ scores could contribute to as many as six comparisons (first and second tests, first and third, second and third, etc.).

McNemar (1940) questioned the statistical appropriateness of this method of inflating *N*s, and from the original data determined—for the three residence intervals and for each child—the mean IQ change from initial to final testing. Based on his recalculations the short-, medium-, and long-residence experimental groups dropped 2 IQ points, rose 5 points, and rose 3 points, respectively. The control group rose 4 points, rose 2 points, and dropped 6 points, respectively.

In their reply to McNemar (1940), Wellman, Skeels, and Skodak (1940) pointed out that their 11 long-resident control children with initial IQs of 80 or above lost a mean of 16 IQ points, while their 11 long-resident experimental children of similar initial mean IQ lost only a mean of 2 IQ points. On the other hand, for 10 experimental and 11 control children whose IQs were initially below 80, and who were in residence 400 days or longer, the experimental group gained 8 IQ points compared to the control group's gain of 4 IQ points (neither gain being statistically reliable). In sum, the mean IQ of the brighter experimental children dropped considerably less than did the mean IQ of the brighter control children, while the mean IQ of the duller experimental children rose slightly higher than did their controls. The major effect of the preschool program was in preventing a drop in IQ, not in raising the IQ, but a portion of the result can be ascribed to regression effects: under either condition the initially brighter children *lost* IQ points, and the initially duller children *gained* IQ points.

We might interject here a reminder that 10 of the 12 contrast children in the Skeels and Dye (1939) study had initial IQs higher than 80, and since those children were also part of the control group in the Skeels et al. (1938) study, it is they who account for most of the differences between the control and experimental groups in the latter study. We have already discussed the characteristics of those children, in particular their ages at initial testing and the evidence for central nervous system pathology. Few psychologists are aware of the fact that these 10 to 12 children made so large a contribution to the results of two of the most influential studies in the history of the study of intelligence.

A third series of papers from the Iowa Child Welfare Research Station traced the mental growth of children from "poor stock" who, at an early age or younger, 154 were available for retesting and made up the experimental group. Intelligence test scores were available for 80 of the true age or younger, 154 were available for retesting and comprised the experimental group. Intelligence test scores were available for 80 of the true mothers (mean IQ = 88, SD = 16), and Skodak provided much additional information on both the true and foster parents. For 144 true mothers, mean school grade completed was 9.9 years, but according to the author most of these women did poorly in school. The mean grade completed by 88 of the true fathers was 10.2 (although some of them were still in school). Most of the true mothers and fathers were in lower level occupations. One-hundred-and-forty of the infants were illegitimate.

The foster parents presented a more promising picture, their homes being described as "above average" and "superior." Their mean educational level was twelfth grade and the foster fathers were generally more highly skilled and successful than the true fathers, or indeed than males in the general population.

After they had been in their foster homes at least a year, and when their median age was 1 year, 7 months, the foster children's mean IQ was 116. Two-and-a-half years later, it had dropped to 111.5. As Skodak (1938) indicated, these means compared favorably with those of children from the highest socioeconomic families. However, the decrease in IQ was a reliable one, due primarily to a drop in the scores of the initially highest IQ infants, another example of the pervasive effects of regression toward the mean. Later in her monograph, Skodak's data described a direct relationship between the initial IQ and the direction of change: the lower the initial IQ the larger the increase, while the higher the initial IQ the greater the decrease.

In later tests the mean IQ continued to drop, and for 17 children still available at age 6 it was 108. As with many early intervention studies, the initial impact on IQ scores appears to have been very large, but it decreased over time. In Skodak's study, the unreliability of testing in infancy, along with regression artifacts, apparently contributed to this phenomenon; after its initial impact, continued stay in a beneficial environment resulted in a reduction rather than an increase in IQ scores. Skodak attributed this reduction to children in the foster homes that were "inferior" relative to the other foster homes (p. 82), but elsewhere (p. 63) she emphasized that "inferior" here was relative, and that all the foster homes were above average.

Skodak (1939) summarized her findings in 18 statements, starting with the assertion that the high mental levels obtained by the foster children were above the mean for the population as a whole and were above expectations based on the mental level of their true parents. She buttressed these findings by pointing out that children who had been placed in foster homes where fathers were in the higher occupational categories had, at older ages, higher IQs than did the remaining children, which of course suggests the delicate influence of environmental forces. In the remaining statements she described her other findings. Her overall conclusion was that the strong, well-known relationship of the IQs of parents and children was "very largely the result of environmental impacts on the child" (p. 131), that the hereditary limits on mental development were extremely broad, and that "environmental factors can . . . produce changes which for ordinary purposes may represent a shift from one extreme to another of the present distribution of intelligence among children" (p. 132). (Almost 30 years later, she wrote that "the influence of environmental experiences can be so great as to cover the range from profound mental defect to intellectual giftedness" [Skodak, 1968, p. 17.]) Her viewpoint, along with that of most of her Iowa colleagues, was straightforward: They supported the radical empiricist philosophy that the environment is responsible for creating the normal curve of intelligence, and that, consequently, profound retardation (where there is no central nervous system pathology) as well as intellectual giftedness are the result of variations in environmental stimulation. Little wonder that these studies aroused such heated debate.

Immediate criticism of the Iowa studies came from a number of sources; McNemar's critique, already alluded to, is perhaps the best known. Concerning Skodak's (1939) foster placement study, he questioned whether the true parents were in fact inferior to the general population. Based on his analysis, they were not, and consequently the mean IQ eventually reached by the foster children was not beyond the range to be expected from the probable mental level of their genetic parents. He also leveled charges of selective placement.

The intrusive bias of selective placement is certainly evident in the Skodak study. The children whose true fathers were in the three upper occupational brackets had mean IQs that were higher than the mean IQs of the other children. Skodak accounted for this by noting that for those rare children from superior parentage "an effort was made to place the child in the best home available" (p. 82). She was aware that this type of selective placement would bias her results, but she minimized its effects, and ignored it completely when she emphasized that children placed in superior foster homes had higher IQs than those placed in foster homes that were not quite so good, attributing the results to the different levels of stimulation in the foster homes.

Further evidence of selective placement was provided by the relationship between the mean occupational classification of the foster parents and the mean IQ of the true mothers. Based on Skodak's data, McNemar (1940) found a correlation of .35 between true mother's IQ and foster father's occupational status. Four children with IQs averaging about 72 were placed in homes where fathers had the two lowest occupational classifications, whereas 18 children with an average IQ of 96 were placed in homes where fathers had next to the highest occupational classification. Also, true mothers' educational level was about 10.6 for 52 children placed in homes where foster fathers had the two highest occupational levels. Finally, the correlation between the mid-parent educational level of the true and foster parents was .30. In sum, there was more than a little evidence of selective placement, enough certainly to question any conclusion that it was the differential characteristics of the foster homes that created differences in mental development.

In their reply, Wellman et al. (1940) reiterated that the true parents were neither intellectually, educationally, nor occupationally average, and were certainly below the level of the foster parents in their attainments. They pointed out that unmarried mothers from average or somewhat below average socioeconomic levels frequently place their children privately, not through public agencies; and they noted that selective placement, where it occurred, was inconsistent and variable and could not entirely account for the high correlation between the children's final IQs and the characteristics of the foster homes.

They also admonished McNemar for ignoring the section on children placed in foster homes at older ages. In that section of her study, Skodak followed 65 children who represented the upper levels of the orphanage population (mentally retarded children, remember, were not placed in foster homes). Twelve of these children were illegitimate, and all 65 came from broken homes. Although they were not orphans, they had spent from 2 to 3 years in an orphanage. Age of foster home placement ranged from 2 years to 5.5 years (mean = 3.6 years).

In general, their true parents' characteristics and attainments were inferior even when compared with the true parents of the children in the early placement study. Also, their foster mothers and fathers had a mean grade level of 10.7 and 9.7, respectively, levels that were appreciably lower than those of the foster parents in the younger infant placement study. But no matter; these children reached a similar mental level as the children in the early placement study. Whereas at mean age 3.4 their mean preplacement IQ was 98.5, after at least 1 year in foster homes their mean IQ rose to 104, a reliable increase. For 24 of the children given two postplacement tests, mean IQs rose from a preplacement level of 98 to postplacement levels of 102 at mean age 4.8 years, and 108 at 6.8 years of age. This compares with a mean increase of only 1 IQ point for 20 children given two tests while still in the orphanage, but no ages or retest intervals for this "control" group were supplied.

Unfortunately, selective placement also occurred in this study, with brighter children tending to be placed in superior foster homes; and, again, there was some regression toward the mean, with size of IQ increase being inversely proportional to initial IQ level ($r = -.36$). Consequently, lower IQ children placed in relatively inferior foster homes gained the most, a result that is difficult to understand if one assumes a direct relationship between foster home environment and foster children's mental level. Skodak concluded that even when a good foster home placement is made at later ages, children can gain in intelligence.

In an ancillary study particularly germane for this volume, Skodak (1938) described how, from the 154 children in the foster placement study, she selected 16 adopted children whose true mothers were known to be retarded (mean IQ = 66). The educational level of the true parents was lower than that of the total group, but was available for only 7 of the fathers. For 10 of the true fathers where information on occupational level was available, it was also lower than that of the total group.

The results were similar to those of the larger study. Following a year in the foster home, when the 16 children averaged 2.5 years of age, their mean IQ was 116.4. At 4.3 years of age, it had dropped to 107.6. But very important from Skodak's viewpoint was the finding that the eight children placed in homes having the three highest occupational classifications scored 5 IQ points higher on the first examination, and 8.5 points higher on the second examination, than did the eight children placed in homes classified at the four lowest occupational levels, despite the fact that the true mothers of the former group had a lower mean IQ than did the true mothers of the latter group. These findings led Skodak to suggest that for physically normal infants, the intelligence level of the genetic mother should have no influence on placement of the child because children of retarded mothers will be indistinguishable from children of nonretarded mothers.

In reviewing Skodak's (1939) study, Barbara Burks (1939) made some interesting comments about the entire study and in particular about the subgroup of 16 children. She reminded the reader that in order to be placed, children from the orphanage had to be judged physically normal and in good health, and that before they were legally adopted they were required to spend a year's probationary period in the foster home. Consequently, *only the most promising children would be adopted.* She noted also that at the time of the first test the subgroup of 16 children were about 5 months older than the rest of the children, raising the possibility that they underwent a longer, more precautionary probationary period, and she suggested that precautions may have been more rigorous for those placed in the better homes. Furthermore, on the first test (given after the probationary period), the eight children in the upper level foster homes had a mean age of 3.4 years, or 1.7 years older than the eight children placed in the homes with lower occupational level (see Skodak, 1939, Table 12), giving the higher status parents more opportunity to sift out unpromising children.

Burks made some other astute observations about the Skodak (1939) study, including the fact that the Kuhlmann-Binet yields IQs that are too high, by 3 to 6 points, in the 2- to 4-year-old age range, and even higher under 2 years of age; and the 1916 Stanford-Binet also gives scores that are somewhat too high at the preschool level. This would account for the decrease in IQs, which paralleled the decrease in the Kuhlmann age norms.

Consequently, the more accurate mean IQ of Skodak's sample would be about 7 points above average, in agreement with studies of school-age foster children. On the other hand, the 1916 Stanford-Binet produces adult IQs that are too low when CA 16 years is used to obtain the IQ (MA/CA × 100), a situation that was remedied in the 1937 revision. If this was true, the mean IQ of the true mothers would have been closer to 100 and more comparable with their grade levels (unless they were simply promoted to higher grades because of physical maturity, as Skodak maintained).

Early reactions to the Iowa studies were expressed in many of the papers of the Thirty-Ninth Yearbook of the National Society for the Study of Education (Whipple, 1940), the most revealing single source for understanding the temper of the times and the deep wounds the nature-nurture issue inflicted on psychology. The second section of this two-volume publication contained descriptions and summaries of original studies on the stability of intelligence tests, studies of familial (genetic) and environmental influences on intelligence and achievement, reviews by Skeels and Wellman, studies of retarded and gifted children, and nine studies of the effects of nursery school attendance on intelligence, eight of which were unable to replicate the Iowa findings.

In addition to a section on the physiology of intelligence, the first volume contained reviews and commentaries of the nature-nurture question, including two chapters by Goodenough. In one of these she discussed the interpretive errors that can result from inadequate understanding of test measurement. In the other she critically reviewed a number of studies, reiterated the known facts that infant tests cannot predict later intelligence and that scores are not fixed, and admonished the environmentalists for their extreme claims. Also included in this section of the Yearbook were chapters by Wellman, and by Stoddard and Wellman, defining and defending the environmental position and replying to their critics. The child, they wrote, "is a flexible, changeable, responding organism within wide limits set by heredity and other organic conditions, and within other wide limits set by environmental stimulations and opportunities" (p. 431). What crucially separated the two camps was the width of these limits.

In Terman's comments (also in Whipple, 1940, Part I), there is one curious paragraph (on p. 462) describing how he requested and received the original data of the Iowa orphanage preschool project (Skeels et al., 1938), and by his calculations found that the average IQ change from first to last test was +1.8 for the preschool group and −1.3 for the control group. This is a startling statement, undermining the entire study, but of course there is no way to verify it. On the whole, he made clear his belief that the limits on intellectual change set by heredity were much narrower than were perceived by the Iowa group, except in instances of children reared in isolation or, as he put it, reared "by some kind of robot that provided the necessary care to keep [the child] alive and healthy" (p. 467). Though Terman's comments do not match McNemar's in the acidity of their sarcasm, they were sardonic enough, as the following passage illustrates.

> It happens that the Yearbook contains another contribution on the IQ effects of association with the feebleminded (XXI, Part II). There we find reported a mean IQ of 100 for children who had lived less than two years with their feebleminded mothers, and a mean of only 52 for those who had remained with their defective mothers to the age of 12 years. The difference is 47 points. If we add this 47-point drop caused by association with defective mothers to the Skeels-Dye 28-point increase caused by association with moron nursemaids, we get 75 IQ points as a measure of the difference in intellectual stimulus value between these two classes of defective females. This may not seem to make sense, but it is at least an interesting wonderland that the environmentalists have opened to us. (p. 464)

What bemused Terman was the fact that Speer, in Part II of the Yearbook, had reported that children raised by retarded mothers gradually *lose* intelligence, while Skeels and Dye had reported that retarded orphanage children quickly *gain* intelligence when transferred to a ward for retarded women.

Goodenough and Maurer (1940) observed that improved rapport and lessened anxiety on second testing will shift mean scores upward somewhat, counteracting the downward regression toward the mean in the initially higher scoring children and resulting in little change. On the other hand, the initially lower IQ children will increase even more on second testing because the regression and rapport effects both act in the same direction, upward. These effects had been attributed by the Iowa group entirely to environmental stimulation. In their own study, Goodenough and Maurer found that not only did children in the University of Minnesota nursery school increase in IQ, but so also did a control group of children who had not attended nursery school, a result they ascribed to practice in taking the test. Furthermore, the children from superior home backgrounds made slightly greater gains than the remaining children because, according to the authors, improved rapport increased the validity of the second test. Regression effects were evident even for the control children, leading to the conclusion that "The Iowa statistical laboratory has played a far greater part in affecting the 'intelligence' of children than has the Iowa nursery school" (p. 511).

Skodak and Skeels (1945, 1949) continued to follow the children from the early adoption study. In 1945, they reported that 139 of the children had a mean IQ of 113 when they were about 7 years old, based on follow-up tests administered by the authors. The previously reported IQ differences between children placed in homes classified in the upper three occupational levels, compared with children placed in homes classified at the lower four levels, all but disappeared by age 7; the result, according to the authors, of the sudden stimulating effect that attending school had on the children from the lower level homes, in contrast to the school's leveling influence on the children from the superior homes.

A most interesting aspect of the follow-up was the emergence of an increasingly higher correlation of the foster children's IQ with their true mothers' IQs. Skodak and Skeels stressed that these correlations throw no light on the important finding that these adopted children's mean IQ was 26 points higher than that of their true mothers. It was in this study, also, that a mean IQ of 83 was reported for 12 of the true fathers.

In the final follow-up (Skodak & Skeels, 1949), 100 of the adopted children were still available; at mean age 13.5 years their average IQ was 107 on the 1916 Stanford-Binet. (On the 1937 Stanford-Binet, which had not been used previously, it was 117.) There is no doubt, then, that most of these adopted children maintained their average or above average mental level.

There are three series of correlations in the final follow-up study that are of special interest. They are given in Table 4.

The eight highest correlations of children's IQs with true mothers' IQs and educational levels are all statistically reliable. As the children matured there was an increasing relationship between their mental levels and the intellectual characteristics of their true mothers, but not with the intellec-

TABLE 4
Correlations Given in the Skodak and Skeels (1949) Follow-up Study

Adopted Children's IQ	*Foster Mothers' Education*	*True Mothers' Education*	*True Mothers' IQ*
At 2.2 yrs.	−.03	.04	.00
At. 4.3 yrs.	.04	.31	.28
At 7.0 yrs.	.10	.37	.35
At 13.5 yrs. (1916 S-B)	.04	.31	.38
At 13.5 yrs. (1937 S-B)	.02	.32	.44

tual characteristics of their foster mothers.[1] The foster fathers' educational levels, not given here, were also unrelated to the children's IQs (ranging from .00 to .06).

The comparison of the mean IQs of children placed in homes rated in the upper three, as opposed to the lower four, occupational categories took a different course with these children than it did with the sample of children analyzed in the 1945 follow-up. If we look only at ages where there were at least 20 in each of the two groups, we find the following: a difference of 4 IQ points at age 1 in favor of the children placed in the upper level occupational homes, a difference of 1 IQ point at age 6 in favor of the children in the lower level adoptive homes, and differences of 2 points and 1 point in favor of children in the upper level homes when they reached ages 12 and 13. Concerning these negative results, Skodak and Skeels observed that the cultural opportunities and intellectual stimulation did not always directly reflect the occupational classification of the families, an observation that was quite different from their previous explanation implicating the differential stimulating and leveling influence of the schools. They concluded that although the results "show persistent slight differences in favor of homes in the upper three categories" (p. 106), they would not attempt a detailed analysis of the results because the number of cases was small.

When the dust had settled, there were two major findings from the early adoption study: (a) the adopted children's mean IQ was much higher than their true mothers' mean IQ, and (b) the children's latest IQs correlated moderately with their true mothers' IQs and educational levels, but were unrelated to the foster parents' educational and occupational levels. Skodak and Skeels judged (a) to be the more important finding because it demonstrated that environmental effects can raise the IQ of children who they believe would have been limited to a borderline or retarded intellectual level. This interpretation, however, neglects some crucial facts. For one thing, in order to be adopted the young children had to pass a rigorous selection procedure set up by the agency to guard against the adoption of mentally retarded children. This procedure included psychological testing

[1]See Honzik (1957) for comparisons of these correlations with gradually emerging parent-child correlations of children reared by their own parents. Not given in Table 4 are the test-retest correlations, which were .54 for the first and second tests, .44 for the first and third tests, and .35 for the first and final tests (1916 Stanford-Binet). Where applicable, these correlations are compatible with those subsequently found for nonretarded groups by other investigators (see our Table 1, Chapter 4), and with the general principle that intelligence tests given at an early age, and separated by longer retest intervals, are not as good predictors of later scores as are tests given when the child is older and when retest intervals are shorter. Correlations between the second and fourth tests, and the third and fourth tests, were .58 and .71, respectively.

and consultation, physical exams, and at least a year's probation in the prospective home. Consequently, there was very little possibility that the children who were adopted would be mentally retarded. It is not especially surprising that there are many children who have average or above average intelligence even though their mothers have below average or even retarded intelligence, and it is even less surprising when the children are in some way *selected.*

The only objective way to judge the effects of early adoption would be to randomly place children either for adoption or for continued residence in the orphanage. For very good ethical and moral reasons, this could not be done in the Iowa studies. Consequently, the only controls available to the Iowa investigators were the children who were not adopted for a number of reasons, reasons that also made it highly probable that they would not develop normally.

Finding (b) raised difficulties for the environmentalist position, for it indicated that the intellectual and educational levels of the true mothers, who had not seen their children since shortly after birth, had some relationship to the IQs of the children when they were about 13 years old, while the educational and occupational levels of the foster parents were unrelated to the children's IQs.

In response, Skodak and Skeels turned once again to the children of mothers judged to be definitely mentally retarded. They turned also to an artifact they had previously minimized: selective placement. First, they showed that at the fourth testing the mean IQ of the 8 children of retarded mothers (mean IQ = 63) was 104, compared with a mean IQ of 129 for children whose parents were of average IQ or higher (mean IQ = 111). Why was there this 25-point discrepancy between the mean IQs of the two groups of children? The reason, according to the authors, is that the children of the higher IQ mothers had been placed in homes that Skodak and Skeels here described as superior in every way to the homes in which the lower IQ children had been placed, *despite the fact that there were no differences in the educational or occupational levels of the foster parents of the two groups.* They concluded, therefore, that the reliable correlations cannot be attributed to genetic determinants alone.

Despite the obvious difficulties and biases in the Iowa studies (see especially Munsinger's 1975 critique of these and other adoption studies), they have been cited repeatedly in many textbooks and journal articles as the source of solid evidence that early stimulation exerts an enduring effect on intelligence, and they are routinely introduced as a basis for studies of early intervention. Longstreth (1981) quotes some of these glowing references.

In his presidential address to the American Association on Mental Deficiency, Kuhlmann (1940) was apparently alluding to the Iowa studies when he gave this general assessment.

> More spectacular than this is the recent claim by a few psychologists that mental deficiency can after all be much improved and even cured by what is essentially special training. In the distant past this claim could not be supported by before and after results of intelligence tests. Now, however, we are presented with I.Q.'s that have changed forty points or more, claimed to be the result of no more than an improved home environment and special training. It would be of interest to have these investigators explain why they succeeded where Seguin and so many others doing a much more thorough job of special training and often in the best of home environments failed so dismally. It will undoubtedly take psychology several years to discover and fully explain that most of these results can be accounted for in four or five other ways than by assuming that any material real change in intelligence has taken place. (p. 19)

Among the studies Skodak and Skeels (1949) cited as evidence of the modifiability of intelligence was a study by Bernardine Schmidt. We now take a close look at that remarkable study.

THE CLAIMS OF BERNARDINE SCHMIDT

When I was in graduate school we heard a great deal about a study by Bernardine Schmidt (1946). Her doctoral dissertation was concerned with the educational, social, and vocational development of mentally retarded students, but data on changes in intelligence test scores were added for the publication of her study in *Psychological Monographs,* a prestigious journal of the American Psychological Association. A Prefatory Statement by Schmidt, two members of her committee, and the journal editor noted that because of the intense interest raised by a preliminary publication (in *School and Society,* 1945, *62,* 409–412), the study would be published despite the fact that the results were in sharp contrast to "conventional professional opinion" and provided an "element of controversy" that might have merited independent repetition prior to publication. Apparently part of this controversy stemmed from a letter that Lloyd M. Yepsen, the president of the American Association on Mental Deficiency, had written to the editor of *Psychological Monographs* alerting him to the fact that there were important questions being raised about whether Schmidt was "competent in the field of differential diagnosis," and noting the dangers of raising the hopes of parents of retarded children. The editor replied that, after considering the problem for nearly 2 years, the decision was made to publish the paper, and he called attention to the Prefatory Statement in Schmidt's monograph (see Yepsen's section of Nolan, Westfall, Stothers, Terman, Goodenough, Newland, & Yepsen, 1949).

Because the Schmidt study was published shortly after the initial reactions to the University of Iowa studies, and followed the landmark series of papers in the National Society for the Study of Education's Thirty-Ninth Yearbook, *Intelligence: Its Nature and Nurture* (Whipple, 1940), the debate over the elasticity of the IQ was then, as it is even now, in full swing. Schmidt's findings were so impressive that if they were valid there could be little question that intelligence was indeed extraordinarily flexible, and the Iowa studies would have been vindicated.

The subjects in Schmidt's study were 322 retarded boys and girls, 12 to 14 years of age, with IQs ranging from 27 to 69, who were in five special centers of the Chicago school system. The 254 children who were in three of the centers comprised the total experimental group. However, for purposes of statistical analysis, from this total a sub-group of 64 girls was used as a comparison group for the 68 girls in the remaining two centers who served as the "nonexperimental" group. The 64 were chosen so as to closely match the 68 controls in terms of CA, IQ, years of schooling, socioeconomic status, and academic achievement. There were two other control conditions, involving pairs of twins, which are not discussed here.

The duration of the study was 8 years. During years 1 to 3, students participated in either the experimental or nonexperimental schools, while years 4 to 8 consisted of a follow-up of the students' activities after they had left the school. A battery of tests was given at 18-month intervals to assess the students' progress, but this review is concerned only with the results of the Stanford–Binet intelligence test.

The method of training was as follows. First, case histories were developed for each child, on the basis of which an experimental educational program was planned. This program was then carried out by special education teachers in classes having pupil/teacher ratios of 19–28/1. The training program can only be described as unspectacular. The 254 experimental students were (a) taught personal hygiene and grooming, and given job responsibilities, (b) given academic training in reading, writing, spelling, and arithmetic, (c) given training to develop their "hand skills," such as sewing, carpentry, electrical repairs, cooking, housecleaning, and arts and crafts, and (d) provided with better work and study habits and experiences, along with the provision of occupational and vocational information and guidance. The curriculum emphasized a relaxed atmosphere, group planning and experience, social and vocational competence, and economic self-sufficiency. All this was planned and supervised by Schmidt, who described herself as the "head teacher." Presumably, the nonexperimental children received their usual special education instruction.

No doubt these teaching procedures and goals look familiar to the special education specialist now, as they must have then. But the results could hardly look familiar. For 254 children in the experimental group, after 18 months the mean IQ went from 52.1 to 65.1, and after another 18 months to a mean of 71.6. The gains did not stop there. At the fourth testing, the 254 subjects had a mean IQ of 79.1, by the fifth testing, 199 subjects still available had a mean of 82.7. At final testing at the end of the post-school period, the average Stanford-Binet IQ for the 109 students available for testing was 89.3, for a total IQ gain over the 7.5-year period of 37 points. In fact, according to Schmidt (although this isn't evident in her data) the mean overall gain for the entire group was 40.7 IQ points! By the end of the post-school period, 60% of the group was classified as at least of low-normal intelligence, 27% as dull normal, and only 7% as still retarded. Needless to say, startling gains were also made on many other tests, and in personal adjustment. The comparison of the sub-group of 64 experimental girls with the matched group of 68 controls was equally impressive. At the end of 5 years the experimental group went from a mean of 55.3 to a mean of 79.1, while the control group went from a mean of 60.0 to a mean of 56.4.

Is it any wonder that this study, published in the scholarly *Psychological Monographs,* caused such a stir, or that the *Reader's Digest* and *Woman's Home Companion* reported that at last the retarded could be changed into nonretarded persons (see Kirk, 1948a)? But disillusionment followed. Samuel Kirk, among others, found the results difficult to believe. In 1948 he published a critique of Schmidt's study. His main points were as follows.

1. Although Schmidt's subjects were said to be unselected (that is, she used all the students in the specified special centers), she reported their mean initial IQ to be about 50. However, according to the *Annual Report of the Superintendent,* the practice was to assign to ungraded classes children with IQs ranging between 50 and 75. In fact, from 1937 to 1940 (at the time of Schmidt's study), the average IQ for children referred to special classes in Chicago was 68 to 69. Why was the mean IQ of the unselected students in Schmidt's study so different from the mean IQ of all students in special classes? Kirk could not check on the individual IQs because Schmidt would not release the names of the students who participated in her study. Consequently, Kirk visited the Chicago school system and found that the mean IQ of the special class (not the special centers) which Schmidt taught was 69.

2. No one in the Chicago system knew that Schmidt had been a "head teacher" or that she had been supervising a number of classes. In fact, no "head teacher" was appointed for the special centers, and the teachers were surprised to hear that Schmidt had planned and supervised their work.

3. Schmidt reported that her subjects were initially reading at just

below the middle of the first grade level. Nevertheless, she administered the Bernreuter Personality Inventory, which requires a high school reading level.

There were a number of other discrepancies listed by Kirk, including disparities in the data, which I also found very confusing. One gets the feeling, after reading Kirk's paper, that Schmidt's study was largely a figment of her imagination, and Schmidt's (1948) reply does little to disabuse one of this notion.

In her reply, Schmidt claimed that: (a) there were four duplications of her program under way; (b) a number of studies in the literature prior to her own study had reported results that were not appreciably different from her own; (c) the records in the *Annual Reports* were unreliable and inconsistent and the teacher's record book (from which Kirk drew much of his data) did not reflect the actual placement of the children; (d) undocumented, oral statements cannot be trusted.

Except by vague references to the unreliability of the *Annual Report* and oral reports, she made no attempt to explain why the initial IQs of the students in her experiment were so much lower than the average for the special class students, nor why she claimed to be a "head teacher" who planned and supervised other teachers, nor, especially, how her subjects could have taken the Bernreuter Inventory. She defended the preservation of the privacy of her subjects, pleaded for responsibility in the conduct of such research, and urged replication.

Attempts were made to follow up the four duplications of her program. Of the four persons mentioned, three made statements (included in Nolan et al., 1949). One of these denied that he was doing a study. The second reported that in his study there were many indications of a "vast improvement" in the pupils, but there was no change in IQ. The third did "not have time to analyze the publications in order to make any statement regarding Bernadine [*sic*] Schmidt's publications" (p. 226). The fourth did not reply.

Concerning the Bernreuter, Schmidt later explained that since the children could not read it, she read it to them and recorded their answers [see Newland section in Nolan et al. (1949) as well as Schmidt's statement on p. 13 of her monograph that on tests designed for self-recording by students, such a deviation might be required]. This could easily have been checked, but apparently the tests were unavailable. Even if it were so, however, it is unlikely that her students could have understood the questions.

Goodenough (1949b), in a review of Schmidt's monograph, also remarked on the dearth of not only basic data but also of information concerning the means by which such remarkable improvements were accomplished, considering that the methods that *were* described were not particularly unusual. She was also disturbed by the plethora of arithmetical errors and discrepancies in the tables.

In volumes 14 and 15 of the *Journal of Exceptional Children,* Hill (1948), Kirk (1948b) (in a digest of his longer review), Nolan et al. (1949), and Stevens (1948) effectively applied the *coup de grace.*

The best estimate of the Bernardine Schmidt study is that it was largely, if not entirely, fraudulent and that in fact there was no miracle in Chicago.

BERNARDINE SCHMIDT REVISITED: THE CLAIMS OF MARVA COLLINS

Some 35 years after Bernardine Schmidt published her extraordinary findings, there emerged in Chicago a teacher whose claims were fully as remarkable, if not more so, as those made by Schmidt. Full page ads in the *Wall Street Journal* (April 24, 1980) and in *Newsweek* (April 28, 1980), paid for by the SmithKline Corporation, described the extraordinary success that Marva Collins has with "unteachable" grade school children from the poor section of the West Side of Chicago. In a slogan-filled statement, Collins tells of the work she does in her private Westside Preparatory School. Children do not fail, she writes, "educators" fail children. "Today the world beats a path to our door to gawk at the 'bright' and 'gifted' children who came from public schools a year ago labeled 'retarded,' 'troublesome' and 'disturbed'." They are transformed not by miracles, she goes on, but simply by love and determination. Also hard work, "heaping doses of student-teacher dialogue," drill, and daily reading and writing assignments. "Anything works if the teacher does," writes Marva Collins.

At ages 5 to 10 her students read and discuss the classics, and she tells them they are the brightest children in the whole world. The banal Dick and Jane books are useless, so she substitutes Tolstoy's *Fables and Fairytales* or Plato's dialogues or Shakespeare's *Romeo and Juliet.* Because she views the public school system as a failure, she favors replacing it with publicly funded tuition vouchers that parents could use to send their children to teachers and schools of their choice, a sort of free market educational system.

In a footnote, the SmithKline Corporation comments that Marva Collins is proving the bankruptcy of conventional education; that in 1975, after 14 frustrating years in the public schools, she opened her private school, and now inner city students from Westside Preparatory School are "sought by the most prestigious high schools in the nation." It is humbling, the SmithKline writer notes, to see "retarded" youngsters expound on Thoreau,

Dante, Aristotle and Chaucer, and to realize that this one-room school has actually turned down a $16,000 federal grant in order to remain independent.

On television there was a "docudrama" on Marva Collins, the news program 60 Minutes did a feature on her, and she has been invited to lecture throughout the country (at $10,000 a lecture, according to Albert Shanker in his *New York Times* ad of March 7, 1982). Westside Prep moved to larger quarters and its waiting list expanded.

As in the Bernardine Schmidt affair, careful investigative work revealed the exaggeration and fraud that epitomize these miracles. The initial exposure was made by George Schmidt (as far as I know, no relation to Bernardine), in an article in a little-known newsletter of a group of Chicago public school substitute teachers, called *Substance* (sub-stance). I have been unable to get a copy of his article but according to an article in the *American Teacher* of April, 1982, Len Walter, an anchor reporter for Chicago's WBBN news radio, initially used the *Substance* article to bring to the public's attention the serious questions being raised about Marva Collins' assertions. For one thing, despite her claims that she rejected federal funds, she had in fact received $69,000 in CETA funds from the government (she later said that she did not know this money had originated in Washington). According to Walter, who interviewed a former Westside Prep teacher, half of Collins' students "failed" the California Achievement Test. Furthermore, Collins had written an article in the September 16, 1981 issue of the Chicago *Sun-Times* that was very similar to an article by the psychologist Neil Postman, which had been reprinted in the fall, 1981 issue of the *American Educator* just weeks before Collins' *Sun-Times* article. She made no reference to Postman, who expressed surprise at the "remarkable coincidence."

Further investigation by other reporters forced Collins to disclaim any knowledge of a vita, reportedly sent to parents, which listed her as having a degree from Northwestern University. She has, in fact, a degree in secretarial science from Clark College. During the course of a two-part appearance on the Phil Donahue television show, she complained that she had become the victim of a witch hunt. An article in the March 8, 1982 issue of *Newsweek* digests the history of this sadly familiar affair, which demonstrates once again how the wish to believe can cloud our critical faculties.

KIRK'S OWN STUDY

Although critical of Schmidt's study, Kirk had no reason to doubt that a properly designed experiment would demonstrate that early intervention will raise retarded intelligence. In 1958, he published the results of his own study, begun in 1949 and specifically designed to determine the effects of preschool training on the development of retarded children. All children were initially between 3 and 6 years of age and had IQs between 40 and 80. There were two experimental groups: (a) The Community Experimental Group of 26 children was provided with a daily enriched nursery school environment from 9 to 3 o'clock. At about 6 years of age these children were placed in a regular first grade or special class. (b) The Institution Experimental Group consisted of 15 institutionalized children who, as part of the experiment, were enrolled in a preschool in the institution from 9 to 3 o'clock daily.

There were also two contrast groups ("contrast" rather than "control" because it was impossible to find enough children at one time or in one location to provide the usual randomized control). (a) The Community Contrast Group consisted of 26 community children who did not attend a preschool. (b) The Institution Contrast Group was composed of 12 children from another institution who were given no preschool education, plus a "subcontrast" group consisting of 10 institutionalized retarded children whose tests and retests at the preschool level were available in the institution's files.

The preschool program had a ratio of one teacher to four or five children. The teachers individually tutored children who required special attention in certain areas, and adapted their materials and activities to the children's mental level. Intelligence tests and a number of other tests were regularly administered to all children, usually at 9-month intervals.

Kirk provided case histories of the experimental children, plus comparisons of the results of objective testing and rating scales. We discuss only the results of the periodic testing on the Stanford–Binet Intelligence Scale. Complete data for 25 Community Experimental and 26 Community Contrast Group members were available. The mean IQ of the experimental children, which was 72.5 prior to the preschool experience (when the children were an average of 4.4 years of age), rose to 83.7 at the end of the preschool period some 2 years later. After a year of regular school, their mean IQ was 84.2. Over the same testing periods, the mean IQs of the contrast children were 75.8, 75.2, and 82.7. Note that the groups differed by 8.5 points in mean IQ at the end of the preschool period, but after a year of regular school the differences all but evaporated.

For the Institution Groups, on the other hand, the differences persisted. For the 15 experimental children the IQ rose from a preschool mean of 61 to a mean of 73 after 2 years of preschool, and remained at about that level a year later. The mean IQ of the 12 contrast children dropped from 57.1 to 49.9 over the same period, and also remained at about that level a year later. The mean IQ (63) of the 10 cases drawn from the files remained the same from the mean ages of 4.5 to 6.0 years, in contrast to the loss in IQ of the contrast children, a result that is difficult to understand and for which Kirk had no explanation.

In sum, then, the major result is that the two preschool groups of retarded and borderline children, one from institutions and one from the community, gained an average of 11 to 12 IQ points during the course of the preschool experience, an order of increase that would soon become typical of many early intervention studies. However, the fact that the Community Contrast Group later overtook the Community Experimental Group led Kirk to suggest that for retarded and borderline children in adequate homes, a regular school experience will allow them to overtake peers who have had the advantage of attending a preschool. The early superiority of the Experimental over the Contrast Group, as well as the diminishing difference on the follow-up test, also presaged the findings of subsequent intervention studies, particularly those of the Head Start program (Clarke & Clarke, 1976).

Kirk (1958) was cautious in his conclusions, stating only that "rate of development can be accelerated or depressed within the limits set by the organism" (p. 213). Yet in referring to this study years later, Kirk (1970) mentioned only the results for the Institution Groups. And in a 1982 interview, he asserted that his data, along with the data of Skeels, Heber, and others, indicate that early education increases children's IQs, while lack of its slows the rate of mental growth (Kirk, 1982). As always, a careful look at the original studies will sensitize the reader to the amendments and qualifications that such summarizing statements usually require.

PROJECT HEAD START

On May 18, 1965, President Lyndon B. Johnson publicly announced a new program in his war on poverty. More than 1,600 federal grants were awarded in order to establish 9,508 preschool centers so that hundreds of thousands of underpriviledged children would be given a "head start" during the summer months before entering kindergarten or first grade. Additional awards were to be made, so that a total of 2,500 projects would reach some 530,000 children in 11,000 centers. Full-year programs would also be instituted. Project Head Start was designed to halt the vicious cycle of poverty and parental neglect that breeds children who, as adults, continue to live in poverty and in turn produce socially and culturally disadvantaged children. At this writing, this commendable program is still functioning, and in 1984 received a budget of 995.8 million dollars. Not only does it provide early intellectual and educational stimulation, it also provides nutritional and medical assistance, involves parents in the education of their children, and attempts to foster social competence and improved motivation (Zigler & Valentine, 1979). Surely it is the kind of program that deserves support and encouragement.

A major goal of Head Start is improved education, but implicit in its conception was the prevention and/or amelioration of what was referred to as cultural-familial mental retardation. If this most prevalent form of mental retardation was due to poor environment, then improving the environment should raise the intelligence of culturally deprived children.[2]

It is important to separate the practical, caring aspects of this program from the philosophical and theoretical issues surrounding it, just as, in a parallel manner, it is important to separate the goal of improving scholastic and social competence from the goal of raising intelligence. To understand how Project Head Start fits into the chronology of events that constitutes the continuing debate about the origin and nature of human intelligence and the curability of mental retardation, we must turn to the project's theoretical foundation.

Theoretical Foundation: Hunt, Hebb, and Piaget

In his introduction to Zigler and Valentine's (1979) edited book on the history and status of the project, Cooke wrote that "the fundamental theoretical basis of Head Start was the concept that intellect is, to a large extent, a product of experience, not inheritance. The remarkable studies of Harold Skeels in the late thirties, followed by the work of J. McVicker Hunt and others, gave support to this belief" (p. xxiii).

We have already reviewed the Skeels studies. Cooke's other reference was to the extremely influential book, *Intelligence and Experience* (Hunt,

---

[2]The term *cultural deprivation* was frequently used but infrequently defined. According to one description, culturally deprived children receive adequate stimulation (by many siblings) but the stimulation lacks a clear focus. They interact less with their mothers (or mother surrogates) than do middle class children, and are more likely to be reinforced for inhibitory than for exploratory behavior, with reinforcement being diffuse rather than directed toward the quality or adequacy of the child's response (Gray & Klaus, 1968). Bereiter and Engelmann (1966) equated cultural deprivation with the lack of opportunity for a conceptual type of language expression, stemming from the fact that in lower class homes the cognitive use of language is severely restricted.

1961), in which Hunt critically examined the belief in fixed intelligence and predetermined development, while marshalling much evidence, including animal experiments, in support of the view that "heredity, while it may still be an important factor [in determining differences in intelligence], can no longer be assumed to have major responsibility for these differences" (p. 265). According to Hunt, "genes set limits on the individual's potential for intellectual development, but they do not guarantee that this potential will be achieved" (p. 7). Hunt was not simply referring to the findings that children brought up in extreme isolation, or infrequently attended to in understaffed orphanages, will behave in a retarded manner. He included less extreme circumstances, and later stated that he "viewed the effects of cultural deprivation as analagous to the experimentally found effects of experiential deprivation in infancy" (Hunt, 1964, p. 242). Animal experiments were relevant, and in fact "the difference between the culturally deprived and the culturally privileged is, for children, analogous to the difference between cage-reared and pet-reared rats and dogs" (1964, p. 236).

Hunt did not view physical isolation as the major problem, nor did he believe that living under the crowded conditions typical of life in poverty should be a handicap during a child's first year. He suggested that it begins to adversely affect development in the second year, when the child's outward expressions are curbed by "adults already made ill-tempered by their own discomforts" (1964, p. 238), and continues into the third year, when children brought up under such circumstances have poor linguistic role models and receive either no responses to their questions or outright rebuffs. With few playthings available, there is "little opportunity for the kinds of environmental encounters required to keep a two-year-old youngster developing at all, and certainly not at an optimal rate and not in the direction demanded for adaptation in a highly technological culture" (p. 238). Nevertheless, retardation resulting from these circumstances "can probably be reversed to a considerable degree by supplying proper circumstances in either a nursery school or a day-care center" (p. 238), preferably at 3 years of age.

On the basis of this kind of "armchair analysis," as Hunt called it, many influential workers considered that cultural deprivation was a major source of mild mental retardation, and consequently they prescribed early intervention as a preventive measure.

Hunt labeled his approach "Interactionism." No one would argue with the statement that genetic-environmental interaction is essential for an organism's development, but what epitomized Hunt's viewpoint was his contention that environment was more influential than genes in producing individual variations in intelligence. He drew from many sources, including

Hebb's neurological theory of cell assemblies and, in particular, Piaget's stage theory of development.

According to Hebb (1949), the *cell assembly* is a brain process that corresponds to a sensory event, and that continues to reverberate after the sensory event has ceased. One such assembly will form connections with others and can be made active with others, illustrating the mechanism of association. A series of cell assemblies is a *phase sequence.* Hebb set his theory against Gestalt field theory by postulating that the neural activities of cell assemblies and phase sequences that are produced by eye movements and eye fixations underlie the perception of figures. Perception, then, is a learned skill. From initially perceiving only an amorphous mass with several foci (such as the corners of a triangle), the infant develops—as a function of eye movements—the ability to clearly see an entire figure at a glance. This concept was extended to general learning and to intelligence, which Hebb (1949) discussed in the last pages of his book, *The Organization of Behavior.*

The development and activation of cell assemblies placed a premium on motor activity and experience, and fit neatly within the empiricist tradition, providing it with an impressive-sounding neurological base. However, to my knowledge there has never been any evidence that cell assemblies and phase sequences actually exist as learning engrams. To the contrary, in the area of perception—the foundation stone of Hebb's theory—the best evidence is that the capacity to perceive objects is an inborn faculty (Hubel & Wiesel, 1979), and that sensory neurons require stimulation only so that they do not deteriorate and so that the innate program can be expressed. Environmental stimulation does not produce the capacity to perceive; rather, it allows the genetic program to express itself. Of course the evidence now available was unavailable to Hebb, so that he could not have known that his extensions to general learning and intelligence were based on a faulty conception of the development of perception. But the leap from visual deprivation in young animals to the cultural deprivation described by Hunt was a prodigious one, and produced a kind of detached, self-reverberating "cell assembly" that continued to have a life of its own even when deprived of the basis for its existence.

By far the largest proportion of Hunt's book was devoted to the work of Jean Piaget, which Hunt thought would "eradicate the preformationism which still often lingers in psychology" (p. 111). Most readers are no doubt familiar enough with Piaget's theory of the stages of human development so that it need not be repeated here. Hunt stressed the Piagetian concept that the thought structures and processes of each stage become incorporated and reorganized in the subsequent stages, and he noted particularly Piaget's description of adaptive interaction between organism and environment, expressed in the constructs of assimilation and accommodation. In Hunt's interpretation of Piaget, children's encounters with the environment are continually changing their thinking and behavior as a consequence of accomodation and assimilation, and consequently intelligence cannot be fixed. Experience builds into human beings a "hierarchically organized system of operations" (Hunt, 1961, p. 247), similar in some ways but more complex than those built into computers. According to Hunt (p. 258), Piaget did not deny the role genes play in development, only that genetic influence fell far short of being the entire story.

Hunt was certainly correct in writing that Piaget did not believe in a structural preformationism in which the stages of development are already in the genes at birth. But Piaget was quick to point out that although he was not a preformationist, neither was he an empiricist. He believed, for example, that the organism's internal schemes of action must assimilate external data; as he put it, "No knowledge is based on perceptions alone, for these are always accompanied by schemes of action," and, further, "when we say that natural numbers are innate, what is innate is not the numbers but the process that constructs the numbers" (in Piattelli-Palmarini, 1980, pp. 23-24, 197). He appears to have replaced *structural* preformationism with *functional* preformationism in which innate neurological and organic functioning must lead—by means of organically rooted autoregulations (self-organizations) and equilibrations acting on incoming stimuli—to new internal schemata that create new constructions and elaborations (Piaget, 1968, p. 979). Consequently, Piaget believed that whenever you teach children something you prevent them from inventing or discovering it, and that it is unwise to attempt to rush them through the stages (Bringuier, 1980, pp. 128-130).

Both preformationism (innatism) and structuralism require that there be interaction with the environment for the child to develop normally, in the former in order to trigger and shape genetically programmed instructions and predispositions, and in the latter to provide the material for the development of more advanced internal schemata. Retardation resulting from severe environmental isolation cannot differentiate the two theories.

Furthermore, if the developmental stage concept is applicable to all humans, it is difficult to see how it cannot, in one way or another, be an expression of a maturational process universally present in the human central nervous system, a process that produces a predisposition to respond in certain ways. In theory, there are an almost limitless number of ways to react to environmental stimuli, yet according to Piagetian theory all humans pass through exactly the same stages, though at different rates and with some individuals not reaching the more advanced stages. How then can

Piagetian theory banish preformationism, which continues to exist as a productive theory in one form or another? Indeed, so fixed is the order of development that Hunt himself based a scale of infant development on the infant's progress through the sensorimotor period (Uzgiris & Hunt, 1975).

In the end, though, the most serious difficulty with the theoretical foundations of the Head Start program was not simply the questionable internal validity of the Hebbian constructs or the incomplete anti-preformationism of the Piagetian constructs, but rather their inapplicability as support for the belief that intellectual retardation can result from cultural deprivation. Children from minority groups, who constitute a large proportion of the Head Start population, are from environments that are culturally *different,* not culturally deprived, for they have their own very vital culture—as a number of workers have pointed out (Cole & Bruner, 1971; Ginsburg, 1972)—within which there are children who are very bright, or who are mentally retarded, or who (the vast majority) are somewhere in between. In sum, there was very little contact between the research and theory used as background support for Project Head Start and the nature of the deprivation that the program was designed to remedy.

The Westinghouse Evaluation

Of the many evaluations of Head Start, by far the most influential was the 1969 Westinghouse Learning Corporation/Ohio University report. In turn—in an infinite regress—the Westinghouse evaluation became the subject of innumerable evaluations (see for example Datta, 1976, who cites a number of these and provides a brief summary of the Westinghouse Report). Of the 12,927 Head Start Centers serving various geographical areas in 1966-67, the Westinghouse group ultimately chose 104 for their assessment. The target population consisted of the children who had completed Head Start programs and were entering first, second, or third grade in the fall of 1968. Comparisons were made with children—from the primary grades of the same schools—who had been eligible for Head Start but who had not participated. Approximately half the 3,963 children tested had been in one of the Head Start programs.

Ten assessment instruments were used: four that gathered background information, three that were considered measures of cognitive ability, and three that were measures of affective development. Neither the Stanford-Binet nor the Wechsler was given, but one of the Cognitive Measures was the individually administered Illinois Test of Psycholinguistic Ability (ITPA) (Kirk, McCarthy, & Kirk, 1968), chosen as a measure of receptive and expressive communication, school readiness, and general intellectual development. It consists of 10 subtests (plus 2 supplementary subtests, not given in the evaluation), and is highly correlated with individual, standardized intelligence tests (Kirk & Kirk, 1978). In fact, when corrected for restricted range (the normative sample of the ITPA was limited to children of average intelligence), the ITPA correlates about as highly with the Stanford–Binet as does the WISC (Silverstein, 1978). Because it can serve as a measure of general intelligence, the ITPA results will be examined.

An analysis of covariance (an index of socioeconomic status was the covariate) in a random replications model was used to analyze ITPA performance differences of experimental and comparison groups on each of the 10 subtests and on the total score. For children who had summer Head Start experience only, there were no reliable differences between experimental and comparison groups. The children who had participated in full year programs also did not differ reliably on ITPA total scores, although Head Start children in the second grade were reliably higher than were comparison children on two of the ITPA subtests, a finding not duplicated by the first or third grade children. The mean scores for the full-year Head Start children ranged from 6 to 12 months below the standardization norms for their age levels.

Partitioning the data according to geographic area of the programs did produce reliable total score differences in favor of the second grade Head Start children who were in the Western and Southeastern geographic areas (too few centers were available for analysis at the third grade level). However, in the Northeast area the differences favored the second grade comparison children, at a marginal level of reliability ($p = .06$).

Partitioning in terms of population (cities, towns, or rural areas) produced no reliable differences in ITPA total scores.

A review of 31 follow-up studies (Grotberg, cited in Datta, 1976) showed that any immediate gains of the Head Start groups relative to the comparison groups were transitory. After leaving the programs, the rate of gain of the preschool children leveled off and then declined, while the comparison children showed a growth spurt upon entering school. Soon the two groups were indistinguishable, a typical outcome for intervention studies.

The Westinghouse report concluded that summer programs should be phased out, and recommended strategies for improving the full-year programs.

The early years of Project Head Start had been plagued with problems. Starting dates for the various programs followed quickly after the decision on funding, leaving little time for planning and preparation; the intervention period was relatively short and the teachers often poorly trained. Under such conditions no one could expect clean experimental designs and dramatic results. Yet Head Start provided so much support and assistance to poor children and their families that it survived its disastrous inception and even produced numerous satellites, including the Handicapped Children's Program, the Child Development Associate Program (for teachers), Health Start, Home Start, the Child and Family Resource Programs (to provide information) and—most famous of all—Project Follow Through.

PROJECT FOLLOW THROUGH

In 1967, as a response to the preliminary evidence that Head Start children were not maintaining their early gains, Project Follow Through Planned Variation was introduced as an experimental project to extend into the primary grades the special training given to Head Start children, in the hope that a more sustained effort would produce a more permanent effect. Because funding from the United States Office of Education (USOE) was limited, it was decided to try a number of innovative curricula that were different from each other in terms of educational philosophy and teaching technique (the "planned variation").

Classes were implemented in 1963 by 13 "sponsors" who had been selected to introduce their programs to most of the 90 participating school districts.[3] The sponsors were primarily social scientists who had some experience in applying their views to the classroom and who were deemed capable of producing a comprehensive, theory-based teaching program, including related materials, for kindergarten and primary level children and their parents (Rhine, Elardo, & Spencer, 1981). These sponsors, who worked with as few as 6 to as many as 20 school districts, represented diverse orientations, ranging from behavioral, cognitive-developmental, and psychoanalytic, to humanistic psychology. Some based their programs (models) on their classroom research, others on their general experiences as educators or psychologists. Consequently, some models emphasized the systematic use of reinforcement to improve the children's classroom behavior or the home behavior of the children and their parents, whereas others aimed for the development of positive attitudes by the use of materials

[3]Although there were 13 sponsors in 1968–1969, 10 additional models were added later, and some were discontinued. A list of 19 Follow Through models operating in 1980, and the 153 communities in which they were implemented, is given in Rhine (1981, Appendix). Note that in 1969–1971, the planned variation strategy was adopted by Project Head Start.

geared to each child's interests; some sponsors designed relatively open classes, while others designed more structured environments, and so on. Likewise, different approaches were used to involve parents in the mandated Policy Advisory Committees.

A recent listing of the titles of some of the models gives the flavor of the different theoretical orientations: Behavior Analysis Model, Cultural Linguistic Model, Culturally Democratic Learning Environment, Direct Instruction Model, High/Scope Cognitively Oriented Model, Individualized Early Learning Model, Open Education Model, Parent-Supported Diagnostic Model, and Responsive Educational Model.

The Abt Association Evaluation

Of all the evaluations of Project Follow Through, the most influential assessment was begun by the Stanford Research Institute in 1968, and in 1972 was continued by Abt Associates, Inc., who analyzed the results of tests given to Follow Through and non-Follow Through comparison children, as well as questionnaires administered to their teachers and interviews obtained from their parents. The tests given to the children were classified as either measures of basic skills (four tests), cognitive conceptual skills (four tests), or affect (three tests). The evaluation was extensive, comparing up to 22 Follow Through models and thousands of children who were in Follow Through programs or in untreated comparison groups over a 4-year period. A substantial portion of the assessment was presented in a multivolume publication prepared by Abt Associates for the USOE, but we focus primarily on the results presented in one of the volumes (Bock, Stebbins, & Proper, 1977).

Bock et al. presented the results for 17 Follow Through models. The number of sites at which each model was used ranged from 1 to 12, with a median of 5. For example, the Self-Sponsored Programs model was implemented at five sites: Detroit, New York, Philadelphia, Portland, and San Diego. A Summary of Effects Table was given for each model, listing significant differences in favor of the Follow Through or non-Follow Through children, or instances where there were no significant differences between the groups. For a difference to be considered significant it had to be both statistically reliable ($p < .05$) and "material" (the positive or negative effect had to be equal to or greater than one-fourth the standard deviation of the relevant outcome measure). Results were available from a total of 99 sites, at many of which more than one wave of children was assessed.

Neither the Wechsler nor the Stanford–Binet was part of the evaluation, but it did include the shortened version of Raven's Coloured Progressive

Matrices Test, a test that can be given to groups and which many psychologists consider to be a good measure of general intelligence (e.g., Jensen, 1980). Based on the tables in Bock et al., I tallied 139 comparisons, in each of which the Follow Through and non-Follow Through groups were from the same city or town. I excluded 32 comparisons where very large covariate adjustments had been made to compensate for pre-treatment group differences (keyed in Bock et al's. tables as "untrustworthy effects"), or where the preschool experiences of the two groups differed by 50% or more; although inclusion of all of these data would not have affected the results of the tally.

Of the 107 comparisons on Raven's test, 5 significant differences favored Follow Through groups, 11 favored non-Follow Through groups, and in 91 there were no reliable differences. It is very clear that experience in Follow Through programs had no effect on intelligence, as measured by the Coloured Progressive Matrices Test.

Assessment of the "planned variation" aspect of Project Follow Through also produced unexpected results. A major goal was to compare the effectiveness of different educational models, but the results indicated that differences between sites using the same model were much greater than differences between the models! Apparently our theories are relatively insignificant compared with the practical effects of the interaction of particular children with particular teachers in particular school settings.

In discussing the Abt evaluation, House, Glass, McLean, and Walker (1978) asked: "Can it be that so much effort had no measurable outcome?" (p. 155). Apparently it can, although workers interpreted the results of Head Start and Follow Through in vastly different ways. Success has been claimed for various aspects of different models, with negative results blamed on unrealistic goals, inadequate preparation, government short-sightedness and interference, non-optimal age of children at intervention, inadequate duration and/or intensity of the programs, inappropriate evaluative criteria, improper use of statistics, and the teachers and programs themselves (e.g., Abt, 1976; Caruso & Detterman, 1981; Hellmuth, 1968, 1970; House et al., 1978; Kennedy 1978; Rhine, 1981, 1983; Zigler & Berman, 1983; Zigler & Valentine, 1979). Continually under attack was Jensen's (1969) general statement that the negative results of compensatory education were foreordained because the variance in intelligence is largely genetically determined.

THE CONSORTIUM FOR LONGITUDINAL STUDIES

The task facing anyone hoping to review Projects Head Start and Follow Through is intimidating; in their book on Head Start, Zigler and Valentine (1979) listed 1,070 references for the period 1965 to 1975. Rather, three preschool programs are examined here because they were geared particularly for children at risk for mental retardation, and also because they were included in the Consortium for Longitudinal Studies (henceforth referred to as the Consortium).

The Consortium was formed in 1975 to measure the long-term effects of early education programs, in order to counter such evaluations as the Westinghouse report. A group of researchers, headed by Irving Lazar of Cornell University, was provided with limited federal funds to assess the long-term effects of a number of the intervention programs started in the 1960s. Original and follow-up data from 11 different early intervention programs were reanalyzed and statistically pooled. Results have been presented in a book (Consortium for Longitudinal Studies, 1983) and in prestigious journals (Darlington, Royce, Snipper, Murray, & Lazar, 1980; Lazar & Darlington, 1982). Only one of the Consortium programs was a Head Start program and one was a Follow Through program. According to Condry (1983), the programs included in the Consortium assessment were more closely supervised and carefully documented than were the Head Start programs, and were models of what Head Start programs should be. The major conclusion of the Consortium assessment was that high-quality early education programs had positive effects on children's school experience. These programs also produced increases in children's IQs (relative to controls) which lasted for several years and then dissipated; but the Consortium emphasized that improving children's intellectual skills was less important than the more practical goal of school success. The Early Training Project, the Micro-Social Learning Environment, and the Perry Preschool Program were 3 of the 11 preschool programs followed up by the Consortium.

The Early Training Project

Six years before Project Head Start was announced, a group of workers was preparing a preschool project aimed at offsetting the progressive retardation observed in poor children as they progress through school. By providing special experiences during the 2½ years prior to first grade, they hoped to develop in these children characteristics that would promote school success, and also intellectual and social competence. Following a preliminary pilot study, the major project began in 1962 (Gray & Klaus, 1968,

1970; Gray & Ramsey, 1982; Gray, Ramsey, & Klaus, 1982; Klaus & Gray, 1968).

There were four groups of children. All were black, born in 1958, from extremely low income families, and lived in Tennessee. There were two experimental groups, one (E1) which started in the program in 1962 (2 years, 3 months prior to entering first grade), and a second (E2) which started in the program 1 year later. A third group served as one control (C1), described as a local control because they were from the same small city as were groups E1 and E2. The second control (C2) was a "distal" control because it was composed of children from a different small city in Tennessee.

Group E1 was given three summers of special experiences and weekly home visits from the summer of 1962 through the summer of 1964. Group E2 started in the summer of 1963. For 10 weeks during the summers the experimental groups spent 4 hours a day, including lunch, at the school, engaging in small-group activities with assistant teachers (graduate and undergraduate college students). Each of the groups was led by an experienced, black first grade teacher. A great deal of positive reinforcement was dispensed, including hugging and verbal praise, in the hope that motivation would become internalized and the children would learn to be more persistent and better able to delay gratification.

Specifically, the experimental program was oriented toward (a) perceptual development, (b) acquisition of basic concepts, and (c) language development. Training emphasized the ability to discriminate, to perceive likenesses and differences, and to understand the concepts of color, shape and form, number, and position. Verbal fluency was encouraged, vocabulary was increased, and the children were taught to name many objects and to correctly pronounce words. Materials included, among other things, picture books, paints, cubes, peg boards, formboard puzzles, and wheel toys.

During the 9 months when the summer preschool was not in session, a teacher (who was black) paid weekly visits to each child's home and worked with the child and mother. Emphasis was placed on using materials available in and outside the home to demonstrate to the mothers the educational value of everyday objects. When the children attended first grade in 1964, the home visitors saw the mothers twice a month.

The control groups were given no special training but were tested whenever the experimental groups were. To maintain their interest in the program, members of Group C2 were paid a modest amount, but because the school system of Group C1 objected to cash payment, C1 children were given small gifts, an occasional picnic or party, and later, a play period twice a week.

Attrition was quite low and therefore subsequent assessments included a substantial proportion of the children who had started the program. Because this survey is concerned with changes in intelligence, we focus on the two most widely used intelligence tests. One of these, the Stanford–Binet (1960 revision), was among the tests initially given in 1962, when the children ranged from 3.5 to 4.4 years of age. It was subsequently administered at least annually through 1966 and then again in 1968, at which point the number of children who had contributed scores every year ranged from 18 to 23 per group.

Based on an analysis of variance of these IQ scores, Gray and Klaus (1970) reported a reliable groups effect and groups by testing interval interaction. It would perhaps have been more appropriate to have used the *differences* between the original pre-intervention scores of 1962 and the subsequent scores, in view of the fact that the experimental groups had slightly higher initial IQs than the control groups, but in any case the interesting finding was the course of the scores over the 6-year period. In both experimental groups the scores rose after the intervention, then fell after the children entered public school. For example, in 1962 the mean IQ for E1 children was 88, in 1964 it rose to 96, and in 1968 it was down to 87. The E2 mean started at 93, was 97 in 1964, and dropped to 90 in 1968.

The mean IQs of the two control groups followed a different course. C1 started at 85, in 1964 it dropped to 83, and in 1968 it was 85 again. C2 started at 87, dropped to 80 in 1964, and continued to drop to 78 in 1968, the only one of the four groups that was appreciably lower in 1968 than in 1962.

The Wechsler Intelligence Scale for Children (WISC) was administered annually from 1964 through 1966, and the WISC–R was given in 1975, providing the final IQ scores. Gray et al. (1982) supplied only the WISC Verbal and Performance scores; the Full Scale IQs given here are derivations. Also, they combined the scores of the two experimental groups because they did not differ (despite the fact that one group had received a year's longer intervention than the other). The mean scores of the combined experimental group went from about 87 in 1964 to about 97 in 1965, then dropped to 79 on the WISC–R in 1975. (The WISC–R at these age and IQ levels gives a Full Scale IQ that is at least 3 to 5 points lower than the WISC, see Flynn, 1985; Spitz, 1983). Group C1 went from 80 to 91, and then dropped to 77 on the WISC–R in 1975. Finally, Group C2 went from 79 to 86, and had a final mean WISC–R IQ of 79 in 1975.

In summing up the intelligence test results, Gray et al. (1982) concluded that "changes in performance . . . lasted through the fourth grade" (p. 254). However, the data suggest that the differences between experimental and control groups lasted until the children entered first grade. All groups dropped subsequently, the distal control group more rapidly than the others, and by 1975 all groups were at approximately the same IQ level. The Early Training Project had no lasting effect on intelligence, as measured by standardized individual intelligence tests.

A discrepancy in the manner in which some results were reported should be mentioned, even though our major interest is not in school performance. In the published paper of a conference report, Gray and Ramsey (1982), commenting on whether their control children were more frequently placed in special education classes than were their experimental (early training) children, wrote that their results "showed striking differences. Only 2 among the 36 experimental children spent some time in EMR classes, while among the 19 (local) control young people, 7 did so." But these placements must have been for a very short time, based on data that were given separately for males and females and that included the distal control group (Gray et al., 1982, p. 47). For the category: "EMR placement of 1 or more years," only one of six experimental/control comparisons was statistically reliable: the comparison between the combined experimental females versus the local control group females. None of the experimental girls were in an EMR class for a year or more, but then neither were any of the girls from the distal control group. For the category "Total retained (held back) or EMR placement," the proportions for the experimental, local control, and distal control groups were, respectively, 55%, 67%, and 54%.

In their contribution to the Consortium for Longitudinal Studies, Gray, Ramsey, and Klaus (1983) dropped the category "EMR placement of 1 or more years," and the relatively good school progress of the distal control group was no longer given because "the school policies in our two towns appeared to differ somewhat in matters of retention in grade, of social promotions, and of policy and availability of special education classes" (p. 52). Apparently, then, the relevance and generality of special class placement as an outcome variable are limited by the vagaries of individual school policies.

The Micro-Social Learning Environment

According to Professor Lazar (1982), the Micro-Social Learning Environment (MSLE) was "the most—perhaps the only—really original preschool curriculum in the last 30 years." Designed and directed by Myron Woolman, the project began in 1969, supported by funds from the New Jersey State Department of Education. Eight months later it was declared a success by New Jersey's Commissioner of Education, and by James Farmer, Assistant Secretary of Health, Education, and Welfare, who praised the project and promised that the Nixon administration would encourage additional such programs (reported in the Feb. 1, 1970 issue of the *New York Times*).

The MSLE was a 5-year demonstration project designed to prepare 4- and 5-year-old disadvantaged children to meet successfully the demands they would face when they entered first grade. Woolman's theoretical stance, unabashedly empiristic, was based on his interpretation of the reinforcement theory of Thorndike and Skinner that learning takes place as a consequence of satisfactions derived from reduced tensions. In the MSLE the tensions would be created by each child's desire to satisfy the norms of the group. The classrooms were designed to produce a "society of learners" sharing the same basic goal, with each child striving to master the material in order to maintain and improve his or her position in the group, immersed in a simulated miniature social situation (micro-social) organized as a fail-safe learning environment. Thus prepared to enter and complete first grade, the children would progress through subsequent grades and ultimately into an adulthood much improved over what it would have been without the preschool experience.

Most of Woolman's (1971) report to the New Jersey State Department of Education is a discussion of the philosophical and pedagogical background for the MSLE, but for the Consortium book he supplied a good summary (Woolman, 1983). At the outset, most of the children were disruptive and badly behaved. More than half spoke Spanish as their primary language, and 55% could not speak English. Of the 135 who participated in the initial program, 114 were from families described as either settled or seasonal migrant workers, about half of whom were on welfare but supplemented their income by picking crops and working in food processing and canning plants. Nine of the children were from higher socioeconomic families but were included because they had psychological or social problems, and three participants were children of project teachers. The program was scheduled for the full year, and during the 4 years of classes 300 children participated. The average stay was 2 years, with a range of .5 to 3 years.

The site was an abandoned supermarket converted into offices, one playroom, and three classrooms. Each classroom had a Modular Learning Area and a Life Simulator Area. In the Modular Area there were five large tables (modules), each of which was partitioned by vertical boards into three sections. Two children worked in each section so that six children, working in pairs, were at each module. In the same spacious room with the five modules was the Life Simulator Area, separated from the Modular Area by an open railing, and divided into a simulator section, a free time section, and an art section.

The four teachers changed assignments every 2 months. Their job was to shift the children around, start the activities, evaluate performance, supervise the teacher and parent assistants, "and, above all, [they] maintained the dynamic flow of the children so that they perceived themselves as being in an active state of growth" (Woolman, 1983, p. 279).

Behavioral adjustment and speech and reading were developed primarily in the Modular Area, where the children used workbooks either alone or with their partners. Upon completing their workbooks they moved to the next module to complete another workbook, and so on, presumably gaining status by this tangible evidence of improvement. When they reached a pre-designated module they became "monitors," which permitted them to help partners below their level. Partners stayed together for no more than a week, and the children were free to walk about and even to enter the Simulator Area.

The Life Simulator Area contained an assortment of toys, miniature replicas of animals, people, vehicles, and food, plus materials related to the Modulator workbooks. From this area, site visits were made to diverse local establishments after the language base for a particular establishment (e.g., store or industry) was mastered. The Life Simulator Area was designed to provide real or simulated experience of the symbolic workbook material, including real representatives of newly learned words.

To evaluate his program, Woolman had planned a pre- and posttest design, with a matched control group to be selected by the New Jersey Department of Education. Unfortunately, only 13 control children were tested when—without notifying Woolman—testing of control children stopped. Short-term evaluation data were collected from the experimental children while they were still in the program, but for the 1976 Consortium study Woolman apparently collected data on school competence only. To create some kind of comparison group he used a random sample of children who had entered first grade a year earlier than the experimental children. As far as I can determine, the only contribution of the MSLE project to the Consortium findings was that the percentage (32%) of program children retained (left back) at least once was no different than the percentage (35%) of the general Vineland school population, and considerably less than the percentage (63%) of Hispanic-surnamed children in the comparison group who had been retained at least once.

Our special interest is in the changes in IQ that were found in the Consortium follow-up of 1976, but these data are impossible to find for the MSLE project. In his original report, Woolman (1971, Vol. II) provided data on 78 pre-program WISC IQs for his experimental group. Because these data were given as frequencies of score intervals, I derived an approximate mean IQ of 76. Of the 78 scores, a random sample of 29 was also posttested 8 months later, and their mean score rose reliably from 79 at pretest to 89 at posttest.

Darlington et al. (1980), in their table of the characteristics of the Consortium follow-up sample, gave an *N* of 297 for the Woolman study, 66 of whom attended pre-school. The mean pre-program IQ was given as 71.5 for 297 combined experimental and control children. However, according to Lazar and Darlington (1982, Tables 2 and 3) the 1976 follow-up produced data on at least one instrument for 611 children in the Woolman project (presumably both experimental and control), with IQs available on 95 of them. Subtracting the 66 experimental children would leave 29 who were in a control group.

Finally, Woolman (1983) implied that 135 children initially placed in the Micro-Social Learning Environment had been pre-tested on the WISC. Nowhere in his chapter, however, does he mention posttest IQs obtained in the 1976 follow-up. It is impossible to determine from any of the published data how many of the experimental children provided both 1976 posttest and pre-experimental IQs, what their scores were, or how they differed from control scores. Despite the fact that Lazar and Darlington stated in their Table 3 that 95 of Woolman's subjects (66 of whom were apparently experimental children) received pre-experimental and follow-up scores, in their Table 2 they noted that a mean pre-test IQ was not available for these children. This is very baffling, to say the least.

The report of an increase of 10 IQ points on the WISC for 29 experimental children over an 8-month period makes no mention of whether any of these children were among the 55% who, when they entered the program, could not speak English. One wonders how valid the pre-program tests were, considering the children's language problems, and how much of the 10-point rise was attributable to improved English and test-related training. (However, in a phone call to me on January 25, 1984, Woolman recalled that where necessary the test was given in Spanish by Spanish-speaking testers.)

In view of the paucity of data in the 1976 follow-up and the fact that Dr. Woolman—an earnest and dedicated psychologist—was deprived of a proper control group by unfortunate circumstances, it is difficult to understand why this project was included in the Consortium. It was surely not one of the projects that were purportedly such models of experimental design that Head Start programs would do well to emulate.

When the project ended and Woolman left, the MSLE program was abandoned and to my knowledge was never tried again, in Vineland or anywhere else.

The Perry Preschool Program

After several years of preparation, the Perry Preschool Program was begun in Ypsilanti, Michigan, in 1962, supported by a USOE grant. The participants were 3- and 4-year-old disadvantaged black children, and the project was notable for its careful use of experimental and control groups initially equated on cultural deprivation ratings and mean Stanford–Binet IQ scores. The progress of the children was reported in a series of monographs, the most recent of which contain assessments made when they had reached 14 and 15 years of age (Schweinhart & Weikart, 1980, 1983), and when they had reached 19 years of age (Berrueta-Clement, Schweinhart, Barnett, Epstein, & Weikart, 1984)

The project was designed to include only educable retarded children, with IQs in the 50 to 85 range. Note that 85 was a full standard deviation above the 70 IQ that had been used as the upper limit of mental retardation until 1959, when the American Association on Mental Retardation raised it to 85, only to return it again to 70 in 1973 (Grossman, 1977). In any event, the average entry IQ for the project children was about 79, so that most of them tested at what we now consider the borderline and dull normal intelligence levels. The mean entry age was 3.5 years.

During the 5 years of the project, 58 children served in the experimental groups and 65 in the control groups. Five pairs of experimental and control groups produced five replications (5 "waves," labeled 0 through 4), with the first two waves entering in 1962 (wave 0 being 4-year-olds, wave 1 3-year-olds), with a new group entering each year through 1965. Consequently all but the first group of children participated in the preschool program for two years prior to entering kindergarten. Annual assessments were made of both the experimental and the untreated control children.

Half-days classes were held 5 days a week over about a 30–week period each year, supplemented with weekly, 1.5–hour home visits to involve the mothers in the project.

Originally the theoretical rationale was fully empiristic. The project leaders quoted approvingly the statement that "it is now possible to entertain a new *tabula rasa* theory which hypothecates that at conception individuals are much alike in intellectual endowment except for the few rare hereditary neurologic defects" (Pasamanick & Knobloch, 1961, as quoted by Weikart, Deloria, Lawser, & Wiegerink, 1970, p. 9). It is life experiences and sociocultural milieu alone that produce individual differences in intelligence. As the project progressed, Piagetian theory provided the foundation for a curriculum in which "emphasis was placed on visual-motor skills, number concepts, and language enrichment activities" (Weikart, Rogers, Adcock, & McClelland, 1971, p. 1). Consequently, the focus was on the process of learning rather than on facts or subject matter.

Piaget's concepts of "logico-mathematical" and "spatio-temporal" relations underlay the curriculum's four content areas: grouping, seriation (ordering), spatial relations, and temporal relations. Material could be presented at increasingly more abstract levels, from the level of real objects or events to the level at which cues refer to the objects or events (index level), to the level at which representations stand for objects or events (symbol level), and finally to the highest level where the representations bear no resemblance to the actual object or event (sign level; written words, for example, although reading and writing were not part of the curriculum).

Numerous examples of how training in the four content areas could be implemented at the index and symbol level were provided in a teachers' Activity Guide, from which I have chosen only a few examples. For classification (grouping), a teacher might show models of a train, train tracks, an airplane and an airport and ask the children to match the objects that go together and to explain why certain objects are grouped together. In another example, the children are asked to find objects in the room that have different shapes, and to name the objects and shapes. Toy vehicles, furniture, and clothes are categorized, as are colors.

For seriation, the children might decorate three sizes of coffee cans and order the cans according to size, verbalizing the sequence. Groups of objects are used to illustrate same, more, and less; objects are arranged in ones, twos, and threes; and so on. Contrasting terms, such as dark/light, rough/smooth, and loud/quiet are discussed.

For spatial relations, children might be asked to point out which parts of the body are missing from incomplete pictures. Mirrors and pictures of the children can be used to identify body parts. Concepts of between, in front of, in back of, and behind are described and enlarged upon whenever an appropriate opportunity arises. Concepts of distance and direction are illustrated.

For temporal relations, the teacher might use planning experiences to emphasize the concepts of start and finish, beginning and end. Teachers are advised to take every opportunity to verbalize sequences, e.g., "First a big block, next a little block." If-then conditionals are elaborated. Magazine pictures can be cut out and set in a sequence that tells a story. Stories are read that emphasize the sequence of events, and the growing of plants and seasonal changes are used to illustrate changes over time.

Many such examples were given by Weikart et al. (1971), including illustrations of how teachers have incorporated these concepts in the course of a school day, for instance by emphasizing the size relations of the objects being put away during clean-up time. Role-playing and field trips were included in the curriculum.

The reader familiar with the Stanford–Binet Intelligence Scale will recognize that many of its subtests at the 4-, 5-, and 6-year level are similar to the activities in the Perry curriculum. The interested reader should compare the long list of curriculum activities given by Weikart et al. (1971) with the Stanford–Binet subtests at those age levels.[4]

In their follow-up through ages 14 and 15, the project workers obtained IQs on 89% of the original sample. The results are shown in Figure 1, where apparently the "waves" have been combined. The IQs at ages 3 to 10 are derived from the Stanford–Binet, 1960 form, whereas at age 14 they are from the WISC. These results are typical of the course of IQs in many early intervention programs: There is a sharp initial rise in IQ for the preschool children, followed by a gradual decline until there are no longer any differences between control and experimental groups. Notice that here, as in the Early Training Project, the experimental/control difference begins to diminish when the children enter first grade. Differences vanish by age 8. At age 14, both groups have a mean IQ of about 81, which should be adjusted upward because the WISC generally measures lower than the

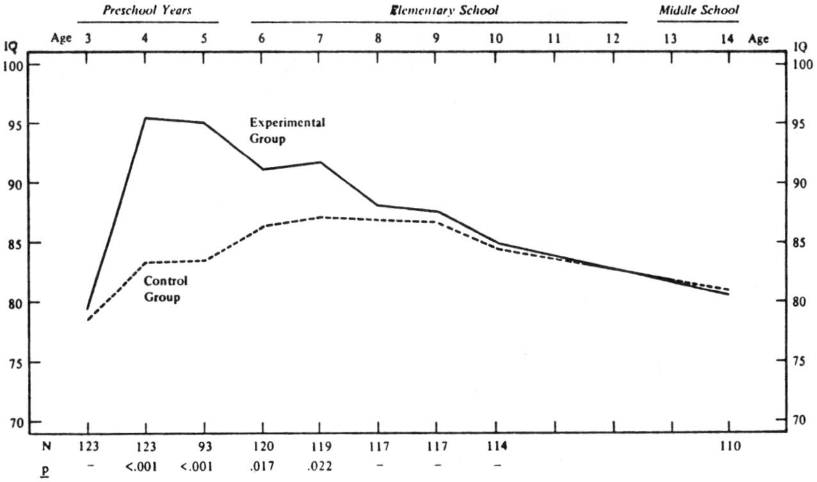

FIG. 1. Example of the temporary effect of early intervention on IQ scores. Results of the Perry Preschool Program (Schweinhart & Weikart, 1980); reproduced with the kind permission of Dr. Schweinhart.

[4]The Weikart et al. (1971) monograph is available from the National Association for the Education of Young Children, 1834 Connecticut Ave., N.W., Washington, D.C. 20009.

Stanford-Binet, by about 5 IQ points (Flynn, 1984). In view of this, there would appear to be a leveling off of both groups from around 9 or 10 years of age.

But the more interesting aspect of this project is that from this small base sprouted a large organization, changing its orientation along the way. Whereas in 1962 the Ypsilanti group had used an approach in which the teachers directed the children's learning, in 1964 a less directive, more cognitively oriented approach in the Piagetian tradition was introduced. In 1968, the USOE funded two Ypsilanti proposals, one in which the Cognitively Oriented Curriculum Model was implemented with kindergarten and primary level children as part of the Follow Through Project, and the other in which the Ypsilanti Preschool Curriculum Demonstration Project studied the long-term impact of preschool education, and compared three different educational programs (one of which was their Cognitively Oriented Curriculum).

But this was only the beginning. Some 2 years later, the Ypsilanti group created an independent agency, the High/Scope Educational Research Foundation. The modest Perry Preschool Project grew into a hydra-headed, independent Foundation—a metamorphosis occasionally duplicated by other preschool projects. It receives grants from private and public agencies, publishes books, monographs, films, and a newsletter called *High/Scope Resource* in which, among other things, articles describe the cost effectiveness of "high quality" preschool programs. It offers workshops, summer camps for teenagers, and many training programs, including one in which individuals are formally endorsed as trainers in the Cognitively Oriented Preschool Curriculum.

In sum, it has become a successful Foundation in the business of education, a vocal and effective advocate for early education. No one can object to this; indeed, the successful enterprise should be applauded, but the High/Scope Foundation and others like it can no longer serve as unbiased sources for the assessment of preschool programs in which they have so large a vested interest.

An example of how the mantle of advocacy displaced the presumed objectivity of science is provided by the presentation of their latest results. Believing that the usual professional channels of journal articles and conference presentations were not the most effective ways to reach policy makers, and convinced that their results merited widespread public interest, Weikart and his High/Scope colleagues decided to "create" a news event (described by Weikart in the Spring, 1985 issue of *High/Scope Resource*). They would hold a news conference in Washington, D.C. on September 14, 1984, to announce the publication of *Changed Lives,* a privately published monograph describing the progress of the Perry Preschool Program participants through age 19 (Berrueta-Clement et al., 1984). To stimulate interest in the press conference, they provided advance information to a number of influential newspapers, and hired a public relations firm in Washington, D.C. to manage the local aspects of the conference and generally coordinate the news releases. Unsuccessful in persuading a V.I.P. to announce the results, they nevertheless did get the Assistant Secretary for Human Development Services in the Department of Human Services (the supervising agency for Head Start) to attend the press conference and receive the privately published report.

The results were very gratifying. CBS *Evening News* devoted a 3-minute spot to their report, and the day before the conference the *New York Times* wrote a lead editorial about it. National Public Radio, all the wire services, and most major newspapers carried the story that the Perry Preschool Project had produced important evidence that preschool programs improve lives, save money, and effectively contribute to the reduction of poverty and its associated problems. The effects of this media event continue to reverberate.

Thus did this group of researchers, supported for varying periods of time by the U.S. Office of Education, the National Institute of Mental Health, and a number of private foundations, broadcast their latest findings. The usual safeguard of peer review was circumvented by the press's dissemination of uncritically accepted statements to a public that had neither the information nor the expertise to make an informed evaluation.

Was all this hoopla justified by the findings? Readers will have to buy the monograph (available for $15 from the High/Scope Press) and judge for themselves. I found little to get so excited about, other than the major annoyance that unwarranted conclusions were repeatedly drawn, and the minor annoyance that standard deviations (SDs) or other measures of variability were never given. The monograph emphasizes, among other things, the effects at age 19 (an age reached in 1977 by Wave Zero and in 1981 by Wave Four) of preschool attendance on school, occupational, and criminal behavior, and provides a cost-benefit analysis of the program. A few of the findings and a number of conclusions, some of which I found debatable, are given below.

The mean high school grade point average was 2.08 for 38 members of the preschool (experimental) group, reliably higher than the 1.71 for 39 members of the control group. The preschool group had a C average compared with the control group's C minus average, a difference that would seem to have little practical value.

Only 15% of the preschool group was ever classified as mentally retarded compared with 35% of the control group, despite the fact that at age 14 the two groups were no different in mean IQ. On the other hand, "children who went to preschool spent more time [than control children] receiving remedial education" (p. 25). In other words, instead of being placed in special classes, more experimental children received remedial help, suggesting to the authors that the preschool children appeared to their teachers to have more academic promise than those who did not attend preschool. However, one must wonder whether the decision not to label these children as mentally retarded was influenced by the fact that they were in the well-known Perry Preschool Project. There were, nevertheless, no reliable differences in the number of children ever classified as handicapped, in the percentage of children ever receiving special services of all kinds, nor in the mean number of grades repeated.

The results of a 16-item "Attitude Toward High School" scale led the authors to conclude that the members of the preschool group "expressed more favorable attitudes toward high school than the other group" (p. 78). However, a look at the actual scores indicates that on only two items are there reliable (p at least .05 or less) differences between the groups (one of which was a question about how important high school was as a place for sports and athletics). On the total score, the difference between groups was 1.1 point, which was marginally reliable ($p = .083$, but again, no SDs were given).

Significantly more (67%) of the preschool group graduated high school than did the control group (49%). Eight of these graduates (all from the preschool group) received a graduate equivalency diploma (G.E.D.). Why these students, but none of the control students, required the G.E.D. is not explained.

Much is made of the superiority of the experimental group on an Adult Performance Level Survey (APL), a multiple-choice test developed by the American College Testing Program "to assess skills needed for economic success in modern society" (p. 32), and also described as "a measure of competence in skills of everyday life" (p. 78). Although the subjects were read each item (a departure from standard procedure), reading skills were still required for the supplementary information accompanying some of the items. The total score of the preschool group averaged 24.6, compared with 21.8 for the control group, a reliable difference. In other words, out of 40 items, preschool children answered an average of 3 more items correctly than did the control children. However, it should be noted that of eight persons who said they would not take the test because they could not read, five were from the preschool group. Of four others who gave other reasons for refusing to take the test, one was from the preschool group. What these reasons were is not given.

The employment records of the groups are also compared. Forty-five percent of the preschool group, compared with 25% of the control group, reported that they were supporting themselves by their own or their spouse's earnings, but there are no separate data for how many of the members of each group were supported by their spouses. Reliably more members of the preschool group were working (50% compared with 32%), but the average salaries of the two groups were not reliably different. However, the preschool group's *median* salary of \$2,772 was higher than the \$1,070 earned by the control group (marginally reliable, $p = .06$. These are the *only* medians given in the monograph). Although low salaries for young, unskilled black workers from a poor environment are not unexpected, these figures provide no evidence that, as yet, preschool attendance has broken the cycle of poverty. The authors recognized that the participants' reports of self-support are questionable in light of these low earnings, but reasoned that "regardless of whether respondents are in fact self-supporting, the point to be made . . . is that the extent to which respondents perceive themselves as self-supporting differs by treatment group" (Barrueta-Clement et al., 1984, p. 50, footnote 17).

Indeed, many of the group differences are derived from interviews with the participants that, as indicated above, may not be entirely dependable. There are no group differences in car ownerships or drivers licenses, which are objective measures, and social service records show no differences in persons ever assisted, or in the use of medicaid or food stamps, although fewer members of the preschool group received General Assistance funds or had teenage pregnancies. Members of the control group had significantly more arrests, but the groups did not differ in number of convictions. The self-esteem of the members of the two groups, as measured by a questionnaire, was about the same.

The cost-benefit analysis is necessarily imprecise because of the difficulty of assigning monetary value to education, reduced crime, and numerous other variables, but according to the figures, by age 19 the per-child benefits of 1 year of preschool outweighed the costs by \$2,515. On the other hand, for 2 years of preschool the costs were greater than the benefits by \$1,180. Because of continued and increased earnings, the authors assume that future benefits will far outweigh the costs, based largely on the *expectation* that the experimental group will earn more money than the controls. An interesting sidelight is that because of the higher cost of the preschool program, the second year is cost-inefficient. That is, it would be more cost-effective to substitute a new group in place of a second year of preschool education. One year would be sufficient in any case, as it "produced the same effects as two" (p. 85). One wonders why, if 1 year was good, 2 years weren't better.

When the significance of effects is marginal, correlations can provide a better idea of the extent of relationships and the size of effects. In the Appendix of their monograph, Berrueta-Clement et al. provide a revealing correlation matrix for 12 variables. The dichotomous variable *preschool education* (member of experimental or control group) correlates significantly ($r = .42$) with only one other variable, *IQ at school entry* (IQ before the group differences had faded). The correlation of *preschool education* with *school achievement* is .18, with *years of schooling completed* is .16, with *misbehavior* is –.09, with *special education placement* is .17, with *arrests* is –.05, with *months worked* is .19.

These are all low and nonsignificant, and indicate that there is no meaningful relationship between attending or not attending preschool and a number of important later behaviors. Consequently, the authors postulate an indirect relationship in which *preschool education* produced a higher *IQ at school entry* which in turn led to (was correlated with) better *scholastic achievement* (r = .48), which in turn led to more *years of schooling* completed (r = .49), and which in turn led to *fewer arrests* (r = –.44) (with many of the variables multiply related). But this kind of analysis is unbounded. For example, *family socioeconomic status* (SES) correlates (r = .44) with *scholastic achievement,* at which point we can tap into the above causal chain. In fact, *pre-intervention IQ* correlates reliably (r = .37) with *IQ at school entry,* so a case might be made for *pre-intervention IQ* and *family SES* as important variables related to later behavior. But this kind of speculation is futile. The one thing that stands out is that there is no direct correlation between preschool attendance and later behavior.

Most advocates of early education no longer claim that intelligence can be permanently raised. They claim instead that good preschool education is a socializing force, improving adjustment to school and society and allowing many children to escape from delinquency and poverty. The Perry Preschool Project has produced some suggestive trends that encourage the hope that preschool education will help some children to live a better life. But the trends are marginal and dictate a cautious attitude. Indeed, the Project personnel do express caution: "Early education is *not* a panacea. . . . It does not solve the nation's crime problem. . . . It is *part* of the solution, not the *whole* solution" (Berrueta-Clement et al., 1984, p. 115). Yet these justified cautions are often missing from press releases. History teaches that this kind of salesmanship—although it may initially advance a noble cause—often destroys an entire movement when exaggerated claims are followed by disillusionment. There is no escaping the banal requirement that findings must be carefully and objectively analyzed, and that claims must not so indiscriminately escape from the data.

TWO OTHER INTERVENTION PROJECTS: PORTAGE AND ABECEDARIAN

The projects reviewed above represent a small sampling of the large number of programs designed to either prevent or raise deficient cognitive behavior. I do not have a comprehensive list of such programs, but of the many that I am aware of I mention just two others in order to give some idea of their diversity.

The Portage Project was (and still is) a parent-based early intervention program in Portage, Wisconsin. It received funding from the Bureau of Education for the Handicapped from 1969 to 1972, after which local and state agencies assumed the support. Funding to disseminate the project's activities was later supplied by the Office of Special Education, Head Start, and the Agency for International Development. It began modestly enough, enrolling rural, preschool, multiply handicapped children ranging from infancy to 6 years of age, who had one or more of the following: mental retardation (nearly half the children), a behavior problem, a physical handicap, impaired vision or hearing, cultural deprivation, and impaired speech or hearing. Over a 9.5-month period a teacher visited each home for 1.5 hours once a week (Shearer & Shearer, 1972, 1976). In addition to using a standardized developmental assessment instrument, the Portage staff used their own developmental checklist, in part to determine the behaviors targeted for training each week. However, the training was implemented not by the visiting teacher but by the parents.

The major focus, then, was on "teaching parents what to teach, what to reinforce, and how to observe and record behavior" (Shearer & Shearer, 1972, p. 210), using the principles of behavior modification (e.g., Lindsley, 1966). Presumably the parents too were reinforced by their success in teaching their children and recording their behavior.

Cochran and Shearer (1984) reported that in the first year of operation (1970–1971), Portage children with a mean IQ of 77.1 on the Stanford–Binet gained 18.3 IQ points over a 9-month period. However, there was no control group, and I can nowhere find details of the study, including who did the testing. In another study, a new group of Portage children made reliably greater gains than those made by children attending a local Head Start classroom. For detailed data on this study, project publications refer readers to an unpublished report by Peniston (1972).

The Peniston paper describes a 10-month pre- and post-evaluation (during 1971–1972) of 36 randomly selected multiply handicapped children in the Portage Project, and a contrast group of 27 randomly selected children in the Head Start program. Unfortunately, pre- and posttest evaluation instruments were administered by the home teachers, who were not trained psychometrists and who cannot be considered unbiased. But even more curious, the design apparently was not longitudinal. "Instead, the investigator is taking cross-sectional aspects of different multiply handicapped preschool children at different times and inferring change" (Peniston, 1972, p. 26). In the posttreatment comparison, the mean of the combined Cattell and Stanford–Binet Tests (it's not clear why they were combined) was much higher for the *contrast* than for the Portage group but this result was completely *reversed* by "adjusting" the means to take into account differences in pretreatment means, despite the fact that this was not a longitudinal study. This frequently cited study fails to meet even minimal standards for the assessment of intervention effects.

In 1980 the Portage Project declared that "the Project has gone beyond our wildest dreams and expectations" (Portage Report, 1980, p. 1). By then, the Portage staff had trained and provided assistance to more than 70 sites across the country, had assisted numerous Head Start programs, trained Peace Corps volunteers, and developed or assisted in developing dozens of Portage Projects throughout the world. The Project has even been lured into the classroom, combining classroom and home-based programs. Training manuals, guides, and information pamphlets are published and sold by the Project. As recently as 1984, publications of the Project staff continue to cite the Peniston (1972) report, as well as the Shearer and Shearer (1972, 1976) papers (which in turn cite the Peniston report), as evidence that their program has a beneficial effect on intellectual development (e.g., Shearer & Loftin, 1984).

* * *

Another well-known and frequently cited intervention program is the Carolina Abecedarian Project (Ramey & Campbell, 1981; Ramey & Haskins, 1981a, 1981b; Ramey, Holmberg, Sparling, & Collier, 1977).[5] This admirably designed project, begun in 1972 at the Frank Porter Graham Child Development Center at the University of North Carolina, was aimed at preventing mental retardation. The project staff selected pregnant mothers from families whose children were at risk for developing mental retardation, and when the children were born they were pair-matched on a number of variables and then randomly assigned to either an experimental or control group. Both groups were provided with a number of supportive services, and both were given nutritional supplements, but only the experimental group attended the project's day care center.

Briefly, the rationale for this project was that high risk children receive "vague or competing sensory messages" (Ramey et al., 1977, p. 107), which they cannot use at the moment they receive them. Consequently, the staff designed "an organized resource bank of unambiguous experiences or activities" that are made available "to the child at a time and in such a way that he can use and master it successfully" (p. 107). For the infant, this resource bank consisted of more than 300 curriculum items—each designed

[5]Abecedarian pertains to the alphabet, and an abecedarian is a person who is learning the alphabet or who teaches the alphabet and other rudiments of learning.

as a game or activity—which are individually prescribed for each child as he or she develops.

The experimental children were transported to the day care center for a full day, 5 days a week, 50 weeks a year. There was one setting for infants from 4 weeks old till the time they could walk, and another setting for 1- to 3-year-olds.

Results for the first two cohorts of 27 experimental (E) children and the first two cohorts of 28 (reduced gradually by attrition to 23 by age 5) control (C) children were presented at an international symposium (Ramey & Campbell, 1981). Means IQs of E and C groups at 1 year of age (Bayley Mental Development Index), 2 to 4 years of age (Stanford-Binet), and 5 years of age (Wechsler Preschool and Primary Scale of Intelligence) are given below.

Age (yr.)	*E*	*C*	*Difference*
1	106	105	1
2	93	84	9
3	95	81	14
4	96	84	12
5	98	91	7

Because three different tests were used, the fluctuations in IQ must be viewed cautiously, but the widening differences between experimental and control groups followed by a later narrowing of these differences is typical of early intervention studies.

Ramey and Haskins (1981b) attribute the typical evanescence of IQ gains in intervention studies to inadequate public school programs, but this explanation cannot apply to their study, where differences were due to the decline and rebound of the mean IQ of the control group rather than to a gain and subsequent drop in mean IQ by the experimental group. They attribute their own results in part to the fact that at some time during the study 19 members of the control group entered a day care program (not theirs), and they mention also the selective effects of attrition. Alternative explanations are given by Jensen (1981).

In 1984, one publication (Ramey & Campbell) presented the test results of *all* subjects, whereas in another publication (Ramey, Yeates, & Short) scores were not included if the children had not contributed to test results at every testing or had not lived with their mothers through the first 4 years of life. Neither publication included results at 5 years of age. However, Dr. Frances Campbell kindly sent me a computer printout of the annual intelligence test results of all subjects (as in Ramey & Campbell, 1984), including results at 5 years of age. The mean scores are given below.

Age (yr.)	*E*	*C*	*Difference*
1	111	105	6
2	96	85	11
3	101	84	17
4	102	89	13
5	101	94	7

Number of test scores in the combined experimental group was 51 at age 1 year, and 49 at age 5 years, while in the combined control group the *N* dropped from 53 to 46.

Aside from the fact that the experimental children in cohorts 3 and 4 had a rather high mean Bayley MDI of 116 (thereby raising the mean IQ of the entire experimental group), the full results pretty much parallel the results for the first two cohort groups; that is, group differences expand until age 3, but by age 5 they are once again very similar to what they had been at age 1. Note that Ramey et al. (1984) found that at 1 year of age developmental functions had not yet been affected by intervention, so that differences between their experimental and control groups at that age were presumably due to sampling artifacts.

THE TRANSITORY IQ EFFECT

Hereditarians and environmentalists propose rather different reasons for the pervasive finding that the superior IQs of experimental children, when compared with control children, is transitory (Brown & Campione, 1982; Campbell & Frey, 1970). Environmentalists claim that because intelligence is malleable it can be raised even when a favorable environment is provided during only part of the child's day. They also assume that intelligence tests underestimate the intelligence of poor children who have not been exposed to the same materials and opportunities to learn as have middle- and upper-class children, so that providing these experiences will raise their scores. When the child is no longer provided with a proper environment, IQs will decline.

Hereditarians propose that preschool programs train the child on the very skills that are required by test items. For example, at ages 5 to 7 years the Stanford–Binet contains subtests on vocabulary, number concepts, folding paper, similarities and differences, picture absurdities, copying, and so on. On these types of items the children will perform well, but when they are older and are presented with different test items they are thrown back on their own resources and their scores decline. In this view, the training did not change their basic intelligence, it merely provided them with skills that will not generalize to novel tasks. Familiarity with the material, unaccompanied by training, is not enough, and in later years even specific training of dull children is insufficient because the increasing difficulty of the tasks can be dealt with only by children and adolescents whose genetic endowment provides them with the necessary skills.

The Abecedarian Project is an example of intervention/nonintervention differences resulting from the fact that the IQs of the intervention children remain relatively constant while the IQs of the control children show a greater decline, only to climb back to that of the experimental children at a later age. But there also have been instances in which IQ gains of experimental children have not only been transitory but have dropped much *lower* than the IQs of a control group after a few years in public school, a sort of negative rebound effect (Miller & Bizzell, 1983; Miller & Dyer, 1975). This raises the possibility that for some children formal preschool experience can in some ways be harmful. Elkind (1969), who has a Piagetian orientation, suggests that up to certain limits, the longer we delay instruction the better, because there is greater plasticity in older children. Moreover, from a Piagetian perspective it is useless to try to rush children through the developmental stages. This is not to say that children should not be given preschool enrichment, which can be a positive experience for most of them, but only that there is no evidence that it has long-term benefits. In fact, it can be detrimental for preschool children of less than average ability to be given formal instruction, as in early reading programs, because—having not yet acquired the required competencies—they will tend to blame themselves rather than the material for their failures (Elkind, 1982).

Despite the tumult swirling around intervention studies and their evaluations, there can be little doubt that results thus far provide no support for the influential empiricist position that there is a critical period during which enriched environmental input will permanently raise a child's level of intelligence (Bloom, 1964). Nor do they provide satisfactory evidence that the incidence of cultural-familial mental retardation can be reduced by early or compensatory education programs, recognizing nevertheless that the interventions have been of relatively short duration (Clarke & Clarke, 1977).

The failure to permanently raise intelligence has prompted a shift from IQ to social competence as a primary criterion for evaluating the success of intervention programs (Rheingold, 1973; Zigler & Berman, 1983; Zigler & Trickett, 1978). This is a sensible change in emphasis, more in line with original recommendations of the Planning Committee for the Head Start Project, but at the same time it is a tacit admission that intelligence is not as modifiable as many people would have us believe. Based on the writings of Hunt and Bloom, and the reports of Skeels and his coworkers, there were many educators and psychologists who took it for granted that early enrichment would permanently raise IQ. On the other hand there were many workers, including some of the consultants and experts involved in planning Head Start and Follow Through, who had no such illusions, but whose voices were drowned by the enthusiasm of the times (Zigler, 1973/1979).

6 The Disturbing Case of the Milwaukee Project[1]

Ellis B. Page
Duke University

In the 1960s, during the social push of President Lyndon Johnson's Great Society, Dr. Rick Heber and others at the University of Wisconsin initiated an early intervention program referred to as the "Milwaukee Project." The story of this project may be the most unusual in the history of education. Considering its size, the project was grotesquely costly, eventually running some $14 million. Not long after the project's inception the directors claimed that they had raised the IQs of 20 children by some 30 points, but the nature of this change, if real, was impossible for outsiders to verify. The Director himself, Rick Heber, had a startling career: close to powerful political figures, he had been given a high Presidential appointment, but subsequently was convicted for fraud and personal misuse of federal funds and consigned to a federal penitentiary. Two other colleagues were also convicted.

Even more disturbing than these events were the reactions of the national media and certain political lobbies. Without any public proof the media took as fact the miraculous changes in IQ, lauded the project as giving the final rebuttal to hereditarians, and in subsequent years frequently cited the project as a major achievement. When corruption and fraud in the project's leadership were revealed, however, the major media turned deaf ears. These became non-events, in startling contrast to the media's pursuit of other fallen heroes.

Perhaps most disturbing of all have been the reactions of the community of social scientists. The Milwaukee Project, with its extraordinary claims of

---

[1]We appreciate the kind permission from *The Journal of Special Education* to quote extensively from the article published there by Page and Grandon (1981).

change in intelligence, was rarely criticized by scientists, despite its absorption of scarce resources or the implausibility of its outcome. To the contrary, some social scientists reported the project uncritically in college textbooks, where it would reach its most vulnerable targets.

As noted in the previous chapter, many plans for the social and educational betterment of low-achieving groups emerged out of the social optimism of the 1960s. Together, social planners and many behavioral scientists agreed that group differences in intelligence resulted overwhelmingly from differences in environment. It therefore seemed plausible to choose selected low achievers and to intervene in their preschool life, stimulating and training those early behaviors that would presumably lay the groundwork for later equality in schools and careers.

IMPORTANCE OF THE MILWAUKEE PROJECT

In any comparison with Head Start or with many other related federal projects, the Milwaukee Project (Heber, Garber, Harrington, Hoffman, & Falender, 1972) was small indeed. Rather than training tens of thousands, it aimed at just 20 children from a Milwaukee slum. Yet it was an extraordinarily expensive program with intensive one-on-one adult–child interaction and parent training, and it extended for many years. Most unusual for such a study, it was to have a Control group (C) of another 20 children who came from the same neighborhood as did the 20 Experimental (E) children. The C group would be tested regularly, but would otherwise share in none of the activities of the E children.

An ideal of science is the articulation of theory and the discovery of causal relationships, but the scientific enterprise ultimately depends on the open presentation of data and the possibility of refutation. Yet from its beginning the Milwaukee Project, despite its experimental structure, has seemed more a media event than a scientific enterprise. After 18 years it has seldom appeared in refereed journals, and details remain clouded. Nevertheless its fame has been extraordinary, particularly for its central claim of "a remarkable acceleration of intellectual development on the part of [children] . . . exposed to the infant stimulation program" so that "the discrepancy between Experimental and Control [children] . . . varies from a minimum of 25 IQ points at 24 months to 30 IQ points at 66 months" (Heber et al., 1972, p. 50). In other words, children who presumably would have been of low average or dull normal intelligence were, because of intensive environmental intervention, functioning at a superior intellectual level.

If this claim was true the Milwaukee Project deserved its apparent image as the high-water mark of environmentalist accomplishment, and, repeatedly, writers advocating interventions *have* cited this project as such. An event of this kind can take on a mythic quality and become a pillar of one's ideology about the origins of human nature and the proper directions for social reform. When large social upheavals are in progress, whether their causes are scientific, economic, or political, it is essential to be able to point to some widely known and celebrated event as providing a rationale for actions. This was particularly true for the interventionists when, as we have seen, extensive evaluation had cast long shadows across the largest compensatory programs. Controversial data seemed to leave us asking not whether such programs raised IQs by 30 points, but whether there were any lasting detectable effects at all.

That the Milwaukee Project provided a major pillar to shore up the nation's empiricist viewpoint is suggested in the press reports of that time. As detailed earlier (Page, 1972b; Page & Grandon, 1981), the President's Committee on Mental Retardation (1971) wrote that "the intelligence of the parent is a vital factor in the intelligence of the children—*mainly because of the environment* that the parents create for the young children" (p. 6, italics added). The Committee referred to Heber's project and stated: "By 43 months, the children in the enriched environment are scoring an average of 33 IQ points higher than the control group [and are] on the average exceeding the norms generally established by peer groups of the majority culture" (pp. 10–11). It is clear that the President's Committee, charged with determining facts about mental retardation and with helping to shape federal policy on programs, took the Milwaukee Project at face value.

Apparently the press caught the message from the President's Commission. *Time* (May 8, 1972) discussed the class differences in mild retardation and stated flatly to its 20 million readers that such retardation was environmental in origin. How did *Time* learn this truth, and leapfrog over all the difficulties and controversies of the nature–nurture debate? A *Time* staffer assured the present writer of its accuracy, pointing to the recent President's Commission and alluding, once again, to the Milwaukee Project (Field, 1972).[2]

Its ideological importance is confirmed in numerous other stories in the popular periodicals, and is emphasized by writers in the nontechnical psychological literature. George Albee, a clinical psychologist and former APA President, is quoted as saying:

[2]The press appears to lean in an environmentalist direction in most such coverage. *Time* had anticipated doing a review of Jensen's (1980) *Bias in Mental Testing*, and had scheduled its publication. But after calling a number of experts, *Time* "postponed" the review because it could not gather "any solid negative criticism." That review still has not appeared.

> I think the Milwaukee Project is very exciting. It challenges the notion that IQ is fixed. It has been criticized by the group around Jensen and Eysenck because it represents such a threat to their position. . . . But if there is a criticism, *and I think it's not very serious,* it is that Heber used a total push effort in which he threw everything in. So you really can't know from this first study which of the many different things they did with the children actually had an effect (Trotter, 1976, p. 46, italics added).

And in the same article J. McVicker Hunt is cited as underlining the crucial status of the Milwaukee Project in the ideological scene: "It's unique, and I think it's extremely important, particularly in the debate between those who feel that the life history is important and such people as Shockley and Jensen" (p. 46).[3] The journalist Trotter (1976) described its status as "unique, exciting and spectacular," and as "amazing" (p. 4).

Despite this acknowledged importance, the Milwaukee Project has hardly ever been exposed to scientific analysis by an outsider, or to any detailed criticism. The major exceptions have been earlier articles by Page (1972b) and by Page and Grandon (1981), which contained a series of technical criticisms to which the project investigators have made no direct response. However, soon after the first of these (Page, 1972b), the project officers released the first technical report of any reasonable availability, and promised a "final and comprehensive report" in 1974. As of the spring of 1986, the Final Report had not yet been released.

STRUCTURE OF THE MILWAUKEE PROJECT

The project began in the massive tide of social effort in the mid-1960s, characterized as the Great Society. The project's originator, Dr. Rick Heber of the University of Wisconsin—Madison, had a history of work in the field of mental retardation, notably in the area of classification. In the 1960s Heber began to investigate an urban slum:

> We surveyed a residential area of the city of Milwaukee characterized by 1960 census data as having the lowest median family income, the greatest rate of dilapidated housing, and the greatest population density per living unit. Over

[3]In fact, Eysenck and Shockley apparently did not directly examine the Milwaukee Project. Jensen had earlier speculated that the claimed IQ changes in Milwaukee might reflect some "reaction range" to maximum environmental stimulation—an effect which in principle might be consistent even with a high heritability of intelligence. And Heber, before any published criticisms and despite the nature-nurture emphasis in his study rationale, stated that his early findings were not a disproof of the nature side: "Professor Jensen and I both agree that, regardless of the outcome in terms of data, the Milwaukee Project is in no sense a test of his position on heritability" (Heber, 1972).

> a six-month period, all families residing in this area with a newborn infant, and at least one other child of the age of six, were selected for study. (Heber et al., 1972, p. 4)

The purpose of the study was to identify families with a high probability of producing retarded offspring (Heber, Dever, & Conry, 1968). Findings indicated that among the 88 families located, 40 had maternal IQs of 80 or higher, and 48 were below 80. Paternal IQ was not included at that time.

The researchers found that four-fifths of the children with IQs of 80 or under had mothers with IQs of 80 or under. They also found that the "generally acknowledged statement that slum-dwelling children score lower on intelligence tests as they become older" (Heber et al., 1972, p. 5) held true only for offspring of mothers whose IQs were below 80, suggesting to Heber and his colleagues that the lower the maternal IQ the higher the risk of offspring with low IQs, especially when maternal IQs were in the mid-retarded range or below.

In the 1972 report, they commented:

> At first glance, these population survey data seem to suggest direct support for the genetic hypothesis of etiology of cultural-familial retardation. However, simply casual observation suggested that the mentally retarded mother residing in the slums creates a social environment for her offspring which is distinctly different from that created by "ghetto-dwelling" mothers of normal intelligence. These observations and our survey data engendered our concern with an approach to rehabilitation of the family, rather than, simply, the individual retarded adult. (Heber et al., 1972, p. 9)

Note that there is no reported evidence of environmental differences between homes of normal as compared with retarded mothers, only a "simply casual observation." But there is an important shift in theory—from retardation caused by the larger community environment to retardation caused (one way or another) by the family itself.

The Milwaukee Project, then, was designed to treat the "whole family" in order to improve the chances for normal intelligence of ghetto youngsters. According to the investigators, the project was:

> composed of two components: 1) the infant, early childhood stimulation program and 2) a maternal rehabilitation program. Intervention into the experiential environment of the Experimental infants began as soon as was feasible after birth (within 6 months) and has continued to the age of regular school entry, approximately 6 years. (Garber, 1975, p. 289)

Families for this experiment were chosen on the basis of "black cultural" extraction and maternal IQs of less than 75 on the Wechsler Adult Intelligence Scale (WAIS). There were to be 40 such families in the study, and the original intention was that these would be "randomly" assigned to two groups (whether they were so assigned was a point of contention). Only the E group was given the massive intervention, but the same schedule of criterion testing was employed with both groups to provide a measure of experimental effect.

As we have seen, the early findings of the project indicated massive differences in measured IQ between children from the E and C groups, differences that approximate 2 standard deviations (Garber & Heber, 1973; Heber et al., 1972; Heber & Garber, 1972). Other differences in infant test performance were reportedly of the same astonishing magnitude.

PUBLICATION AND REACTION

The first formal report of the Milwaukee Project appears to have been a short paper delivered at a conference in Warsaw (Heber & Garber, 1972), followed by a brief progress report that was given some private circulation, (Heber, 1971). The difficulties of obtaining this progress report and the obscurity of its origins are described elsewhere (Page, 1972b). Following Page's criticisms in the open literature, a somewhat more public document, with considerable technical detail, was circulated (Heber et al., 1972).

Following the Warsaw report, many newspapers picked up the happy news of the miracle (as it was sometimes called) that had taken place in Milwaukee, stressing the 33-point gain in IQ. The project had taken potentially retarded individuals and produced superior intellects! It therefore became the rallying point for social planners who may not have recognized the technical nuances of the project but who agreed with Garber that "in good conscience, we could not allow poverty and inequality to exist in our nation" (Garber, 1975, p. 287).

It remains unclear who was responsible for the general publicity given the Milwaukee Project. Dr. Heber (1972) has stated that "there have been no press releases" issued by his staff or by the City of Milwaukee. He suggested, rather, that the press releases were prepared from reports by the Social Rehabilitation Service (SRS). But the SRS Research Director equally affirmed that his office never issued a press release or held a press conference. The official considered the great publicity to be an outgrowth of a popular article published in 1971 in *American Education,* and written by Stephen P. Strickland of the U.S. Office of Education, who apparently had served as private educational consultant to the project group. In early 1972, after there had been enormous press celebration of the project but no technical accounting or criticism, both Heber and Dr. Joseph Fenton (an officer of the SRS) took the view that the October, 1971 report (Heber, 1971) was not intended for broad distribution, despite the fact that it was the only extant summary of a well-known study that had been federally supported for 5 years (Page, 1972b, p. 9).

Principals of the project have by now published a number of papers and articles. A bibliography (supplied by the project staff in 1979) listed 10 such references, and commented that the 1972 technical report was no longer available. One investigator (G.M. Grandon) located six more papers by project officers, these similarly thin, broad, and nontechnical. A search of the *Social Science Citation Index* (*SSCI*) showed that the relatively unavailable 1972 report was cited over 40 times, and the very early population-survey piece (Garber & Heber, 1973) 15 times. The total SSCI count, from 1972 to 1980, was of 70 articles referencing one or another report of the study, usually in a noncritical fashion. Almost all of the referencing articles seemed to accept the reported findings without methodological or substantive reservations.

As noted, however, two researchers have taken public exception to the methodology of the study (Page, 1972b, 1973; Page & Grandon, 1981). Based upon available data, Page (1972b) argued as follows:

> The Milwaukee Project, then, is here viewed as deficient on three counts: biased selection of treatment groups; contamination of criterion tests; and failure to specify the treatments. Any one of these would largely invalidate a study. Together, they destroy it. Further serious questions have emerged about the availability of technical information for the scientific community. (p. 16).

This criticism was published in the *Educational Researcher,* and Dr. Heber was invited by the editor to respond, but chose not to. Nor did the later Project Report allude or respond to the criticisms, except indirectly on the point of randomization.

Similarly, the criticism by Page and Grandon (1981) was published in *The Journal of Special Education,* whose editor offered Dr. Garber an opportunity to respond in the next issue. This offer, too, was declined.

While no writers actually endorsed the project methodology in detail, some have discussed related issues (Kershner, 1973; Kruskal, 1975; Layzer, 1974, 1975; Thompson, 1975; Throne, 1975a). Layzer's comments were part of his attack on the usual mathematical techniques for the estimation of heritability coefficients. However, he applied no such rigorous standards to the Milwaukee Project, and was taken to task for this double standard (Thompson, 1975, p. 1126).

In general, then, we must conclude that the Milwaukee Project has had little exposure to scientific criticism. Its fame stems, rather, from repeated news releases and from brief, broad descriptive materials of the sort presented in the proceedings of nontechnical professional meetings.

METHODOLOGICAL CONCERNS

After the first criticism (Page, 1972b), some new material emerged on each of the three central methodological points: uncertain randomization, possible contamination of criterion tests, and failure to specify treatments. I review the status of each of these concerns, so far as they can be made out at the present time.

Randomization

The question of whether the children were randomly assigned is, as experienced researchers will recognize, not at all a minor matter. To the contrary, it is essential to any assumption of pretreatment equality, which in turn is essential to any confidence that later differences are the result of the treatments. For example, as the researchers had earlier noted, child IQ is correlated with maternal IQ. However, it is equally true that child IQ is correlated with paternal IQ. Any bias in either parent's IQ will have a predictable effect on later child IQ. On the other hand, minor and unbiased deviations from true randomness should not affect experimental validity.

Clearly, the directors of the Milwaukee Project intended it to be received as a field *experiment.* Their writings emphasize an appearance of comparability of Experimental and Control groups. And as Kerlinger (1973) pointed out: "Lacking the ability to randomize, the experimenter must abandon the research, modify it to suit the situation, or seek another situation where randomization is feasible and permissible" (p. 404). Unfortunately, the sampling for the Milwaukee Project is not consistently described. Let us examine some key statements. Heber and Garber (1972) had written:

> As a consequence of the survey data, we have utilized maternal IQ as a basis for selection of a group of newborns, with confidence that a substantial percentage would be identified as mentally retarded as they grow older. By screening all mothers of babies born in our survey area over a period of about one year, we identified mothers of newborns who had IQs less than 70. We have drawn 40 of these mentally retarded mothers from the subject pool and assigned them randomly to either our Experimental or our Control group. (p. 32)

On the other hand, Heber and Dever (1970) wrote that they "identified mothers . . . who have IQs less than 75. . . . [and] have drawn 50 of these mentally retarded mothers from the pool and assigned them randomly to either an experimental or a control group" (p. 421).

But elsewhere, Heber et al. (1972) stated:

> Because of consideration of logistics of preparing infant intervention staff, transportation of infants to the infant center, etc., it was decided to assign infants to experimental and control groups on a monthly basis rather than on an alternating one-by-one basis. . . . Our projections that this would result in an accumulation of three to four subjects per month did not hold so that in some periods a two month interval was required to produce an increment of three or four to the control group. (p. 10)

One notes the shifting numbers in which the limit on maternal IQ was either 70 or 75, the number of participating families was either 40 or 50, and the families were assigned to groups either randomly (i.e., alternating at each entry between the two groups) or with three or four successive families being assigned to one group. Yet each statement is intended to describe the same event of some years before. In later accounts, 40 was given as the number of participating families, 75 as the top maternal IQ, and the deviation from strict random assignment was no longer mentioned: "The 40 families were randomly assigned to an Experimental or Control condition" (Garber & Heber, 1981, p. 74).

Physical Measurement

When there is reason to doubt pretreatment equality, one possible check is to examine other measures taken early, including physical measures. Page (1972b) analyzed ten graphs for height and weight presented in Appendix A of the 1971 report. The earliest data were for 24 months. While the relevant tables were missing, it was possible to estimate the height and standard deviations from the graphs. With a presumed N of 20 each for Es and Cs, there was a very large and statistically reliable difference in height, equal to more than 2 standard deviations. Under the assumptions made in this examination, then, the E and C children could not have been drawn from the same population. When the project officers were shown this analysis there were, over time, three distinctly different and mutually contradictory explanations.

First, Heber (1972) wrote that the data "suggest a treatment effect." But as pointed out by Page (1972b), the differences of over 3 inches at 24 months would imply the most wretched sort of malnutrition or poisoning—and this done to the E group!

The second explanation, following the published criticism, was given in a well-attended public address on November 10, 1972, at the Gengras

Center in Hartford, Connecticut, where Dr. Heber was describing the study. Part of that address:

> The data that Page based his conclusion on, the differences in height, were based on a figure included in the Appendix to our Progress Report, which was based on a sample of 8 experimental and 8 control kids at 24 months, who differed to a degree that he thought was larger than would occur by chance statistically.... He obviously assumed that the Ns were 20 in each group, and computed his test on that basis. But I can say here that we just completed a computer analysis... and there are no differences between either height or weight, etc.

In view of this response I reanalyzed the data that were estimated from the graph, this time with *N*s of 8 and 8, and again found a significant height difference at 24 months, favoring the C group.

But the Milwaukee Project directors had still a third explanation, this one contradicting the second. In the December 1972 Progress Report (released in 1973), there were new tables of weight and height, including the number of children composing each mean. In a footnote, the authors commented: "In actual fact, . . . the *n*'s for which we had data at 24 months were two and five respectively for the two groups and, of course, provide no basis for meaningful statistical comparison" (Heber et al., 1972, p. 45).

From their tables, in fact, it turns out that for physical data the *N*s fluctuated between 2 and 20 for the E group, and between 5 and 18 for the C group. It is clear that no tests of group comparability were designed into the project.

Height Variances

Commenting on this adjustment of *N*s for 24 months, the project directors asserted:

> Statistical analyses of height-weight data at all subsequent age levels where the n's are more nearly complete produce no significant differences between groups. One index of the comparability in terms of physical status of the two groups at birth is provided through hospital and birth records. . . . Again, the differences between groups are non-significant. (Heber et al., 1972, p. 46)

Apparently, the project statisticians tested the reported data only for differences in *means*. But comparability of groups is diagnosed just as effectively through other distributional differences. The reported birth data are provided in our Table 5.

From this table, it is easy to make an *F*-test of the *variances* by squaring

TABLE 5.
Mean height and weight of the
Experimental and Control Groups at birth

	Experimental $N = 20$	*Control* $N = 18$
Height	19.4 in. (SD = 1.2)	19.8 in. (SD = 1.9)
Weight	6 lb. 15 oz. (SD = .94)	7 lb. 2 oz. (SD = 1.1)

Data from Heber et al., 1972, Table 3.2.
Reprinted from Page and Grandon (1981), Table 1, p. 247, with permission of *The Journal of Special Education.*

and dividing the SDs ($F = 3.61/1.44 = 2.51$, $df = 17, 19$). Caution must be taken when multiple comparisons are possible, but this F-test suggests that, at a marginal level of reliability, these variances in height may not be from the same population ($p < .06$). (A similar difficulty with variances plagues the mental-test data, as reported later.)

Of course field experiments are almost inevitably messy enterprises, especially when conducted over a long time, with shifting project personnel, inadequate records, and forgetfulness about procedures. Still, what records do exist raise doubts about the comparability of the E and C groups of the Milwaukee Project, particularly because of acknowledged irregularities in the sampling and assignment of children.

Attrition

Any longitudinal study is threatened by attrition, especially when reasons for dropping out may be related to the project treatment. First mention of attrition is made in the Heber et al. (1972) report:

> Up to the present time two Control families have been lost and all efforts to locate them have failed.
>
> The Experimental group lost two subjects very early; one infant died as a result of a sudden crib death, and the second was lost by withdrawal of the mother from the program. . . . Since both of these losses occurred while the samples were still being accumulated, they were replaced, bringing the total N to 20; however, more recently three Experimental families have been lost due to relocation to southern states. In two of these cases, the families left after the children had reached four years of age, and in the third case, after the child was 4½. Contact has been maintained with these three families however, and the children will receive the same comprehensive evaluations at age 7 scheduled for all subjects. In addition, subsequent to accumulation

> of the basic samples, additional infants born to Experimental mothers were also introduced to the intervention program and there are five such younger siblings. Intelligence test data on these siblings is (sic) reported separately from basic samples. (pp. 44–45)

In general, none of the difficulties created by these shifts is identified or acknowledged in the Project Reports. The composition of the curves of E and C intelligence, as often presented in reports, is obscured by such anomalies. The exact numbers of E and C children are clouded, with no clear statement of who was lost through attrition and how such loss affected the reported data. Further, the group data for intelligence or other test measures are seldom presented with *N*s or with variances.

The Nature of the Criterion Tests

The classic picture of the outcome from the Milwaukee Project is seen in Figure 2 (reproduced from Heber et al., 1972, p. 49a). The C children slide down into the lower normal range; the E children rapidly achieve superior intelligence and maintain this remarkable lead (about 30 IQ points) until 5½ years of age, with nothing to suggest that the

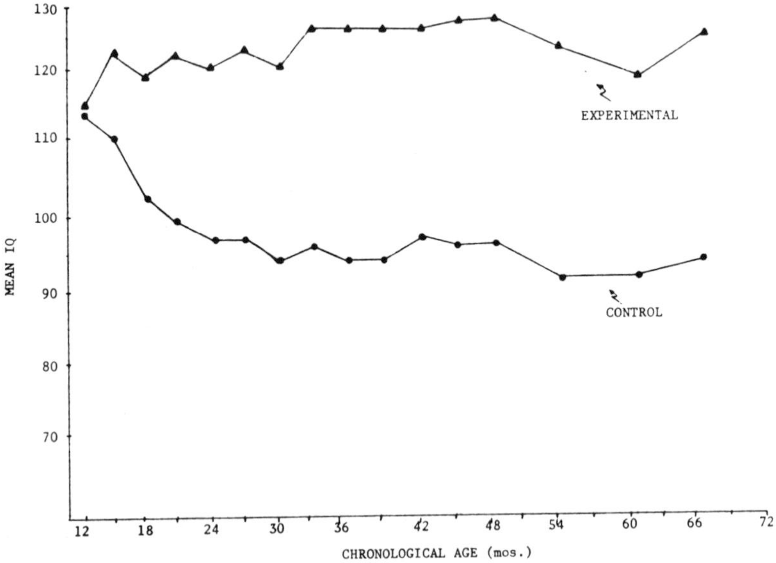

FIG. 2. Mean IQ scores at increasing ages for the Experimental and Control Groups of the Milwaukee Project. From Heber et al., 1972, p. 49a, Figure 3.18.

disparity will not persist. Heber and his colleagues gave the following explanation of the tests:

> The data presented uses (sic) scores derived from the Gessell schedules from 12-21 months, and Cattell and Binet scores from 24 to 66 months. . . . Of those Controls tested, only three have ever scored over 100 on the WPPSI and they are included, while the remainder are below 91. On the other hand, not one Experimental child has scored as yet below 100. (pp. 49–50)

The same report gives very little information about the shifting *N*s that produced the 3-month data points in Figure 2, or the variances at any one point, except for the following:

> The Experimental group at 60 months, had a mean IQ of 118 (s.d. = 6.3) compared to the Control group's mean IQ of 92 (s.d. = 12.5): a difference of 26 points. The mean IQ of the Experimental group at 66 months is 124 (s.d. = 8.6), compared to the Control group's mean IQ of 94 (s.d. = 10.7): a difference of thirty points. (pp. 49–50)

There is no report of any individual records or of test reliability from one test to the next. WPPSI scores, which show as much as 14 points lower estimates, are mentioned but are not included in the chart.

Development vs. Intelligence

As noted, the instrument used for the first 2 years of testing was the Gesell Developmental Schedule, composed of about 20 types of behavior. Some of the measured behaviors are: reactions to a dangling ring, rattle, or bell; to social stimulation; to motor behaviors such as standing or sitting; to one, two, and three cubes. As noted often by psychometricians, these behaviors are better measures of sensorimotor precocity than of intellectual ability. Except for cases of gross handicap, correlations with later measured intelligence are very low, and it is quite clear that something different is being measured in older children. On the other hand, by around 4 years, mental ability ordinarily correlates some .70 with mental ability at 16 (Cronbach, 1970, p. 231).

But the dramatic differences in measured IQ are already obvious in the second year of life for the Milwaukee children. Some explanation for this difference is contained in the Heber et al. (1972) Progress Report, where a nine-page description of the Infancy Program is given, and where the Appendix provides a six-page "Developmental Check List," a one-page "Item Explanations of Developmental Check List," and two pages of "Activities to Emphasize," the only comprehensive report to date of the diagnostics and program that produced the infant portion of the graph shown in Figure 2. Consequently, this program should be carefully examined.

The checklist has items that are likely to appear in developmental measures, such as "Can pull pants down" and "Uses spoon unassisted" (Self-help); "Sits alone steadily" and "Walks upstairs without aid" (Motor, gross); "Builds tower of three blocks after demonstration" and "Copies circles" (Motor, fine); and "Imitates sounds made by teacher" (Language, expressive). Perhaps the items most related to early mental tests are items such as "Knows 'how many' up to 2," "Names one color," "Matches items as to form," "Knows body parts," "Draws a man with head, legs, body, and features," "Understands concepts of 'more' and 'less'," and "Understands 'right' and 'left' " (Basic knowledge).

However, each of these seems to be part of the curriculum, so far as can be made out from the two-page example. The "Activities to Emphasize" section is illustrated for a 12-month-old child named Michelle, and the activities are apparently those of which she is not yet in command. Under "Self-help," among other items, she is to "practice handling spoon." Under "Gross-motor," she is to practice "sitting in chair alone." Under "Expressive Language," she is to practice "imitating sounds made by teacher." Under "Basic Knowledge," she is "continuing to learn body parts" (pp. 135–136).

What does the "Infancy Stimulation Program" consist of, then? Apparently of training in the items surveyed by the project's "Developmental Check List." And in a tidy circle, these checklist items are also those in the Gesell Developmental Schedule. Apply this circle of frequent diagnosis (which practices items) to curriculum (which practices and trains items) to the test (which measures acquisition of the items), and it is no longer surprising that, in the first 2 years, there is a remarkable divergence between the E and C groups, as exhibited in Figure 2.

Item Sample vs. Item Domain

One of the more crucial distinctions in research design is that between the specific items on a test and the background population of items, or domain, of which the test items are only a sample. The value of a norm-referenced test lies not in determining whether the child can perform *these* items, but rather in estimating how well the child is in command of the huge, possibly infinite, domain of abilities that are our real concern.

In the 1960s the distinction was blurred as behaviorists worked to demonstrate their skill in eliciting, shaping, modifying, and reinforcing specific behaviors. This blurring was especially evident in the ill-starred experiments in Performance Contracting (PC) conducted by the Office of Economic Opportunity (OEO). Through PC, psychologists expected to train disadvantaged youths in the skills of reading and arithmetic. Spectacular earlier gains through PC had been marred by the discovery that there had been *teaching of the test.* Indeed, observers noted that students were commenting to each other about familiar items. The OEO, in demanding that the major demonstration of PC be beyond reproach, conceived a remarkable, massive experiment across a wide national sample of low-achieving groups, geographical areas, grade levels, and criterion tests. There was unprecedented rigor in design, with neither students, teachers, nor PC implementers knowing which tests would be used, and with strict prohibitions against their including any test material in the instructional programs. Most unusual, the evaluation was handled by a separate agency (Battelle Memorial Institute) employed directly by the government.

The results were shattering, and showed how much the previous investigators had been deceived by the contamination of the instruction with test material, by the blurring of item sample and item domain, and by the biases created by friendly, self-serving, in-house evaluations (Page, 1972a). Some of the behavior-oriented psychologists in the OEO experiment at first tried determinedly to continue as before. For example, one performance contractor wanted to gather all vocabulary from six reading tests into a programmed unit for the repetitive drilling of just those items! Eventually, he had to be warned severely against doing so. But his adamancy was a symptom of a confusion that is fairly widespread among educators—and that may well have appeared repeatedly in the Milwaukee Project, not only in the first 2 years but across the preschool period covered by the graph. In the later testing programs the curriculum is not clear enough for us to be sure about this circularity. But there are a number of other lines of evidence pointing to it, as we shall see.

Project vs. Outside Evaluation

As noted with the PC experiment, evaluation may be radically different when conducted by outside, truly independent, competent researchers. Preschool individual mental tests, like those that make up the points of Figure 2, are notoriously subject to effects of mood and rapport (Anastasi, 1961, pp. 297-300; Cronbach, 1970, pp. 262-264). Anastasi wrote (1961, p. 297) on the scoring of some preschool tests: "Subjectivity is likely to enter, since many test responses at this level leave no permanent record." Unfortunately, similar tests contributing to Figure 2 were apparently conducted by friendly project personnel, using the same tests that would become familiar to the children, surely to the project directors, and possibly also to the paraprofessionals in daily interaction with the children.

Now with many small, explicitly detailed experiments, it is quite permissible to have only in-house criterion testing, since it is expected that replication by others will thereafter verify or fail to support the findings.

But as all testify, the Milwaukee Project is "unique," both in intensity and in outcome. No one else has claimed similar results, and the methods described are broad enough so that, even with unlimited funds, one could not replicate the project. Therefore, some outside, truly independent evaluation becomes essential as a matter of course. No doubt sensitive to this criticism, the project directors did the following:

> In order to evaluate the effects of the examiner in the production of group differences in test performance, one test administration was conducted by a qualified examiner brought from a neighboring state for this purpose. All subjects were tested in an environment totally unfamiliar to them and the examiner was not appraised of the subject's group membership. At that time, all four-year scores were complete and comparison of these scores with the independent tester showed no significant differences. (Heber et al., 1972, p. 50)

The data referred to are here presented in Table 6.

As close inspection reveals, the data of the tables show that something is amiss. True, as the project directors state, there are no significant differences between the *means* of the two appraisals. Indeed, both comparisons reveal *t*-tests of less than 1.0. But there is strong evidence that these mean similarities are based on test scores which themselves must vary from project examiner to outside tester, for as Table 6 shows, the *variances* for the E children differ widely in the two testings, $F = 2.98$, $p. < .05$.

PROGRAM DESCRIPTION

Earlier articles (Page, 1972b; Page & Grandon, 1981) criticized the Milwaukee Project for lacking one of the principal requirements of any scientific experiment: a clear description of the treatment. We have already examined the "Infancy Stimulation Program." In addition, the Heber et al.

TABLE 6.
Comparison of project examiner and independent examiner IQ-test scores

	Project	*Independent*
Experimental	126 (SD = 5.5)	127 (SD = 9.5)
Control	95.7 (SD = 10.8)	92.1 (SD = 12.6)

Data from Heber et al., 1972, p. 50, Table 3.5.

Reprinted from Page and Grandon (1981), Table 2, p. 252, with permission of *The Journal of Special Education.*

(1972) progress report included nearly 100 pages of descriptions of various programs beyond infancy, which were intended to suggest the additional curriculum. In this, the project directors went farther than before to increase our understanding of the cognitive work.

Even with 100 pages of illustrations, of course, the described program would not fill the years of intensive interaction, and one should therefore regard these materials once again as samples. Yet there is enough information to draw the conclusion that these materials are, indeed, modeled closely after the typical content of *preschool mental tests.* There is intensive drill on concepts such as (for Evaluation): number, size, shape, quantity, position, and weight; and (for Perception): perception of number and of similarities (e.g., "Here are *two* beads, *two* blocks, *two* fingers, *two* cookies, *two* pennies; which box has *two* toys in it?").

With intensive daily practice in such materials, marked improvement in test scores for the same concepts and relations can be expected. But it is impossible to determine to what extent such materials resemble the test items.

LATER PERFORMANCE

The real object of the project, and its greatest interest to psychologists, is not the differences shown in Figure 2, no matter how dramatic. Rather, we are interested in the possible transfer of this trained intelligence to other, newer performance when the youngsters are no longer engaged in the experiment on a daily basis. If the differences are real they should be evident in those regular correlates of such test scores: new measures of later intelligence and school performance given under other conditions. Indeed, such later testing may be the appropriate ultimate measures of project effects.

IQ Testing Under Project Control

Fortunately, there is some information, though scanty, about the later test performance of the E and C children (Flynn, 1984; Garber, 1982; Garber & Heber, 1981; Heber & Garber, 1975). The project was apparently discontinued as an instructional program when the youngsters entered school, but was not ended as a testing/research agency. Four years after the intervention, the project still had "immediate contact with nearly 75% of our original families." The directors continued:

> We have continued IQ testing of the children with the WISC, roughly 1, 2, 3, and 4 years after school entry.

> One major question is, of course, the extent to which the gains of intervention, if any, will be maintained as time goes on. It is apparent that up to this point, at least, WISC differential, on the order of 20+ IQ points, has been maintained over a 4-year follow-up to age 10. The Experimental group has a mean IQ of 105, as compared to the Control group mean of 85. (Garber & Heber, 1981, p. 80)

These tests and testers were, once again, under project control. While it was disappointing that the E children were no longer in the superior range, there was apparently a continued advantage—so far as such early cognitive tests are concerned—over the C children.

The most public information for the E children comes from Flynn (1984), who was studying apparent gains in the U.S. IQ means from 1932 to 1978, and who examined certain Milwaukee data in doing so. Flynn's relevant table is reproduced here as Table 7.

In Table 7, the "Results as presented" are what Flynn was able to obtain from three sources, including personal communication from Garber in December, 1982. We note the additional information about the later testing, including the changes in intelligence tests used, from the Stanford-Binet through the WPPSI to the WISC. Apparently, only the early Stanford-Binet had been in the "superior range," and only for measurements taken before students had entered public schools. We find, in these reported results, an apparent decline of 22 IQ points.

As psychometricians are well aware, there are always questions of

TABLE 7.
Heber's Experimental Group:
Mean IQ performances with increasing age

	Age (years)				
Test	*2–3*	*4–6*	*7–9*	*10–11*	*12–14*
		Results as presented			
SB-LM	122	121			
WPPSI		111			
WISC			103	104	100
		Results adjusted			
SB-LM	108	107			
WPPSI		105			
WISC			95	96	92

Reprinted from Flynn (1984), Table 7, p. 40, with permission of the author and of the American Psychological Association.

comparability across tests (e.g., Spitz, 1983). After studying United States data, Flynn constructed tables for translating one test's score into another. When applied to Milwaukee's Experimental children, Flynn's tables produced the "Results as adjusted," also shown in our Table 7.

Flynn's conclusion about the E children is interesting: "These children never did have a mean IQ above the normal range and their performance was essentially stable just so long as they remained in Heber's program" (p. 40). Flynn's "adjusted" scores show a decline of 16 IQ points. According to these adjusted scores, from about the time they entered school and left daily project control, the E children had a mean IQ that was somewhat below the national average.

Achievement Testing

For the testing of school achievement, in the (usually) highly related areas covered by the Metropolitan Achievement Test, the results appear to have been far less satisfactory, so much so that the project directors do not give much interpretable data, let alone graphs like Figure 2. Here is their cryptic description:

> [On] the Metropolitan Achievement Test the Experimental group was significantly superior to the Control group on all subtests through the first 2 years. For the first year the distribution of the Experimental group approximated the national profile and the performance of the Control group was markedly depressed. The performance of the Control group since then has further declined, first to the lower level of the city of Milwaukee, and then to the still lower one of their inner-city schools. (Garber & Heber, 1981, p. 80)

Here again, the data are remarkably scanty. As with most of the project reports, there are no stated *N*s, variances, or citations of other sources of information. But significantly, there are not even any *means.* Apparently, despite the early introduction and drill with reading and arithmetic, even in the first year the E group was about at the national average.

There is one other source of information about school performance. Clarke and Clarke (1976, pp. 224–225) reported that there was no longer a difference between E and C children in reading ability. Reading ability is, of course, the principal goal of the elementary school, and the most central to all other school learning. Furthermore, reading comprehension is the achievement most highly correlated with measured IQ and with the general factor (*g*) derived from large mental-test batteries (Jensen, 1980).

THE TEXTBOOK MIRACLE

Textbook authors have a difficult role in translating technical literature into a form that is accessible to the student reader. They must satisfy (some) professors that their text is sufficiently rigorous, but must also cope with a world of belief about psychology and education brought to us through the media: gullible, trendy, and politicized, especially the TV and national press.

In covering the Milwaukee Project, textbook authors have not distinguished themselves as guardians of established truth. In the words of Flynn (1984):

> Who can forget the great days of the early 1970s when the first reports emerged: that from ages 2 to 4, the experimental children were not merely normal but superior, that their mean IQ on the Stanford–Binet was above 120. The news spread beyond America to the whole English-speaking world. . . . Heber's results quickly found their way into the textbooks: [One in 1974] was typical with its references to this "exciting" study, its "most encouraging" results, its "impressive" findings—not the usual language of a text. (p. 40)

The textbook treatment of the project was partially reviewed by other investigators (Sommer & Sommer, 1983), who concentrated on texts in abnormal and developmental psychology. They report the "increasing frequency" of reference since 1977:

> [In 1981, we] noticed that [textbook] references (mention of the Heber study was becoming increasingly common) were . . . obscure—conference proceedings, one or two book chapters, progress reports, other people's dissertations, and so forth. (p. 982)

Sommer and Sommer explored the texts in their own two psychological specialties, abnormal and developmental, and found the incidence of mention increasing through 1982, actually appearing in a majority of texts in the latest years surveyed. Their comment: "This analysis yields a picture of research findings becoming widespread in textbooks . . . without ever having been subjected to journal review. Our experience is that *textbooks are regarded as authoritative by the students who read them and the faculty who adopt them*" (Sommer & Sommer, 1983, p. 983, italics added).

The reviewers also comment on the uncritical nature of the citations. They cite one widely used text of abnormal psychology that described the Milwaukee Project as a "rigorously controlled experiment demonstrating the benefits of an early intervention program" (p. 983). They further note the shallow scholarship of the texts, particularly in their failure to cite any earlier criticism of the project. Sommer and Sommer conclude by hoping, "at the least, that this sad episode will cause all of us to be more careful in our scholarship" (p. 985).

In general, from our own observation, a pattern of uncritical citation may also be seen in textbooks in educational psychology and even in general psychology. One widely used text in educational psychology (Sprinthall & Sprinthall, 1981) devoted three pages to the Milwaukee Project. The project was headlined "A CAUSE FOR OPTIMISM" (p. 96), and the authors' laudatory tone was typical of other writers': "Some of the trained group registered IQs of 135—and these were children of mothers whose IQs were 70 or less!" (p. 99).

The authors did cite criticism, and warned that "it is too soon to consider [Heber's] findings conclusive" (p. 99). Yet later in the text the warning was forgotten:

> Rick Heber's study . . . found that massive educational intervention can increase IQs by an average of 33 points. (p. 483)
>
> Heber's program, which begins when the infant is scarcely home from the hospital, may not only prevent intellectual deterioration but may also even give the children an IQ gain. (p. 488)
>
> [The study] indicate[s] rather clearly that intellectual functioning and general development can be positively influenced by a rich, stimulating early environment. (p. 590)

Thus do our textbooks pick up a sort of wish-fulfillment from the current atmosphere of our society, and spread the word—in unexamined, repetitive assertions—that there really was a miracle in Milwaukee.

Sommer and Sommer's (1983) lament about textbooks was published in the *American Psychologist,* which is received by more than 65,000 social scientists. In response, there was published debate about certain of the issues raised: whether it should be mandatory that studies be "replicated," whether refereed publications are really more trustworthy than others, and whether the Milwaukee Project was itself "valid" (Comment, *American Psychologist,* November, 1984, pp. 1315–1319). On the question of validity, Sommer and Sommer (1984) felt themselves "unable to make a judgment" (p. 1318).

And there was some question about one of the touchiest aspects of the Milwaukee Project: whether it was scientifically relevant that there had been a scandal involving the leaders of the Center where the project was housed, leading to convictions and jail sentences for two of them, including Dr. Heber himself. The criticism in the *American Psychologist* was about whether such proved and spectacular dishonesty should affect the public credibility of the project. This is a remarkable question and merits more attention than it has received in the media.

THE QUIET SCANDAL

For his role in alerting the public to the nature of this scandal, we are indebted to the investigative reporting of Rob Fixmer, Staff Writer (and now an Editor) for the *Capital Times* (*CT*) of Madison, Wisconsin. According to the *CT* (Jan. 23, 1981, p. 6), the project was supported for 15 years (up to 1981) with funding of *14 million* dollars. Since the data released have been almost trivial, this expenditure must be counted as largely for the experimental treatments of the children. If 20 children were truly raised 30 points in IQ, then the cost would have been an astonishing $23 thousand per IQ point, per child. Up to that time, information on the public costs, like information about the experiment itself, had been almost impossible to obtain. In addition, Heber "controlled more than $2.3 million per year in grants from a variety of federal agencies" (*CT,* Jan. 14, 1981, p. 1).

As a result of Mr. Fixmer's investigations, Dr. F. Rick Heber and his research associate, Dr. Patrick Flanigan, were charged with one count of conspiracy and 13 counts of converting more than 160 thousand dollars of federal grant funds to their personal use over a 10-year period. They converted to their own accounts the conference registration fees from such organizations as the National Association for Retarded Citizens, the Wisconsin Council of the Knights of Columbus (fund for exceptional children), and the Ohio State University Research Foundation. The money, of course, never appeared on their tax returns. In July of 1981 a jury found Heber and Flanigan guilty and they were sentenced to 3 years in prison and 3 years probation following their release. Each was ordered to repay his share of the stolen money (*CT,* Oct. 31, 1981, pp. 1, 4).

In addition to the federal indictments, the State of Wisconsin also charged Heber and Flanigan on two counts of embezzlement and two counts of tax evasion. Both were convicted, and Flanigan was sentenced to 5 years for fraud, while Heber was sentenced to 4 years on State theft and tax charges, to be served concurrently with the federal sentences. Both were also ordered to pay restitutions and fines (*CT,* Dec. 30, 1981; Feb. 25, 1982).

Interviews with University of Wisconsin personnel revealed that Dr. Heber had been difficult to reach and frequently away from his office during the course of the grant. In fact, when he was relieved of his duties as director of the University of Wisconsin's Waisman Center, the official explanation was that he had been absent from the campus too often (*CT*, April 8, 1981, pp. 1, 16).

In a separate case, Heber's frequent coauthor, Dr. Howard Garber, was brought to court for false payroll entries of more than 23 thousand dollars over an 8-year period. At Heber's direction, Dr. Garber's wife had been placed on the payroll for a no-show job on Heber's grant. The money was intended to reimburse Dr. Garber for his annual summer trips to Sweden to teach a course on mental retardation, there being no grant money allocated for this purpose. Although Garber acquiesced to this arrangement, the judge believed that it was Heber who was primarily responsible for the misapplication of funds. Consequently, when Dr. Garber pleaded guilty to two minor misdemeanors he was sentenced merely to serve 1 hour in the custody of the U.S. Marshall (*CT*, Dec. 23, 1982, pp. 1, 9). At this writing he is still in Madison, at the University of Wisconsin, as the remaining responsible officer for any residual activities of the Milwaukee Project.

Faith In The Milwaukee Project

Apparently there are many professionals who strongly believe in the Milwaukee Project, with its promise of the almost limitless plasticity of intelligence. In their view any shadows on the project's reputation, whether federal indictments for fraud or the major scientific challenges outlined earlier, should be ignored or set aside as irrelevant to "the overall message" of the project. In some of the letters responding to Sommer and Sommer there was a tone of indignation that the article, "Mystery in Milwaukee," seemed to imply some linkage between personal misconduct and the reliability of scientific evidence. One writer challenged "whether an individual's violation of federal law, even for fraud, can be assumed to imply that research data generated by that individual are likely to be fraudulent. . . . Sommer and Sommer have, therefore, done a grave disservice. . . ." (Comment in the *American Psychologist*, 1984, p. 1316).

Evidence vs. Testimony

The scientific proof of any theory must depend on either evidence or testimony. Evidence is much preferred, so long as it is sustained by published data, the provision of sufficient detail, and its general plausibility in light of other findings in the same field. Testimony is a far distant second choice, and must be from respected investigators of established and deserved reputation. Even such testimony is only a transient persuader and is never to be trusted for long if there is disagreement with the major trends of findings and if there is no support from independent researchers and the early release of technical details.

In the Milwaukee Project there has never been any concordance between the claimed results and other research on attempts to raise intelligence. To the contrary, the claims are completely contrary to *verified* research performed under established methods. Furthermore, there are the many contradictions of claimed procedures and data: the shifting stories of the "randomization," the shifting identities of the "forty" claimed subjects, the shifting cutoff scores for maternal IQ, the shifting "numbers" for the reported tables. There are the grave doubts cast by the "independent tester," whose test results produced significantly different distributions from those of project testers. There is the confounding of the IQ-test items with the curriculum training program, the confusion of test content with *domain* content, and especially the continued failure, even after 20 years and $14 million in federal funds, to provide open evidence for the research community.

Under all these conditions, where neither evidence nor testimony is to be relied on, what is the basis for any continued trust in the claimed findings of the Milwaukee Project?

A Double Standard

As we have seen, the Milwaukee Project has assumed a great symbolic and ideological importance. Its Director, Dr. Heber, had been elevated to remarkable levels of governmental influence, including chief advisor on mental retardation to a U.S. President, and the project itself had reached a rare level of news visibility. One would suppose that the tragic collapse of Dr. Heber's reputation would occasion much media attention, to be covered by national TV, radio, and press, and that his court trial would be reported at least weekly in such archival newspapers as *The New York Times.*

After all, we had the example of Sir Cyril Burt, the eminent psychologist and researcher in heritability, whose work also, like Heber's, had ideological significance. After his death, social scientists looked closely at his work on identical twins, and concluded that much of the data was faulty and probably falsified. A chorus of voices was raised to decry this misconduct, and found its way into daily press and TV. There were at least six stories of the "Burt scandal" in the *New York Times* alone. It often appeared as if the entire field of behavioral genetics was placed under a cloud.

Compared with Burt's treatment, the oblivion of the Milwaukee scandal is remarkable. The project's earlier findings had been widely noted. The *Washington Post* believed that it might have "settled once and for all" the question of heredity versus environment for the intelligence of slum children. The *New York Times* had reported that the project "has proved" that IQs could be raised more than 30 points by the methods of Heber and his associates (these quotes cited by Herrnstein, 1982). In contrast, not a word about the Heber scandal appeared in the *Times,* the newsweeklies, *Science* magazine, or on national TV. What is the source of such a double standard? Apparently the major media are warmly supportive of environmentalism and generally condemnatory of genetic attribution for individual differences in intelligence.

Serious students of intelligence must struggle not only against ignorance in their own field but also against the strong winds of bias from the media and the government. It is incumbent upon the scientific community to explore events of high symbolic importance in order to appraise their scientific meaning, and the Milwaukee Project surely has symbolic significance far beyond its scientific merit.

The Missing Final Report

The current status of the long-promised Final Report is quite typical of the project's history. As we have seen, a more complete accounting has been promised ever since scientific criticism was first directed toward the project (Page, 1972b). That criticism apparently motivated the release and limited circulation of the in-house "Progress Report" (Heber, et al., 1972), the deficiencies of which have already been examined. Since then there was an overseas, rather fugitive "Progress Report II" of less than 10 pages (Heber & Garber, 1975). Another report by Garber and Heber (1977) ran less than 9 pages, and also was not refereed.

The article by Sommer and Sommer (1983) drew a published response by Garber (1984).

> A lengthy and detailed report has been accepted by the American Association on Mental Deficiency monograph series for publication. In addition, a shorter interim report to the American Journal of Mental Deficiency has been accepted, is being reviewed, and will be formally available shortly. (p. 1315)

However, more than a year after Garber wrote his promise to the *American Psychologist,* he had still not obtained final acceptance of either report (Meyers, 1985; Robinson, 1985).

Our own recent experiences have been repetitions of the past. Two letters to Garber went unanswered. Two others (one of them registered) produced optimistic responses about the imminence of the Final Report and its general availability. None of the replies included any new material, and promises to send copies were not kept. I also asked for the names of the federal agencies that supported the later work for the Milwaukee Project but Dr. Garber has not responded to questions about sponsors, either. Unfortunately, the "Final Report" remains, as it has for at least 13 years, just around the corner.

The Milwaukee Project is altogether an extraordinary story in the social sciences, and not one of our proudest.

7 Behavior Modification—The Return of Radical Empiricism

In a short autobiographical paper, B.F. Skinner (1967), the eminent psychologist who did so much to advance the behavioristic approach, pointed out that Frazier, the hero of his novel, *Walden Two,* speaks for him when—having failed to predict behavior—he cries out in rage, "Behave, damn you! Behave as you ought!" For Skinner, the essence of psychology is not the prediction of behavior but its control, and only if we obey nature (read: response-reward contingencies) can we control it. Presumably, Frazier also speaks for Skinner when, while lying in a crucifixion-like position, he replies to comments about playing God, "There's a curious similarity," or says angrily, "And I like to play God! Who wouldn't, under the circumstances?" (Skinner, 1948/1962, pp. 296–299).

This God-like demeanor is made palatable by the end result: an idyllic Walden Two where, under the benign influence of positive reinforcement, discord is eliminated and workers are cheerfully carrying out their duties.

The idea that behaviors that are most frequently emitted are the ones that, in the past, had been given immediate and frequent positive reinforcement, and that consequently behavior can be changed by the judicious application of reinforcement, pervades behaviorists' approach to all behavior, including the expression of intelligent behavior. Consequently, behaviorists assume that intelligent behavior has been and can be shaped by the environment. This being the case, then it follows that mental retardation is not immutable, and more adequate (intelligent) behavior can be induced by properly administered reinforcement. Anyone who can play God would not allow retarded children to remain retarded. It is easy to see why such a seductive hypothesis would recruit large numbers of disciples, particularly when there have been so many scientific and popular articles demonstrating the successful shaping of animal and human behaviors.

It is impossible in the space of a single chapter to review all the work in mental retardation that grew out of the Skinnerian position. Much of it has been directed toward training the severely and profoundly retarded in self-care functions, such as using the toilet, brushing their teeth, feeding, dressing, and so on. For this purpose, as well as for reducing self-injurious and destructive behavior, behavior modification is usually the method of choice, and has proved useful (see Whitman & Scibak, 1979, for a review), although some questions about the early enthusiasm for this method have been raised (e.g., Baumeister, 1969). Behavior modification techniques have been used also in the formation of token economies to control and teach retarded persons of varying intellectual levels, both in institutional settings and in classrooms (e.g., Thompson & Grabowski, 1977).

But our interest is in intelligence, and this chapter is confined to an examination of the claims made by some of the principal proponents of the behaviorist position that the intellectual behavior of retarded persons can be raised to a very substantial degree.

RETARDATION AS DEFECTIVE REINFORCEMENT

In the early 1960s Sidney Bijou was (as he still is) among the more active proponents of the behaviorist approach to mental retardation. In a seminal paper (Bijou, 1963), he suggested that it is unwise to conceive of psychological variables in biological terms because this implies that physiological variables will give us all the necessary information to explain psychological phenomena. Rather, "behavioral retardation" should be defined in terms of the interaction of the organism with its environment. In this approach there should be no appeal to unknown hypothetical constructs. A retarded person is viewed as having "a limited repertory of behaviors evolving from interactions with his environmental contacts which constitute his history" (p. 101).

Bijou goes on to specify that "retarded behavior is a function of *observable* biological, physical, and social conditions" (p. 101, italics added). If, for example, there are hereditary anomalies underlying the condition, they are to be ignored for the purposes of psychological understanding and control because hereditary anomalies do not imply defective "mentality," only the production of anatomical and physiological anomalies which in turn affect the individual's interaction with the environment (Bijou is careful to place quotation marks around terms like "mentality" and "native ability").

The primary forces operating to retard development are the kinds and patterns of reinforcement given by the child's parents or parent surrogates. Poor children reared in isolated communities, infants in institutions, and infants with emotionally disturbed parents are especially likely to be limited in the development of adequate behavioral repertoires. As an example of what can result from inadequate reinforcement histories Bijou cites the case of Isabelle, who spent most of her early life isolated with her deaf-mute mother in a dark room until discovered when 6½ years of age (Davis, 1947; Mason, 1942). At the time she was discovered she could not speak, made strange croaking sounds, acted like an infant, and behaved almost like an animal toward strangers. When tested, her mental age was 19 months.

Bijou did not describe how Isabelle developed after she was discovered—although the information is given in the paper he cited (Davis, 1947) and by Mason (1942)—so I digress here to give that information because it seems to me to be crucial to an understanding of the role of native ability (genetic endowment) in human performance, a role that behaviorists wish us to ignore.

After her discovery, Isabelle was given a training program during which she rapidly progressed. About 3 months after being discovered she was saying three-word sentences, and after another 9 months could identify sentences, write, and add to 10. Seven months after that she was asking complicated questions, and by the time she was 8½ she had reached a normal educational level. A year and a half after she had been discovered she gave the impression of a bright, cheerful, energetic little girl, and was considered to be of average intelligence.

The reason why this description of Isabelle's recovery is so important is that this indeed was an example of a severely deprived child in terms of reinforcement (as well as nutritional) history. However, with training and proper care, Isabelle recovered. There are thousands of severely retarded children who at 6½ years of age have a mental age of 2 years, but who—despite the best care and training—never progress the way that Isabelle did.

What is the crucial source of the difference between these children and Isabelle? It seems clear that it cannot be simply the differences in reinforcement history (in fact, the reinforcement history of most profoundly retarded 6½-year-olds is surely more favorable than it was for Isabelle); the source of the difference must be in the central nervous system. The severely retarded children who do not benefit from training, as Isabelle did, have either a damaged central nervous system or deficient genetic endowment, while Isabelle suffered no debilitating brain damage and was endowed with at least average intellectual potential. Of course her endowment was prevented from blossoming by a horribly restricted environment, but once the restrictions were lifted and she was given proper training, she compensated by an extremely rapid rate of growth in her mental development and behavior.

This illustration epitomizes the tunnel vision encouraged by the behaviorists. To concentrate only on the reinforcement history and to minimize mental capacity or genetic endowment is to voluntarily restrict one's field of vision. If the intellectual behavior of mentally retarded individuals is so crucially determined by their reinforcement history, then a change in reinforcement contingencies should transpose retarded behavior into average intellectual behavior, as it did with Isabelle. That this is not possible with the vast majority of retarded persons would appear to be ample evidence that reinforcement contingencies are not responsible for retarded intellectual behavior.

Of course this was not the thinking of behaviorists then, nor is it now. In a follow-up paper published in 1966, Bijou revised and extended his position. The objective remained the analysis of *observable* conditions that produce retarded behavior. Genetic processes may participate in producing retarded psychological development, but only to the extent that they "contribute to pathological anatomical structure and physiological functioning of the individual" (p. 7, footnote 5). Because genetic processes cannot be directly responsible for retarded "mental processes" (which, not being directly observable, cannot be discussed), they affect intelligent behavior through the restrictions they impose on the senses and the physiological capacities of the organism, and by the fact that abnormal physical appearance restricts the child's social interactions (we are not told why physical impairment, but not intellectual impairment, can be directly related to genetic processes).

Five years later, Bijou (1971) pointed out that a mistaken, stereotyped view of behaviorists as "environmentalists" had developed. He reiterated that a behavioral analysis of intelligence starts with the interaction of the biological *phenotype* with environmental variables, and that the availability of physical stimuli and "social arrangers," along with the kinds and schedules of reinforcement of cognitive behaviors, account for the end result: intelligent behavior as measured by performance on a test.

There is, it seems, no place in this system for the *genotype;* nor, apparently, can there be a genetic foundation for specific cognitive behaviors, such as symbolization, abstraction, or language. There is no room, certainly, for polygenic determiners of intelligence.

Conceding that there are limits to the changes that can be made in intelligent behavior, Bijou maintained that these limits cannot be determined until the then current crude intervention and compensatory education programs were superseded by more sophisticated programs. There can be no doubt, in any case, that behaviorists believe that intelligence, even as measured by intelligence tests, is quite malleable and can be substantially raised. From their viewpoint, the degree to which intelligent behavior is retarded is a function of the diversity of restrictions on the development of cognitive repertoires, while accelerated intelligence results from the variety of favorable conditions for their development (Bijou, 1971, p. 233). The difference between gifted and retarded individuals resides in differences in anatomical structure and physiological functioning (but *not* mental functioning) and in the frequency that cognitive behaviors were encouraged (in bright persons) or restricted (in retarded persons) in the individual's past.

In 1981, Bijou and Dunitz-Johnson restated Bijou's extreme behaviorist position that intelligence is not inherent in the central nervous system and therefore that mental retardation is a symptom of restrictions in opportunities for interaction by infants and children with important persons in their environment. They also describe what they consider to be the shortcomings and fallacies of statistical-intelligence theories, organic theories, and learning theories of mental retardation. The role played by biological impairment is to limit children's interactions with their environment, thereby reducing opportunities to learn and to adjust. They state that although the brain integrates and coordinates the individual's activities, "there are no data to indicate . . . that the brain is also a thinking and controlling organ and the locus of intelligence. The brain is no more responsible for an individual's psychological activity than the heart, lungs, stomach, or endocrine system" (p. 309).

Such statements could be considered simply curiosities were it not for the fact that Bijou is an important spokesman and consultant for many of the widely known early intervention programs (e.g., Bijou, 1981).

At one point Bijou and Dunitz-Johnson warn us that: "Cause and effect relationships cannot be determined from correlations between test scores and school achievement" (p. 307), yet the entire structure of the behaviorist position on mental retardation rests on the attribution of causation to a long series of correlations. For example, the fact that lower socioeconomic class mothers do not provide as much verbal communication as do upper class mothers is given as a source of retardation, with no consideration that both dullness in a parent and dullness in a child might be caused by a third variable. Furthermore, one must wonder why, although a disproportionate number of mildly retarded individuals come from lower socioeconomic environments, nevertheless the vast majority of children from poor and deprived families are *not* retarded, and only a small fraction of families in the lower income brackets have a retarded child (Ramey & Finkelstein, 1981). What subtle environmental forces are at work to cause retardation in only relatively few instances?

We must recall also that, from this radical behaviorist viewpoint, the range of intelligent behavior—from retarded to superior—is tied to the continuum of environmental conditions—from unfavorable to extremely favorable. However, prodigious mental achievement (and retarded mental development) often show up very early in life. Halbert Robinson (1981) describes one child prodigy who had begun to speak at 5 months of age and at 6 months had a vocabulary of 50 words. He started to read at 13 months. When Robinson saw him the boy was 2 years, 3 months old, spoke five languages and could read in three languages, understood addition, subtraction, multiplication, division, and square root, and displayed many other interests and abilities. At 4 years, 6 months his Stanford–Binet was in excess of 220. It is incumbent on the behaviorists to find out what reinforcement contingencies went into producing the extraordinary performances of this and other extremely gifted individuals so that the parents of the future can, if they wish, bring to the world large numbers of children with many kinds of remarkable talents.

TRAINING INTELLIGENCE TEST PERFORMANCE

John Throne and his colleagues at the University of Kansas have added some bewildering twists to the empiricism of Skinner and Bijou. Not only can intelligent behavior be produced using operant conditioning (selective reinforcement), but mental retardation—defined as a behavioral disorder—can be reversed by behavioral training (Throne, 1970, 1972, 1975b; Throne & Farb, 1978). Because performance on intelligence tests is the accepted measure of intelligence, and because from a behavioral perspective intelligent performance is identical with intelligence as an abstraction, the way to reverse mental retardation is to train retarded children to perform well on the 12 subtests of the Wechsler Intelligence Scale for Children! The agent of this change is the scientific administration of operant conditioning techniques, and the criterion that mental retardation has been reversed is the production of permanent gains in IQ and generalization of these gains to untrained tasks. Thus far, this program has been applied to the Vocabulary, Digit Span, and Block Design subtests of the WISC (Farb, Cottrell, Montague, & Throne, 1977).

Improved Vocabulary subtest performance of a 6-year, 7-month-old girl with Down's syndrome, who had an IQ of about 49, was described by Cottrell, Montague, Farb, and Throne (1980). In two 30-minute sessions a day, 3 days a week, for a total of 73 sessions, the child was trained by operant techniques to correctly identify and define pictures that were in the same semantic class (category) as the first eight words of the WISC Vocabulary subtest. The reason that they trained the first eight words was that "according to the normative data . . . the first eight words of the Vocabulary subtest of the *Wechsler Intelligence Scale for Children* can be defined by a child of this subject's chronological age" (Cottrell et al., 1980, p. 92). This is not correct, however. According to the WISC Manual (Wechsler, 1949, p. 113), a child who is 6 years, 7 months old should correctly define *18* words. A child of this age who defines only 8 words would receive a Scaled Score of only 4, and if all subtests scaled at 4 it would produce an IQ of 56.

As an example of the training procedure, for the word bicycle the child was trained to identify and define a bus, a plane, and a boat; for hat she was trained to define shoes, a hat, and a shirt; and so on. During training, when pictures of a bus, plane, and boat were spread before her, a picture of a bicycle was included, though not referred to. To bus, she was trained to respond, "Ride in it;" to boat, "Ride in it in the water;" to plane, "Ride in it in the sky."

The reader will perhaps not be too surprised to learn that on criterion testing the child correctly defined the word bicycle ("Ride it" is scored correct), or that she reached criterion on all eight words. Her scores on the Peabody Picture Vocabulary Test also improved, but it might be noted that this test contains some of the same or closely related pictures used during training. Nevertheless, despite all the training, the Vocabulary performance was still in the retarded range. Two additional children were said to replicate these results.

Training for the Forward Digit Span section of the Digit Span subtest was given to a 6-year-old child with Down's syndrome and an IQ of about 50 (Farb & Throne, 1978a). Following training on the more varied of two training conditions, a forward digit span of up to 5 digits was successfully trained, although performance on the 5-digit strings dropped to about 50% correct in a 7-month follow-up. Apparently no effort was made to train the child to recall digits backward, the second part of the WISC Digit Span subtest.

Referring to this study, Throne and Farb (1978) stated that the subject's performance after training was at a level "indicated by the WISC to be normal for a child of her chronological age" (p. 69). But this is no more true for Digit Span than it was for Vocabulary. At the start of the program the girl was 6 years, 7 months old. At that age the average total Digit Span raw score on the WISC is 7, obtained by summing the longest string of digits correctly repeated forward with the longest string correctly repeated backward on either of two trials (Wechsler, 1949, p. 113). We do not know if this child could repeat 2 digits backward. We are not told the duration of training, but based on the figures it appears to have lasted about 90 weeks, so that at the end of training she was about 8 years, 4 months old, and almost 9 years old at the time of the follow-up. A total raw score of 8 is the norm for 7- and 8-year-olds, and at 9 years, 2 months the norm is a total raw score of 9. Consequently, at follow-up or shortly thereafter this child's Digit Span score was a long way from reaching the norm.

Forward Digit Span was also trained in two other retarded children (Farb, Throne, Sailor, & Baer, 1974). One was a 10-year-old boy diagnosed as culturally deprived who had an IQ of around 62. At the time the report was written he was correctly repeating about 75% of 7-digit strings. The total (forward plus backward) raw Digit Span norm for his age is 9. The second child was an 11-year, 9-month old boy who had Down's syndrome and an IQ of about 44. At the time of the report he was getting about 50% of the 4-digit strings correct. For 11- and 12-year-olds the total raw Digit Span score is 10. In sum, training brought the first boy close to his age norm, and if backward digits were given he perhaps would have reached it. The second child remained well below his age norm, and of course the older these children get, the larger the span required.

Block Design performance also has been trained. Farb and Throne (1978b) trained two brain-damaged girls, one 10 years, 8 months old, with an IQ of about 70; the other 14 years, 5 months old, with an IQ of about 50. Operant training was on items similar to the Wechsler Block Design items, and, as in the above studies, generalization tasks were included.

According to the authors, the results indicated that, after training, both girls performed within the normal range, but no data are presented. We do not know what block designs they passed, whether they passed them on the first trial as is required for designs I to VII, or whether they received bonus points for constructing the designs within certain time limits. In view of the careless reporting of the Digit Span and Vocabulary studies, the authors' conclusions cannot be taken on faith.

In spite of the results, Throne and Farb (1978), in reviewing these studies, confidently assure their readers that they have brought retarded children to an average level on three WISC subtests, and they conclude that "we may be on the way to convincing even those inclined to be most skeptical, not only that mental retardation can be reversed, but that steps should be taken to ensure that it is reversed" (p. 73). Needless to say, I for one remain a skeptic.

It is difficult to know where to begin in assessing this project. Presumably, similar training for the nine remaining WISC subtests is under way, but if raising the IQ in this manner is really of any interest, the dubious goal is a long way off, not only because of the failures already encountered (though not conceded), but because a single child would have to be trained on all the subtests, not different children on different subtests. Moreover, the true test of training is how children perform 2 or 3 years later, when they must not simply maintain their performance but improve upon it. But these caveats pale into insignificance compared with the crucial question of whether these workers truly believe that retarded children specifically trained on certain subtests somehow become the intellectual equals of children who score at an average level without specialized training. Will the trained children now compete on equal terms in an algebra class? Throne (1975c) cites the Iowa studies of Skeels and his colleagues as inspiration and support for his view that many, if not most, retarded persons can be brought to the point of normalcy and beyond. The Iowa studies continue to inspire, despite nearly half a century of failure to replicate.

TEACHING MACHINES AND TALKING TYPEWRITERS

In their studies with animals, behaviorists emphasize the shaping of behavior by response-reward contingencies. In order to induce a hungry animal to produce a particular response, immediate reinforcement (food) is given only if the animal more closely approximates the desired behavior. In this way, pigeons can be induced to peck on a lighted response key or even to play ping-pong, if that's what you'd like pigeons to do. According to behaviorists, this and related principles of operant conditioning can be integrated with machines to produce a scientifically based technology of teaching called "programmed instruction." A paper by Skinner in 1954 started things rolling, and during the next 15 years an entirely new field of educational psychology developed (see Lumsdaine & Glaser, 1960, for a compilation of the early studies, including Skinner's 1954 paper).

Because teaching machines are infinitely patient, can be programmed to present material in small steps with frequent repetition, and permit children to advance through a program at their own rate, they would seem to be ideal teaching adjuncts for special classes, and projects using operant conditioning techniques with mentally retarded students proliferated—although not all of them made use of machine technology (Greene, 1966).

Enthusiasm waned somewhat when problems developed, one being that a machine is only as good as its program and although there may be a "science" of operant conditioning there is no prescription available for how to break teaching down into small steps most effectively. It also became evident that different children learn best in different ways and with different materials. Enthusiasm waned even more—always excepting dedicated behaviorists—when returns started coming in indicating unimpressive gains when mildly and moderately retarded children who worked on teaching machines were compared with peers receiving standard instruction (Greene, 1966).

As with other over-sold panaceas, the frequency of publications on using teaching machines to teach classroom subjects to mildly and moderately retarded students rose to a peak and then dropped off. But there is a complicating factor in this description: The crude teaching machines have been replaced by powerful, versatile, and relatively inexpensive computers; programmed instruction has become computer-assisted instruction. Considering the increasing popularity of computers, it is entirely likely that computer-assisted instruction will become a permanent resource for teaching social, vocational, and academic skills to mentally retarded persons (Brebner, Hallworth, & Brown, 1977; Lally, 1981). It is also likely that the exaggerated claims for a teaching technology based on operant principles will not be fulfilled. Teaching machines of whatever description represent an empiricist's dream of environmental control, but individual differences will persist because active construction by the human brain is ultimately necessary for any accomplishment beyond the most rudimentary kind of rote learning. The behaviorist belief that anyone can learn anything if we can just find the proper response-reward contingencies remains unrealized, as behaviorists who have tried to teach reading to severely retarded persons must by now realize (Sidman, 1971). Whether improved learning of modest skills will result from computer-assisted instruction remains to be seen. However, automated devices may prove most useful in providing simple skills to severely and profoundly retarded individuals who have proved resistant to all other attempts to reach them (Stoddard, 1982). One promising development is the use of computer keyboards to provide a means of communication for severely retarded persons unable to speak, a procedure adopted from attempts to train apes to use a symbolic language system (Romski, White, Millen, & Rumbaugh, 1984).

* * *

For Ogden Lindsley (1965/1970), who is a major spokesman for the behaviorists, "Retardation is not the property of the child but of an inadequate child-environment relationship. It is our ability to design suitable environments for exceptional children that is retarded" (p. 232). Consequently, the design and application of "prosthetic" environments will produce efficient behavior, and Lindsley noted that Omar Khayyam Moore had demonstrated that such environments can produce "dramatically efficient behavior" (p. 224) in culturally deprived children. According to Reginald Jones (1970) of the University of California, Moore had taught "reading and related skills to the culturally disadvantaged, the educable mentally retarded, the gifted, the speech impaired, the emotionally disturbed, and those with learning disabilities" (p. 319). Word quickly spread to psychologists, educators, and the media that O.K. Moore was using a "talking typewriter" to teach 3- and 4-year-olds and mentally retarded children to read.

Actually, Moore's theoretical approach was only partially behavioristic, but the usual jargon was there; for example, children were placed in "autotelic responsive environments." Autotelic was defined as activity done for its own sake, not because of external rewards and punishment—a clear break from Skinnerian principles. On the other hand, the responsive environment provided immediate feedback of the consequences of one's actions, and allowed children to proceed at their own rate—a familiar description of the advantages of teaching machines (Moore, 1966; Moore & Anderson, 1968).

The Responsive Environment Laboratory consisted of five portable, soundproofed booths, plus a small classroom and an office with a testing room. In the automated booths a child worked alone for no more than 30 minutes on the Edison Responsive Environment, or "talking typewriter," while observed by an adult through a one-way mirror. Prior to entering the booth, each of the child's fingernails was painted a different color to match the painted typewriter keys; correct color matching produced correct fingering on the typewriter keyboard.

For the first session, the instrument was set for free exploration. When a key was struck it typed the character (letter, number, or punctuation mark) and a voice through a loudspeaker named it (the child was not told this before entering the booth, but had to discover it). This procedure continued over a number of sessions until the child appeared ready to enter Phase 2, which was instituted without warning. In Phase 2, a display window presented a character with a red arrow pointing to it, and the instrument automatically locked all keys except the appropriate matching key, while simultaneously pronouncing the name of the character. When the child struck the correct key the instrument pronounced the name, then covered the display before presenting a new character. Difficulty could be increased by the machine announcing "upper case," and by the booth assistant eliminating either the auditory or visual elements or adding a number of characters with the red arrow pointing only to the target character.

Phase 3 contained two forms, one for reading and one for writing. For reading, after the child had struck the keys for a number of letters that spelled out a real word, the machine told the child to strike the space bar, pronounced the word "space," pronounced each letter the child had struck, then spoke the word made by the letters. Where the word was a picturable noun, it might also project a picture of it. For writing, the child dictated a story that was recorded, then typed the story as it was played back; or, in another version, spontaneous classroom talk was recorded and a list of words that were used was subsequently programmed into the machine for the child to spell out.

In Phase 4, actual stories were programmed into the machine, but we will not go into further detail here. The "Laboratory Transfer Room" was a classroom set aside for the children to engage in cooperative work under a teacher's guidance. Children also used typewriters with cursive type and according to Moore (1966), "Even two- and three-year-olds, including retarded children, can learn to print and write in cursive style" (p. 193).

There were also nonautomated booths, in which assistants sat beside the child. In fact, at the time of the report four of the five booths were not automated, but it was expected that for an optimum program the children would work in nonautomated booths only about 20% of the time.

Moore (1966, footnote 14) wrote that he personally had worked with 102 children on a daily basis, and that 250 children had participated in the project (with, it might be noted, grant support from a number of public agencies and private foundations). No attempt was made to meet the usual criteria of scientific assessment because he intended to operate his laboratories as a demonstration project rather than as a controlled experiment, "for the present and for an additional year or so" (p. 215). To my knowledge he never did run a controlled experiment with retarded children.

Instead, he presented case histories of five children in responsive environment centers in each of five different cities. Two of the children were very bright. One of the remaining three was of borderline intelligence (IQ 72) and had a speech defect. After 172 laboratory sessions, his speech and general deportment improved, he could type five words a minute on the automated equipment, could print, and could read a beginning first grade story. Although he had trouble with arithmetic, he completed first grade successfully, at which time his IQ was 79. According to Moore, he could have benefited from a second year in the laboratory.

The remaining two children were retarded twin girls who had been having trouble in kindergarten. After 150 sessions in the laboratory they could print on the typewriter all upper- and lower-case letters, as well as punctuation marks and other symbols, and could type four words a minute on the automated machine. Their IQs rose to 64 (up 9 points) and 60 (up 4 points). They were assigned to a special class in public school, where they could accurately read an unfamiliar selection from a pre-primer.

Two responsive environment booths containing nonautomated talking typewriters were part of an early intervention project for 45 environmentally deprived 3- and 4-year-old Mexican-American children in Greeley, Colorado, in which the entire nursery school was organized as an autotelic responsive environment (Meier, Nimnicht, & McAfee, 1968). Very cursory results were given because "a comprehensive monograph is being prepared to fully describe and discuss the research which has been going on for four years now" (p. 380). (See also Meier, 1969.) However, the "monograph" turned out to be even less informative than the original paper. Meier (1970) described how teachers were discouraged from forcing children into activities, but were to be responsive to the children's self-initiated and self-directed projects. In responsive environments teachers "do not teach—they facilitate children's learning. The notion of a learning facilitator captures the essence of responsive ability in teaching" (p. 32).

Most of Meier's paper comprised a lecture on how environmental deprivation retards development, and how autotelic activities can reverse the undesirable effects of those deprivations. But the promised full report of the results consisted of a single descriptive paragraph in which we are assured that the experimental children have performed significantly better than the matched controls on standardized tests, although "it is too early yet to draw any firm conclusions" (p. 42). As far as I can determine, no data of the results of this study have ever been published.

The Responsive Environment impressed Blatt and Garfunkel (1969) sufficiently for them to include it in their early intervention project. Initially they had hoped to include 3-year-old children who were, or were likely to become, retarded, but failing in this they selected a sample of children from a culturally deprived environment characterized by high delinquency rates, school failures, low occupational status, and poorly kept homes.

There were three groups: 18 children in Experimental Group 1 received a preschool program—daily from 9 to 4 for 2 years—plus Moore's Responsive environment; 20 children in Experimental Group 2 received the preschool program only; and 21 children in Nonexperimental Group 3 were not involved in the intervention program. Assignment to groups was made by stratified random assignment based on Stanford-Binet IQ, age, and sex. The Nonexperimental Group was not labeled a control because 5 of its members were in some preschool program during the first year of the study, and 13 were in a public school kindergarten during the second year of intervention. Furthermore, according to the authors, not all experimental children attended the program every day and a few "rarely attended the program in the two years of its existence" (p. 49).

As part of the Responsive Environment condition, each of five booths, monitored externally, contained a blackboard, an electric typewriter with an attached Line-A-Time paper-exposing device, and provision for a film-strip projector. The child's nails were painted to match the color-coded keyboard of the typewriter, as recommended by Moore. The teacher said aloud the letter, number, or symbol of each typewriter key struck by the child, who was asked to repeat what the teacher said. Children remained in the booth as long as they desired, up to 30 minutes, and were permitted to keep the carbon copy of their efforts. Daily staff conferences reviewed each child's performance.

At the time of pre-experimental testing the children of each group averaged 3.2 years of age and the mean Binet IQs of Experimental Groups 1 and 2 and Nonexperimental Group 3 were, respectively, 92.6, 92.6, and 89.2. Three years later the respective mean IQs were 96.7, 99.2, and 97.0, leading the authors to conclude that they had "neither significant nor convincing data to substantiate (their) central hypothesis that intelligence is educable" (p. 129). Nor were there any differences between the groups on the other dependent variables, including school achievement tests.

Blatt and Garfunkel made every effort to guard against examiner bias by withholding from the examiners the identity of each child's group membership. As they pointed out, "Most recent studies have been hazy in their reporting of subject attrition, adequate control groups, randomization of subjects . . . , and the utilization of 'blinds' in the assessment of children" (p. 118). Such rudimentary controls are always required if one is not to be deceived by, as the authors put it, the "illusion of change."

Moore moved from Yale University to the University of Pittsburgh, where I have tried without success to contact him. He left a trail of private organizations that are no longer in operation, including the Responsive Environments Foundation in Hamden, Connecticut, and the Responsive Environments Corporation in Englewood Cliffs, New Jersey. If Responsive Environments are alive and well somewhere, they no longer attract much interest. Yet with our penchant for technology we can expect new and more elaborate gimmicks to fill any vacuum created by the demise of the latest magical solution.

8 Medical Intervention

The dream of enhancing intelligence is forever with us. In the future, as science fiction writers see it, intelligence will easily be raised by merely taking a thinking pill. In fact, for Nobel Laureate Linus Pauling the future is here; vitamin C is the magic elixir that will not only prevent colds but will raise retarded IQ. There is a sweeping extrapolation from the legitimate supplements for pathological deficiencies (such as phenylketonuria) or severe nutritional insufficiency, to the use of a generalized, all-purpose potion that will raise low intelligence no matter what the source of the retardation, or even raise intelligence across the entire intellectual spectrum.

Real gains in the prevention of mental retardation have resulted from medical and biochemical research, as for example by rubella vaccination, by maternal desensitization in RH- factor blood incompatibility, by compensating for inborn errors of metabolism, and so on. Surgical treatment in cases of hydrocephalus and the premature closing of the cranial sutures have also proved useful. Although these successes have scratched only the surface of this vast problem, we are encouraged to hope that increasing inroads will be made, particularly by genetic research.

Nevertheless, the history of medical claims is no less checkered than the claims made for psychological and educational intervention. As part of his extremely derogatory review of a book by J.E. Wallace Wallin, Kuhlmann (1914b) castigated Wallin for sloppy methodology in a study reporting the beneficial effects of hygienic and operative dental treatment on intellectual efficiency. His review precipitated one of the bitterest exchanges in the history of mental retardation research (Kuhlmann, 1915; Wallin, 1914). A few years later the removal of tonsils and adenoids from 112 retarded residents at a State Home was said to improve the mentality of 24% of the residents, because obstructed breathing had produced "imperfect aeration of the blood which supplies the brain" (Dawson, 1918, p. 173). Some 30 years later an attempt was made to improve brain functioning by increasing the brain's arterial blood supply by means of revascularization, in which "arterial blood was . . . caused to traverse both vein and the artery" (Beck, McKhann, & Belnap, 1950). This surgery was performed on 125 patients who had mental retardation, convulsive disorders, and brain injury. Retarded children were said to improve, but no objective data were presented.

Various surgical procedures have been tried periodically. In the late 1800s, craniectomy as a cure for mental retardation caused something of a stir. In this operation a transverse strip 8 to 10 inches long and .25 to .75 inches wide was removed from the skull along the coronal suture. Despite the evidence from cases of microcephaly that it is the growth of the brain that determines the size of the skull and not the other way around, the theory was promulgated that premature ossification of the cranial sutures had limited the growth of the brain, and consequently craniectomies were performed on many retarded children, even those who had normal-sized heads. Murdoch (1901) noted that "this operation has been a favorite subject of the lay press . . . and it is surprising with what credulity the exaggerated claims . . . are accepted by very intelligent people." As a result, "parents of many idiotic children . . . often induce the surgeon to operate upon their child, contrary to the dictates of his better judgement" (p. 113). There were the usual claims of success immediately following the operation, but follow-up assessments were routinely negative.

Not only infected teeth, but focal infection of various bodily organs were believed to be the source of many cases of insanity and feeblemindedness. Henry Cotton was a particularly influential adherent of this theory; he and his colleagues were "impressed with the toxic factors found [in many cases of mental retardation] . . . and the marked improvement which occurs when such factors are removed" (Cotton, 1921/1980, p. 168). He presented case histories of three young boys who had been developing normally when for some unknown reason they became emotionally disturbed and mentally retarded. After thorough examinations one of the boys was surgically treated for an abscess of the frontal sinus, after which he improved dramatically, leading to the conclusion that his adrenal gland had been overstimulated by the toxic effect of the abscess and that the boy had appeared mentally retarded because he had been emotionally unstable and could no longer concentrate. In each of the other two cases an intestinal infection and/or obstruction was surgically removed, followed by restoration of normal emotional and mental behavior.

Cotton (1921/1980) was convinced that "many of these so-called feebleminded individuals . . . are retarded, not so much by lack of development of the brain, as through the action of various toxins and the resulting disturbances of cellular metabolism" (p. 172). These results produced a rash of surgical interventions (or, as one wag put it, kept surgeons busy turning colons into semi-colons), but no noticeable decline in the incidence of mental retardation or insanity.

Even more popular than surgery has been the therapeutic use of various chemicals and nutrients, including vitamins, minerals, hormones, and extracts of animal organs. In 1931, in Switzerland, a woman who had developed tetany was dying because her parathyroids were accidentally removed during a thyroidectomy. Brought to a clinic in Geneva for emergency treatment, she was injected with a fluid made from a slice of freshly slaughtered calf's parathyroid mixed with Ringer's solution (as described by Goldstein, 1956). The patient quickly recovered and remained well. The noteriety resulting from this patient's permanent recovery popularized sicca-cell therapy, in which fresh dry cell preparations from the organs of fetal or young animals, usually sheep, were combined with other agents and injected into the patient. This procedure, plus the oral administration of vitamins A, C, D, E, B complex, and mineral and protein supplements, was touted by Hellmut Haubold, of Germany, as improving the physical, intellectual, and social development of children with Down's syndrome. A controlled test of Haubold's claims was undertaken by White (1969, and see her review), who made four trips to Germany to study 13 of Haubold's patients and to give them psychometric examinations. Also included in the study were 31 patients who were given Haubold's treatment regimen by Rosanova in Chicago, and 431 untreated patients with Down's syndrome. White found no reliable evidence for any less decline in IQ for treated than for untreated patients. Wortis (1981) describes how he exposed the unscientific and possibly fraudulent nature of Haubold's claims.

A marvelous example of the unscientific "case history" approach can be found in Goldstein's (1956) report of the remarkable improvement of 11 retarded children, most of whom had Down's syndrome, who were treated by sicca-cell therapy plus supplements. Although Goldstein warned the reader that the results were preliminary and that "We must refrain from being too optimistic" (p. 248), the reported improvements could hardly do less than fire the most extreme form of enthusiasm.

Benda (1969) reported that combined pituitary-thyroid-vitamin B_{12} accelerates the physical growth rate of children with Down's syndrome, and a similar type of treatment may influence their mental development. Fifty Down's syndrome infants were given daily doses of .1 grain thyroid and 1 pituitary capsule as soon after birth as possible, and by the end of the first year the dosage was increased. After 6 years of age the untreated children generally did not develop beyond an MA of 5 years, whereas the treated children continued to develop. However, the treated group was a selected one, other variables were uncontrolled, and no data or statistical analyses were given.

These examples give a general idea of the kinds of interventions that periodically appear and disappear. Two of the more popular movements are next examined in some depth: (1) Glutamic acid therapy, which issued from a prestigious University research setting and became a classic example of the rise and fall of interest in a highly acclaimed treatment, and (2) the continuing claims by Henry Turkel and Ruth Harrell for the beneficial effects of vitamins and minerals (and other supplements) on the mental capacity of Down's syndrome children.

GLUTAMIC ACID THERAPY

Early Enthusiasm and Favorable Results

At about the time Schmidt's study was being exposed as fraudulent, a great deal of interest and excitement was being generated by the reputed power of a chemical agent, glutamic acid, to raise intelligence. The review that follows includes English language publications in which retarded persons served as subjects, as well as animal studies, but not papers published in obscure (for me) reports and journals. Nor do I become involved with the form and dosage of glutamic acid, with whether or not the subjects were in institutions, or with the results of tests other than intelligence tests, but concentrate instead on experimental design. The focus is on how well a study meets rigorous scientific criteria.

Before proceeding, five terms that are important for describing experimental procedures are defined. *Tester-blind* indicates that persons who administer psychological tests in experimental situations are unaware of whether the testee is in an experimental or control group. *Subject-blind* means that the subjects of the experiment are unaware of which group they are in (although it is not always easy to judge when this is the case). *Double-blind* means that both the above conditions obtain. *Environment-blind* means that the people in direct, everyday contact with the subjects do not know to which group the subjects belong, a situation that can only occur under subject-blind conditions. *Triple-blind* means that all the previous procedures are followed.

In 1943, a paper by Price, Waelsch, and Putnam, of the Columbia University College of Physicians and Surgeons, reported a clinical study in which dl-glutamic acid (hereafter this and all variants will be called simply glutamic acid) was administered to eight patients suffering from petit mal and psychomotor epilepsy. There were some untoward side effects in a couple of cases, but also a remarkable reduction in seizures in two of the patients. Most important for the miracle-starved world of mental retardation research was the report that four of the patients showed a marked increase in physical and mental alertness.

Shortly thereafter, Zimmerman and Ross (1944), also at Columbia University, studied the effect of glutamic acid on maze learning of rats. Their results were dramatic. The experimental group was three times faster and more accurate than the control group. From the same laboratory, Albert and Warden (1944), in a one-page note in *Science,* reported the results of a study in which rats were required to step on a series of floor plates in a particular sequence. Eight of nine rats treated with glutamic acid passed a three-plate problem, compared to only two of eight control rats.

These three studies, then, presented encouraging evidence that, at long last, here was a relatively simple way to increase the learning and problem solving performance of rats, and the physical and mental alertness of humans. The flood gates were opened. Two years later, Albert, Hoch, and Waelsch (1946) gave detailed reports of four individuals with secondary mental deficiency who were given glutamic acid therapy, and who were said to be representative of the results obtained from seven of their eight patients. The experimental design can only be described as a randomized-haphazard-within-subjects design in which placebos and glutamic acid were interspersed at the whim of the investigators. There were dramatic increases in IQ following administration of glutamic acid, and dramatic decreases when this was followed by a placebo. The suggestion was made that the treatment did not actually increase intellectual ability; rather, it had removed inhibiting mechanisms that had held down the patients' potentials.

But the real outpouring came with nine consecutive studies by Zimmerman and his colleagues, five of which were by Zimmerman, Burgemeister, and Putnam (1946, 1947, 1948, 1949a, 1949b). The first (1946) was a preliminary report that was encompassed in the second (1947), larger study, where 69 patients were tested, primarily on the Stanford–Binet Intelligence Scale, but also on a number of other tests, before and after glutamic acid treatment. Forty-four of the patients were mentally retarded, 11 of whom had convulsive disorders. The control group consisted of 37 patients who had been given some type of intelligence test (unidentified) 6 months to 8 years prior to the start of this study and were tested again at the beginning of the study, after which they became part of the experimental group. The "experimental" group's change in test scores over a 6-month treatment period was compared (not statistically) with the absence of change exhibited by the "control" group over that initial period of 6 months to 8 years prior to pre-experimental testing. Results indicated an average 7-point gain in IQ, and a rate of development (MA) of the retarded patients that was described as twice as fast as the rate of development of children of average intelligence.

In the third study (1948) of this quintet, 30 of the patients from the second study were retested after an additional 1 year of glutamic acid treatment. There was a gain of 2 additional IQ points, which was not, of course, significant. Of the fourth and fifth studies (1949a, 1949b), which assessed the effects of glutamic acid on persons with Down's syndrome, the fourth was again a preliminary report rushed to publication because of the favorable results on the first seven patients. However, such urgency was hardly called for. It is true that one of the patients gained 20 IQ points (from 74 to 94), but the median gain for the group was 5 IQ points. The full study (1949b) consisted of 30 patients with Down's syndrome and a "control" group of 30 approximately equated retarded children and adults without Down's syndrome. All 60 were administered glutamic acid for a 6-month period, and pre- and posttest scores were compared. No placebo control group was included. Results showed an average gain of 4 to 6 IQ points following treatment. Most of this paper was devoted to the gain in height and weight by the Down's syndrome patients, and it was noted that parents often commented that the child "looks less mongoloid." Such was the magic of glutamic acid.

From 1949 to 1951 four more papers issued from the Zimmerman group. They included a detailed description of the procedures they followed in their treatment and assessment regimen (Zimmerman, 1949), and laudatory reviews of the successes of glutamic acid treatment, particularly in raising individuals from borderline to average intelligence, but with a warning that success is less likely when individuals are emotionally unstable and when there is a Rorschach diagnosis of brain damage (Zimmerman & Burgemeister, 1950a, 1950b). In one of these papers, Zimmerman and Burgemeister (1951) reported a follow-up study of 38 patients (mean IQ of 62) 2.5 to 3 years after cessation of glutamic acid therapy, results of which indicated that the mean IQ was not significantly different than it was prior to treatment. The authors' discussion completely disregarded this finding as they described the factors that influenced the permanency of glutamic acid effects. One's confidence is shaken even more when, having read that Bakwin's (1947) study confirmed their results, it is found that Bakwin's "study" was simply a one-and-a-half-page review.

Quinn and Durling (1950a, 1950b) administered glutamic acid to 31 mentally retarded children over a 6- to 12-month period and in addition gave vitamins to some of the children, which complicated matters irreparably. In general, there was a gain of about 4 IQ points, but the controls were sporadic. Six children served as controls for the six children in the experimental group who had been pre- and posttested on the Merrill–Palmer, while nine other children served as controls for the nine children who had been pre- and posttested on the Stanford–Binet. The control groups did not receive a placebo and there was no tester-blind procedure. I performed Fisher exact probability tests and found that the change in the Merrill-Palmer experimental group was significant ($p = .05$), but the change in the Stanford–Binet experimental group was not. Most of the 5 or more IQ points gained by 13 of the experimental subjects was maintained after a 5-month non-treatment period, but there was no control comparison. In a second study, glutamic acid produced no differential effect on IQ.

Foale (1952) also failed to use a placebo or a tester-blind procedure. She found an average gain of about 3 IQ points in her experimental group after 10 months of glutamic acid treatment, and no gain in the control group.

Among the more exorbitant claims were those made by Kane (1953) in a two-page report of a study of 150 children of various diagnostic categories. According to the author, glutamic acid treatment produced average gains of 16 to 19 IQ points in 106 retarded children who had a history of malnutrition in early infancy, brain injury, and emotional immaturity, but the treatment was of little use in other cases of mental retardation. Neither placebo controls nor tester-blind procedures were used, and no statistical data other than averages were given.

During this period the popular press was quick, as always, to catch the fever. Articles appeared in the *Ladies' Home Journal, Time, Hygeia, Reader's Digest, Science Newsletter,* and *Science Digest* (see Arbitman, 1952). As one example, Bliven (1947), in the title of his article for the *New Republic,* asked, "Can Brains Be Stepped Up?" and gave an affirmative answer, based partly on the "remarkable experiments" which were "carefully conducted over a period of years by Dr. Zimmerman and his colleagues" (p. 20).

The "remarkable" experiments of others were soon added to the list. A similar query in the *Volta Review* (Levine, 1949) asked: "Can We Speed Up the Slow Child?" and answered yes, we can; we can raise the IQ of retarded persons an average of 10 IQ points, and consequently a child of borderline intelligence can be raised to the level of average intelligence. Levine selected six deaf children with IQs ranging from 61 to 81, gave them glutamic acid for 9 weeks and reported that they gained an average of 13 IQ points. There was no control group. In addition to the increase in IQ, there were rather miraculous changes in behavior. On retest after about a 3-month nontreatment period, the average IQ dropped 10 points, along with regression in general responsiveness.

Perhaps the most ambitious study was a doctoral dissertation by Sister Maureen Harney (1950). She used as controls the changes in MAs of 24 of her 31 experimental subjects over an equal period of time *prior* to the experimental pretest, as Zimmerman et al. (1947) had done. For the experiment a large number of tests and assessments were made before and after at least 6 months of glutamic acid treatment, and although positive changes were not reflected in all the tests, the Stanford–Binet rose about 6 IQ points. The MA gain was about 1 year, a much larger gain than during the period prior to therapy.

In the most adequately designed study from the New York State group, Albert, Hoch, and Waelsch (1951) improved on their earlier, preliminary study. They used a substantial number of subjects and attempted a triple-blind procedure, but apparently the placebo was not an adequate imitation. They noted that the children did not pay much attention to the difference in taste between the placebo and the glutamic acid, which was explained to the parents as a difference in strength of the compound they had been receiving. The design was basically an A–B, B–A design. Of the 42 subjects in the low IQ group (mean IQ of about 40), 18 went from 4 months of placebo to 4 months of glutamic acid, 14 received the reverse order, 6 received glutamic acid for 8 months, and 4 received the placebo for 8 months. They found no gain in IQ following the placebo, a significant gain of about 4 points when going from either pretest or placebo to glutamic acid, and a loss of about 3 points when returning from glutamic acid to the placebo. The authors pointed out that although the change was statistically significant, it was of no practical, clinical value.

In 1951 and 1952, three reviews of the glutamic acid experiments were published in journals devoted to mental deficiency and exceptionality. The first was an uncritical, even glowing, review (Gadson, 1951). The other two were much more cautious. Arbitman (1952) pointed out, in simple terms for concerned parents, that a number of glutamic acid studies had violated accepted experimental procedures. Sharp's (1952) short review listed sources of errors and suggestions for future research.

Jaeger-Lee, Gilbert, Washington, and Williams (1953) tested a group of 51 children who had a mean IQ of about 65. The glutamic acid was given to the children by their mothers. At the end of varying periods, glutamic acid was replaced by a placebo, or by no treatment. Because the glutamic acid was described as "distasteful," the placebo was probably ineffective as a control. After 6 months of treatment the mean IQ rose by more than 7 IQ points. After that, subjects gradually dropped out, but after 18 months of treatment, 28 subjects had gained almost 12 points, and by 24 months, 13 subjects had gained almost 14 points. There was no significant placebo effect. Although there was no tester-blind procedure, the possibility of tester bias was discounted because a correlation of .92 was obtained between their Stanford–Binet results and the results of tests given by other psychologists who—for various reasons—happened to test their subjects, and who were unaware of their treatment status.

The effect of 30 days of treatment with glutamic acid on retarded, delinquent, adult males was studied by Kurland and Gilgash (1953). A placebo control was used but apparently a tester-blind procedure was not.

The average IQ of the experimental group rose almost 10 points, as measured by alternate forms of the Wechsler, while the control group remained essentially the same. Three months after treatment was discontinued, there was still a reliable difference between the groups.

In a clinical study with no attempt at controls, Goldstein (1954) reported a 15- to 25% IQ rise following glutamic acid treatment given to moderately retarded children, most of whom had Down's syndrome and an even greater improvement when calf pituitary gland powder was given in addition to the glutamic acid. When a thyroid extract was also added, Goldstein claimed "a rise of 50 to 75 percent mental acceleration and 75 percent physical and social maturity acceleration" (p. 87).

In 1959, there was a final volley from Zimmerman and Burgemeister (1959a, 1959b). In the first study, 150 retarded children and adolescents given glutamic acid were compared with a matched group given reserpine and a group of 50 subjects given a placebo (which matched more closely the glutamic acid than the reserpine tablets), in a double-blind study. It may in fact have been a triple-blind study, but nothing was reported concerning the environment. After 6 months of treatment, the glutamic acid group gained up to 4.5 IQ points more than the other two groups, a gain that was statistically significant. There is no way of knowing how many of these 150 patients were included in the second study (1959b), which reported that 464 patients treated in private practice over "the past several years" gained an average of 5.64 IQ points after 6 months of glutamic acid therapy. There was no mention of a control group, but why should there have been, since, according to the authors, the problem had been taken "out of the academic area of controversy and into the medical realm emphasizing clinical improvement, where it belongs" (p. 656).

Up to this point, most of the studies I have reviewed can be considered favorable to the claims of glutamic acid enthusiasts. Note that only two of these, Albert et al. (1951), and Zimmerman and Burgemeister (1959a), used a tester-blind procedure, and except for the Kurland and Gilgash (1953) and Zimmerman and Burgemeister (1959a) studies, simultaneous placebo controls were poor or nonexistent. However, beginning in 1950 a number of more carefully controlled studies had begun to appear, and attempts to replicate the earlier findings with mentally retarded persons began to meet with failure.

Contrary Results and Fading Hope: Human Studies

Ellson, Fuller, and Urmston (1950) placed an experimental and control group of institutionalized retarded children (mean IQ = 49), matched for age and IQ, under identical conditions except that the experimental group received glutamic acid and the control group received a similar-tasting placebo. Only one person, who did not otherwise participate in the experiment, knew the identity of the groups. After about 9 months of treatment, both groups showed reliable increases in IQ, but were not reliably different from each other. Some extreme gains in IQ—as high as 19 and 21 points—were found in both groups. On a star-tracing task, the experimental group performed faster and less accurately than the control group, suggesting that glutamic acid may indeed result in a higher activity level, but accompanied by a decrease in accuracy. However, on a tapping task, tapping rate did not differ.

McCulloch (1950) matched two groups of institutionalized retarded children and adolescents on age, IQ, and diagnosis. He, as did Ellson et al. (1950), used a triple-blind procedure. That is, a placebo was given to the control group, group members were not separated in the cottages, and neither test-retest examiners, cottage personnel, nor the subjects themselves knew to which group they belonged. After a minimum of 6 months of treatment, there was no significant change in IQ for either group.

Kerr and Szurek (1950) also used a triple-blind procedure, but had only five subjects in their retarded experimental group and no retarded controls. After 6 months of glutamic acid treatment, the five retarded children showed no increase in IQ.

Control and experimental groups were matched by Loeb and Tuddenham (1950) on sex, age, IQ, and diagnosis, and although the match was contaminated by attrition (rarely mentioned in other studies), the final two groups had approximately the same pre-treatment MA. During 17 weeks of glutamic acid treatment for the experimental group and placebo for the controls, the environment was unaltered. However, there is no way of knowing whether their attempt to mimic a tester-blind procedure—the aides who administered the treatment were led to believe that both preparations (the glutamic acid and the placebo) might be beneficial—was successful. Post-treatment retest indicated that both groups had gained 2 to 3 months in MA, but there were no reliable differences between the groups.

Milliken and Standen (1951) split five groups (a group of retarded children, two groups of retarded adults, a group of younger and a group of older nonretarded boys) into closely matched experimentals and controls. Glutamic acid or a similar tasting and appearing placebo was administered to half of each group for 3 to 4 months, then the treatment conditions were switched. Neither the staff nor the subjects were told which solution contained glutamic acid. Results indicated that in none of the retarded groups were pre- to posttest MA changes reliably different for the experimental compared to the control subjects. For the older nonretarded group, the gain in the experimental group's posttest performance on some of the Wechsler subtests was significantly larger than it was for the control group, but for the entire scale the mean sub-test gain was 1.46 and 0.93 for the experimental and control groups, respectively.

An A-B, B-A design was used by Zabarenko and Chambers (1952). About half their moderately retarded subjects received at least 100 days of glutamic acid and then were switched to similar tasting and identically appearing placebo tablets. The remaining subjects received the treatment conditions in the reverse order. Despite the inclusion of a triple-blind procedure, the study was marred by the transfer of about half the subjects to another institution so that the experimenters could study the effect of a more stimulating environment. In any case, results provided no evidence that glutamic acid differentially effected intellectual functioning. A second publication by these authors (Chambers & Zabarenko, 1956) is a slightly different report of the exact same study, with a new title.

Oldfelt's (1952) placebo control failed because it did not have as disagreeable a taste as the glutamic acid, and consequently the blind procedures also failed. Nevertheless, there was no IQ gain after a 4-month treatment period, whether the educable retarded subjects were retested shortly after treatment or 6 months later.

In a triple-blind procedure, Lombard, Gilbert, and Donofrio (1955) provided their control group with a placebo that looked, smelled, and tasted like the glutamic acid given to their experimental group, and only one person in the institution knew that the children were receiving different substances. After a 6- to 7-month treatment period there was no appreciable change in IQ in either group.

As part of his doctoral dissertation, Head (1955) tested 30 educable retarded children, 6 to 12 years of age, over a 90-day experimental period. By random assignment, glutamic acid was administered to 10 of the children, while a placebo with the same taste and form was administered to 10 controls. At the end of 30 days, the placebo and glutamic acid were switched without knowledge of the children or parents. Over the final 30 days, groups were returned to their original treatment. A third group of 10 children was merely tested and retested at the four similar time intervals (pretest, 30 days, 60 days, 90 days), but given no other special treatment. Apparently, there was no tester-blind condition. Head reported that after the first 30 days, the glutamic acid group's gain of 6 IQ points was significantly larger than the placebo group's gain of 3 IQ points. Unfortunately, as Astin and Ross (1960) later pointed out, Head used an incorrect statistical formula. Reanalysis of his data reveals a nonsignificant t of 1.12 instead of the 3.52 that he had reported. Comparisons with the inactive group, or with both control groups combined, are also not significant. When increases in scores following all the 30-day administrations of glutamic acid were pooled, the gain of 4.1 IQ points was obviously not significantly greater than the gain of 3.1 points made by pooled placebo conditions.

Rogers and Pelton (1957) administered a small amount of glutamine for 6 weeks to a group of 10 retarded children, glutamine plus pyridoxine to an equated group, and a placebo to a third equated group, using a triple-blind procedure. Although they reported that the pre- to posttest changes were significantly larger for the combined treatment groups than for the placebo group, their statistical analysis was also in error. Using their published data, the t is 1.87 (not their 2.03), and consequently the differences were not statistically significant. An analysis of variance also indicates that there was no significant effect.

The flood of literature on glutamic acid therapy with humans finally dissipated in one final controversy, typical of all that had gone before. Astin and Ross (1960) placed a large number of the glutamic acid studies in a 2×2 matrix defined by whether or not studies employed control groups and whether results were positive or negative. The largest number of studies fell in the control/negative and the no control/positive cells, resulting in a significant chi square and leading to the conclusion that positive findings resulted primarily because of lack of control groups. Six years later, Vogel, Broverman, Draguns, and Klaiber (1966) declared the Astin and Ross review incomplete and frequently inaccurate. Their own 2×2 table contained what they considered a truer arrangement of studies and produced a nonsignificant chi square. Additional reevaluation led them to conclude that there was in fact more solid evidence for the positive effects of glutamic acid than for more commonly used psychotropic drugs.

This was a clear invitation to persevere, but the invitation was declined. There may have been some isolated studies after 1966, but a search of *Psychological Abstracts* was unrewarding. The flood had subsided.

Animal Studies

The situation in the animal research area was no different. From 1947 to 1951, eight rat studies testing the glutamic acid effect produced generally negative results, although tester-blind procedures were used in only two of the studies. Hamilton and Maher (1947) compared experimental and control groups on a difficult three-table "reasoning" test. The treated rats showed a heightened level of activity and reliably faster performance, but no significant difference in number of errors.

Marx (1948) ran 56 experimental and 33 control rats, plus another group receiving glycine, on a water maze. In a follow-up study he included a group of rats fed the same lab food used by the Columbia University group (Marx, 1949). Tester-blind procedures were always used. In no instance was there any significant performance difference between the glutamic acid and control groups. Marx's suggestion that glutamic acid may have compensated for an inferior batch of food used during the Columbia studies was not corroborated by Porter and his coworkers, who reported that enriching various diets with glutamic acid, or interfering with glutamic acid metabolism, had no effect on water maze performance (Porter & Griffin, 1950; Porter, Griffin, & Stone, 1951).

Steller and McElroy (1948) followed the procedure of Zimmerman and Ross (1944) very closely, as did two studies from the University of Pittsburgh, in which performance comparisons were made using instrumental conditioning as well as a water maze (Pilgrim, Zabarenko, & Patton, 1951; Zabarenko, Pilgrim, & Patton, 1951). All reported negative results.

As of 1951, then, the tally was two positive results and eight negative; enough, one would think, to end the hope that glutamic acid would make rats even smarter than they already are. But then, in 1956 and 1957, Hughes and his colleagues suggested that perhaps the Columbia group was using a duller strain of rats (Hughes, Cooper, & Zubek, 1957; Hughes & Zubek, 1956). Accordingly, they used a strain of maze-dull rats and found that after 40 days of treatment with monosodium glutamate these rats performed reliably better on a maze than non-treatment dull rats. The monosodium glutamate had no differential effect on "bright" rats. Unfortunately, the authors could not replicate these findings (Hughes & Zubek, 1957). In no instance was a pre-treatment test given, and tester-blind procedures were not used. These experiments were the trailing end of the experiments on glutamic acid effects on rats, and there is no evidence of any later revival of interest.

What Went Wrong?

One can never be sure that glutamic acid has no effect on intelligence, but obviously the early hopes have thus far proved premature. Even Zimmerman and Burgemeister seem to have conceded as much. The *raison d'etre* for their last two papers was to play down the IQ effects in favor of other claimed benefits of glutamic acid therapy. A quote from one of these papers (1959b) sums this up.

> Contradictory findings over IQ-point change in the past have been due to overemphasis upon this narrow aspect of mentation rather than on observations of the total change in the individual patient. For this limited approach to the problem in the past, we accept our measure of responsibility. (p. 139)

This is an honest appraisal. As one example of this overemphasis, in one paper, all three tables, the single figure, and almost the entire text had been devoted to the gains in IQ made by various mentally retarded groups (Zimmerman & Burgemeister, 1950a).

This little episode in the history of attempts to change IQ crystalizes

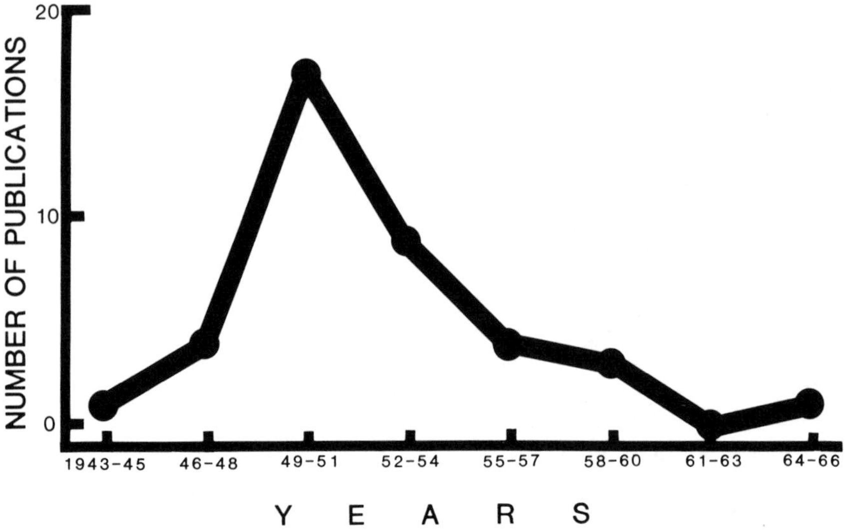

FIG. 3. Twenty-four-year distribution of publications related to the effects of glutamic acid on retarded intelligence.

important problems inherent in this area of research. There is the initial suggestion followed by a number of confirming experiments. Gradually, however, negative results start to accumulate, along with criticisms, and eventually disillusionment sets in, not unlike the course of the polywater episode described in the Introduction. In fact the rise and fall of the number of publications related to glutamic acid and intelligence—shown in Figure 3—can be compared with the publication curve of polywater-related research (Franks, 1981, Figure 9). Although the shapes of the curves are slightly different, they both trace a climb to peak activity followed by a decline to obscurity. It is likely that much of the success that accompanies the initial studies can be attributed to the "experimenter effect," described so well by Rosenthal (1966), in which the expectancies and hopes of the experimenter unintentionally influence the results. In the matter of glutamic acid, there was a complicating factor that cannot be overlooked: the fact that the Columbia group was receiving a grant from Parke, Davis & Co. Nor were they alone. In another positive study (Jaeger-Lee et al., 1953) the glutamic acid was supplied by the granting agent, the International Minerals and Chemical Corporation. One wonders what unconscious influence an award from a drug company has on the experimental testing of a drug. For example, despite the fact that triple-blind procedures to control for the placebo effect have been known for over 130 years (Rosenthal, 1966, p. 367), they were not used in the early glutamic acid studies.

Relaxed standards of objectivity periodically afflict psychology, as in the readiness of some psychologists to ascribe to unknown processes the skillful tricks of Uri Geller (Diaconis, 1978). Of course rosey optimism need not be replaced by immediate, unthinking rejection of anything new. What is required, rather, is healthy skepticism and an awareness of the possibility that changes attributed to the experimentally manipulated variable might have resulted instead from some transitory uncontrolled variable, or even from fraudulent activity.

VITAMIN, MINERAL, AND DRUG THERAPY

To the main title of his book, *New Hope for the Mentally Retarded* Henry Turkel (1972) appended the subtitle *Stymied by the FDA.* Indeed, much of the book consists of a heated protest against the Federal Drug Administration, precipitated by its ban on the interstate shipment of the series of drugs called the "U" Series which, according to Turkel, "acts synergystically to remove accumulations that appear in genetic disorders when a gene or chromosome is lacking, defective, or excessive" (p. 24). One such condition is Down's syndrome, and Turkel makes numerous claims for the effectiveness of the "U" Series in removing excessive metabolites, thereby enabling the patient to lead a more normal life without, however, curing the disease or correcting the abnormal genetic pattern.

To the "U" Series (named from the Greek prefix *eu,* meaning "well-being") Turkel added various supplements, depending on the condition of the patient. The resulting regimen was said to ameliorate some of the physical stigmata associated with Down's syndrome and accelerate physical development; patients were also said to improve on mental and social tests. Turkel presented numerous X-rays and photographs as proof of the physical changes resulting from the therapy and the regression that occurred when medication was withheld. Most of the evidence, however, consisted of inspiring case histories, luminous anecdotal reports, and testimonials to the efficacy of Turkel's therapeutic regimen. After reading these histories only the most hard-hearted skeptic could believe that Turkel wasn't falsely maligned and that any parents who didn't take their Down's syndrome child to Turkel's clinic weren't guilty of gross neglect.

As Turkel describes it, the problems with the FDA began when one of his patients had entered St. Rita's Home for children in Buffalo, New York, where the Sisters were so impressed with the patient's progress that they wanted to give the "U" series to other Down's syndrome children in a controlled experiment. Turkel refused to do a double-blind study because of the importance of adjusting dosages according to each patient's response, and he also wanted to provide patients in the placebo group with the vitamins they required. He recommended instead that the study be a "controlled-blind" study in which neither the patients nor those administering the medication and evaluating the results would know which patients were in the experimental or control group, but in which the principal investigator would know and could adjust the dosage when necessary.

However, the pediatrician at St. Rita's, Thomas Bumbalo, believed that only a double-blind study would be scientifically valid. "This double-blind study was a trial to me," wrote Turkel 1972, p. 76), but he went along with it, supplied the placebo and the "U" Series (the 48 medications that made up the "U" Series are listed in Bumbalo, Morelewicz, & Berens, 1964), and was pleased by what he thought were favorable results. Consequently he was surprised and enraged when Bumbalo et al. (1964) reported completely negative results in the *Journal of the American Medical Association.* These results were instrumental in the FDA's ban on interstate shipment of the drug, and therefore the Bumbalo study became the principal target of Turkel's attack. Among his list of charges was that Bumbalo had given all patients unbound Vitamin D, which "nullifies the action of the "U" Series by causing reaccumulation and deposition of minerals [producing] the same condition that the "U" Series attempts to ameliorate" (Turkel, 1972, p. 78).

Although critical of Bumbalo's study, Turkel nevertheless appealed for a scientific evaluation of the theory that the removal of accumulations present in all genetic defects leads to more normal development. But his dictum that double-blind studies are not feasible in judging his procedures will always provide a ready explanation for negative results. In any case, the messianic fervor with which Turkel has promoted his therapy is unlikely to be dampened by negative results, and a continuous stream of harried parents and their afflicted children will continue to flock to this reincarnated Guggenbühl in his modern Abendberg.

* * *

Turkel is only one of many who have claimed that some type of orthomolecular therapy improves the functioning of persons with Down's syndrome or with other kinds of mental retardation. No doubt supplements will improve functioning when they compensate for a deficiency (in the "U" series, thyroid globuline and organic iodine could help some Down's syndrome patients who have thyroid deficiencies), but the rather exorbitant *general* claims of improved intelligence do not hold up under replication. In the February 1983 issue of the American Psychological Association's *Monitor* (the same publication that in its Sept/Oct 1976 issue published a glowing report of Heber's Milwaukee Project) a headline reported that "Low IQs, Crime Yield to Nutrition." The article cited a recent exploratory double-blind study by Virginia psychologists Ruth Harrell and Ruth Capp, in collaboration with chemist Donald Davis, showing that suitable nutritional intervention can raise the IQs of severely retarded children an average of 15 points over a 9-month period. In addition, there were physical changes in several of the children who had Down's syndrome. Davis cautioned that it would take about 2 more years before their work could be confirmed.

Presumably this report referred to data published in 1981 by Harrell, Capp, Davis, Peerless, and Ravitz. As in some past instances (for example, Skeels & Dye, 1939), a program was launched on the basis of the improvement of one or two children, in this case a mute, severely retarded 7-year-old boy who showed remarkable progress after having been supplied with a nutritional supplement. "In a few days he was talking a little; in a few weeks he was learning to read and write, and he began to act like a normal child" (p. 574). By 9 years of age his IQ was about 90.

Based on this, and more moderate changes in several other children, a nutritional supplement of 11 vitamins and 8 minerals (usually plus a thyroid hormone) was given an experimental test using a partial double-blind procedure. Five children in the experimental group (5 other children in this group had dropped out) were given the supplement for 8 months, whereas 11 children served as a control group for the first 4 months, at which time they too were given the supplement. In other words, this procedure was double-blind only for the first 4 months. Most of the children were in the mild or moderate range of mental retardation.

All children were pretested, then retested at 4 and 8 months. In the report two sets of IQ data were provided, though neither set was complete. One set consisted of tests given by Ruth Harrell, who knew that at the 8-month testing period all of the children had been receiving the supplement. The other set of data was obtained by any one of six psychologists chosen by the parents; we refer to them as "uninvolved" examiners because presumably they had no stake in the outcome of the experiment. The authors referred to these two sets of data separately but this is deceptive because whereas one set of gain scores was derived from tests given by Harrell, the other set was an *average* of the scores obtained by Harrell and the uninvolved psychologists. Both sets of data showed improvement for the experimental group, which gained 5 to 10 IQ points (rounded) at 4 months, and 10 to 16 points after 8 months. The control group showed no change after 4 months, but gained 10 to 12 points after 8 months.

By now we have learned to be cautious of such reports, particularly when the principal investigator is one of the testers. Indeed, from the data provided we note that there were seven subjects who were pretested and retested 8 months later both by Harrell and by an uninvolved psychologist. For these seven subjects, Harrell's results produced a reliable rise in mean IQ of 9 to 11 IQ points (depending on whether we use the IQ of 18 or 30 which Harrell got for one subject tested twice at the 8-month testing). On the other hand, based only on the test results of the uninvolved psychologists these same seven subjects gained only 2 IQ points over the 8-month period, a change that is not statistically reliable. For nine sets of scores obtained only by the uninvolved psychologists, the IQ gain over 8 months was a nonsignificant 4 points. In other words, only the results of tests given by Harrell were significant.

A number of attempts to replicate the Harrell et al. (1981) study have been made. Ellis and Tomporowski (1983) tested severely retarded adults in a double-blind design in which the testers were unaware of the subjects' group assignments. After 7 months neither the experimental group, which daily received pills containing the Harrell vitamin-mineral supplement, nor the placebo group showed any reliable change in IQ.

Two carefully designed double-blind studies of home-reared children with Down's syndrome also failed to replicate. Weathers (1983) provided the supplement over a period of 16 weeks but found no reliable change in IQ either in his experimental group or in a placebo control group, nor were there any changes in visual acuity as had been reported by Harrell and her coworkers. Bennett, McClelland, Kriegsmann, Andrus, and Sells (1983) gave the Harrell supplement to 20 Down's syndrome children over an 8-month period and also reported no change in IQ for them or for 20 placebo controls. Ellman, Silverstein, Zingarelli, Schafer, and Silverstein (1984) supplied the vitamin-mineral supplement to 10 institutionalized retarded young adults for 6 months using a double-blind procedure with a matched control group, also with negative results.

The lesson is very clear. If possible, early reports of dramatic changes should not be widely circulated until replications have been made, because the media are quick to spread the word and parents hasten to have their children participate in the new, unproven therapy (Bennett et al., 1983). Likewise, dramatic improvement by one or two individuals may occur because of the happy match between the patient's needs and the therapeutic regimen, but this match is unlikely to recur in most other patients. Only investigators who are convinced that it will occur can be expected to get positive, though temporary, results.

9 Reuven Feuerstein's Instrumental Enrichment

Recently *Psychology Today* (Chance, 1981) and the *APA Monitor* (Cordes, 1984) informed the American public and the community of psychologists about some exciting new developments emanating from the Holy Land. Israeli psychologist Reuven Feuerstein—white-bearded, forceful, and charismatic under his dark beret—brought forth a theory of cognitive modifiability that has increasingly influenced theory and practice in the field of mental retardation. Referring to the intellectual achievement represented by Feuerstein's two major books, Nicholas Hobbs (1980) wrote: "Few single works in contemporary psychology equal it in originality and ingenuity, in scope, in theoretical importance, and in potential social significance" (p. 566).

Although he had studied for a time with Piaget, Feuerstein's theory departs from Piagetian theory in a decisive way. Whereas Piaget the structuralist taught that children learn and develop by a process of discovery, Feuerstein believes that although interaction with the environment can by itself be a learning experience, it is of limited value unless there is a competent, caring, knowledgeable person to mediate the interaction. The crucial ingredient in cognitive development is the "mediated learning experience" (MLE). Although the development of cognitive structures results from two modalities of environmental-organismic interaction, (1) direct exposure to sources of stimuli and (2) mediated learning, it is the second that is unique to humans and that centrally affects the developing child's cognitive structure. "MLE, therefore, can be considered as the ingredient that determines differential cognitive development (i.e., varying course of cognitive development) in otherwise similarly endowed individuals, even when they live under similar conditions of stimulation" (Feuerstein, Rand, Hoffman, & Miller, 1980, p. 16).

Despite the fact that the term *'similarly endowed'* is included in this description, MLE theory minimizes the importance of native endowment. "We maintain that it is more appropriate to regard genetic factors as producing variations in the level of responsiveness of the individual to learning situations that may require corresponding variations in the quality and quantity of investment necessary for growth" (Feuerstein et al., 1980, p. 8). In other words, when mediated intervention is adjusted for level of native endowment, it will be effective even with poorly endowed individuals. Moreover, the intervention need not occur in early childhood. "Except in the most severe instance of genetic and organic impairment, the human organism is open to modifiability at all ages and stages of development" (p. 9), although "the more and earlier an organism is subjected to MLE, the greater will be his capacity to efficiently use and be affected by direct exposure to sources of stimuli" (p. 16).

Lack of early mediation is the "proximal" cause of retarded performance. "Distal" causes, such as poverty, heredity, injury, and emotional disturbance, will result in retardation only if they are coupled with a lack of mediation, either because of the mediator's absence, refusal, or inadequacy, or because of the child's inability to absorb the mediation.

Feuerstein, Rand, and Hoffman (1979) also distinguish between the terms *cultural deprivation* and *cultural difference,* reserving the former term for individuals who have been alienated from their own culture, and the latter term for the temporarily deficient functioning that can occur when an individual is first faced with an unfamiliar culture.

Although Feuerstein was influenced by Piaget and, in particular, by André Rey at Geneva, one can more readily appreciate the evolution of his ideas when one considers that in the early 1950s he joined an Israeli agency, Youth Aliyah, responsible for integrating immigrant youths into Israel. The youths, who were examined in transit camps in Morocco and southern France, came from disparate and deprived backgrounds in Europe, Asia, and Africa, and in terms of Israel's modern, technological society were severely culturally deprived. For such a population, results from standardized intelligence tests would be invalid, and Feuerstein could give numerous examples of youths who obviously had more intellectual potential than was indicated by their intelligence test scores.

Consequently Feuerstein and his colleague Ya'acov Rand developed the Learning Potential Assessment Device (LPAD) as a more realistic, dynamic measure of intellectual potential and cognitive modifiability. The LPAD requires a test-teach-test format, and only guidelines rather than specific rules are used in its administration. As Feuerstein (1977) puts it, the examiner is a "teacher-observer and the examinee a learner-performer" (p. 112). Students are tested on a series of problems, then taught the strategies necessary to solve the problems, and finally asked to use these strategies on new, more difficult problems. The emphasis is on what the students can learn, not what they already know, and the LPAD provides profiles of the students' strengths and weaknesses. The pilot studies presented by Feuerstein et al. (1979) show some favorable short-term effects and group differences, but the studies are contaminated in many ways, including the subjective nature of the testing. Aside from this, one must be impressed with the difficulty level of some of the examples and the implication that some retarded persons will be trained to do these tasks. Either there is indeed an astonishing program at work here, or many of these individuals are not the typical retarded persons that some of us are used to seeing. In any case, the authors present the results only "as tentative and as useful pointers to further and more detailed research efforts" (Feuerstein et al., 1979, p. 311).

Feuerstein believes that most persons diagnosed as mentally retarded can be taught to function at an average level by enlightened intervention. He concedes that his program has had a few failures, particularly some children who were multihandicapped and who in addition could not communicate. In some instances, resistance from the child or from parents also made intervention difficult. But these are rare instances, quickly dismissed, and the rest of the chapter is devoted to a description of successful case studies, ending with the warning that these cases were deliberately selected to demonstrate the effectiveness of the LPAD (Feuerstein et al., 1979, Chapter 6).

As in many other programs encountered in our review, the case histories are remarkably persuasive and dramatically illustrate numerous examples in which pessimistic assessments were proven wrong. The LPAD ferreted out a potential for modifiability that no one had suspected, and often revealed evidence of cultural deprivation in children who had recently immigrated to Israel. Middle-class children, too, could be "culturally deprived" because of emotional instability and faulty interaction with their parents. Likewise, children with organic disorders may be retarded not primarily because of damage to the central nervous system, but indirectly when such damage affects the interaction with parents, producing a reduced level of mediated learning experience.

No doubt there have been many tragic instances of mistaken diagnoses and prescriptions, as the case histories indicate, but are the kinds of problems usually encountered by the Youth Aliyah agency typical of those encountered elsewhere? In some cases they are, but most of the children and adolescents for whom success was claimed were relatively new immigrants, or at least their families were. Children and families who were culturally deprived in one land, and who became doubly deprived by moving to a new land with a new language and a different culture, are quite distinctive.

Whereas the LPAD is a method of assessing cognitive potential, Instrumental Enrichment (IE), which grew out of the LPAD, was designed to provide one means for reaching this potential (Feuerstein et al., 1980). It consists of 15 instruments, 14 of which are used in the classroom, where the IE program can be inserted into the regular school program for 1 hour a day, 3 to 5 days a week, over a period of up to 3 years. Any of the 15 instruments also can be used separately for individualized remedial programs. There are 500 paper and pencil exercises and learning techniques in the program, providing some 200 to 300 hours of instruction. The teacher becomes the mediator who, with the help of the program, teaches students to think more clearly about various concepts and operations, to use better work habits, to become more self-confident, and to be active generators of information rather than passive recipients. With these newly formed skills and attitudes, students should be better able to understand their general life experiences as well as their regular academic school subjects, which is the major purpose of the IE program.

The IE program is commercially available in the United States from educational firms approved by the Feuerstein group to distribute the material, but enrollment in an inservice training program is a prerequisite for anyone wishing to implement the program. A listing of the 14 programs discussed by Feuerstein et al. (1980) will give some idea of their nature, but for details on the crucial mediating process and the deficiencies that each instrument is designed to remedy, the original book must be consulted.

The *Organization of Dots* teaches students to identify, in an array of dots, certain figures, and to connect particular dots so as to form these figures. The three *Orientation in Space* instruments require students to correctly locate objects relative to each other, and to orient themselves and other objects in space. In the *Comparisons* instrument, students find similarities and differences among pictures, figures, and concepts. *Categorization* teaches the ability to organize material into superordinate categories, and to use various concepts to classify material. *Analytic Perception* requires the disembedding of figures, as in an embedded figures test. *Family Relations* uses kinship to teach students to label and explain various relationships, and to understand a person's changing and multiple roles. In *Temporal Relations* students learn to understand the concepts of time and distance, and the need for all relevant information in solving problems of time and distance. The *Numerical Progressions* exercises include the understanding of intervals, progression, series, and recurring cycles, as in series completion tests. *Instructions* stresses verbal labeling and the ability to understand and follow visual and verbal instructions. *Illustrations* makes students aware of problems, values, and morals, and teaches an understanding of sequences of events. It does so by using pictures that tell a story, as in the Picture Arrangement subtest of the Wechsler Intelligence Scales.

Representational Stencil Design is an advanced level program in which, after some preliminary exercises, students must mentally select the stencils that, if placed on top of each other in a particular order, would produce the target designs. Finally, *Transitive Relations: Syllogisms* is said to foster abstract and inferential thought by requiring students to use deductive inferences and logical rules.

In total, the IE program makes an attractive package that appears to center on the very basic kinds of processes that we think of as forming that amorphous construct we call intelligence. Its sponsors clearly believe that intellectual skills can be learned and, more important, will generalize, for the ultimate goal of the IE program is to improve academic performance and general adjustment. The program is widely used in Israel. In Venezuela, students training to be teachers must study Feuerstein's theories and methods. By 1981 it was being used in 300 school systems in the United States (Chance, 1981). As always, however, the test of a program's usefulness remains the carefully controlled comparative study. Two major studies with poorly performing students have been undertaken, and to these we now turn.

EXPERIMENTAL STUDIES

In 1971, the Feuerstein group began an experimental study in which the effects of the IE program were compared with a regular school curriculum—referred to as General Enrichment (GE)—in a residential as well as a day care setting (Feuerstein et al., 1980). The 218 subjects of this study belonged to what in Israel are referred to as "Oriental" communities, which include immigrants from non-European countries. More than 90% of the subjects' parents were born in Asia or Africa, whereas about 54% of the subjects, who were 12 to 15 years old and mostly boys, were born in Israel. In all, 69% of the subjects were residents before they had reached 6 years of age. They were described as culturally deprived and socially disadvantaged youths who had dropped out of or were doing poorly in school.

The experimental design called for all groups to receive the regular curriculum, except that the IE group substituted IE training for 5 hours a week over the 2-year period. This meant that they received about 300 hours less of the regular curriculum than did the GE group. Intelligence tests were included in the large battery of pre- and posttests given to both groups. The pretest mean IQ of the total group on the Thurstone Primary Mental Abilities (PMA) test was 80; most of the subjects, then, would not be classified as mentally retarded. In fact, 89% were above 70 IQ, and about 60% were above 80 IQ. The groups were retested following the 2-year intervention, and apparently there was no effort to conceal the group identity of the subjects from those who administered the test. Because of some pretest differences between the groups, analysis of covariance was used to adjust pre- and posttest means.

At posttest, reliable differences favoring the IE group were found on four of the eight subtests of the PMA, and on the total PMA score. The largest difference was on the Spatial Relations subtest, the test that was most similar to certain exercises in the IE training program. The scores were given as raw scores, but it is evident that no great change in IQ occurred. The posttest PMA total raw score of the two IE groups was 172, compared with 164 for the two GE groups. A number of other comparisons also favored the IE group, but on only 2 (Bible and Geometry) of the 12 subtests of the Project Achievement Test were the IE groups reliably superior, a result attributed to the fact that the GE groups received 300 more hours of the curriculum learning. In terms of academic improvement, then, differences were minimal.

In general the initial results of this frequently cited first study were encouraging but hardly different from the early results of innumerable intervention studies. Bradley (1983) has critically appraised this study. He pointed out that instead of using a multivariate statistical analysis, the project used a series of univariate F tests, one for each of the 8 subtests and the total score of the PMA, and one for each of the 12 subtests of the Achievement Battery, and so on. This type of analysis does not adjust for the fact that when a number of comparison tests are performed some differences will occur by chance. Additionally, this method of separate analysis used large degrees of freedom for each comparison, which results in statistically significant results even when differences are small and, for practical purposes, quite meaningless. Applying the rule that for differences to be nontrivial they should at least exceed the standard error of measurement, Bradley found that none of the PMA subtest differences approached the size of the standard error of measurement, although the total score difference did.

Preliminary follow-up data on the IE and GE groups provided a test of the hypothesis that group differences will become progressively greater over time (Feuerstein et al., 1980; Rand, Mintzker, Miller, Hoffman, & Friedlender, 1981). Two years after completing the program, when the older subjects were drafted into the army, they were given a number of tests including the Dapar Intelligence Test and the Hebrew Language Development Test. The verbal section of the Dapar is a derivative of the Otis and the Army Alpha Tests, and the figural section is similar to Raven's Progressive Matrices Test.

Results indicated that subjects who had received 2 years of IE intervention performed reliably better than the GE subjects on the Dapar, but reliably lower on the Language Test. The latter result reflected only the pretest differences in Language scores, which had not been entered as covariates. On the Dapar, students who had received 2 years of IE performed better than those receiving only 1 year, and in fact the 2-year students performed at about the same level as a general Youth Aliyah group and well above individuals who had been rejected by the army, which the authors claim would have been the fate of their subjects had there been no intervention. The authors stress their finding that (using medians) 87% of those in the GE group who had scored low on the PMA pretest continued to score low on the Dapar posttest, whereas 53% of the IE subjects who had scored low on the pretest scored high on the posttest, suggesting enduring changes in the IE group and progressive decline in the comparison group.

However, a careful examination of the raw scores on the Dapar do not present so gloomy a picture for the GE group. The standardization mean for the Dapar is 50, with a standard deviation (SD) of 20. For a total *N* of 218, the posttest mean for the IE group was 52.58 and for the GE group was 45.11 (Rand et al., 1981). When these scores are converted to approximate IQ scores, using the Wechsler SD of 15, they become 102 and 96. When one considers that the pretest PMA IQ of the combined groups was only 80, these results indicate that even though the IE group scored reliably higher than the GE group, the means of both groups were at the average level. Furthermore, the 6-point difference does not seem very large considering that the IE students spent 2 years practicing on tasks that are the same or very similar to items used in intelligence tests.

The Feuerstein group would be the first to point out that the pretest IQ mean of 80 was not a true reflection of potential ability because of the cultural disadvantage of children from "Oriental" families. However, the sharp rise in IQ for both the experimental and comparison groups suggests not that the IE program was singularly equipped to raise intelligence, but rather that the additional years of general schooling and acclimatization to the new culture dissipated most of the debilitative effects of cultural differences.

The IE program is being evaluated at numerous sites in the United States, but the largest project is the North American Research Project on Instrumental Enrichment, based at the John F. Kennedy Center of George Peabody College, Vanderbilt University, and implemented at five major sites and several other affiliated sites. The project's director, H.C. Haywood (1977), described Feuerstein's achievements as "the most exciting occurrences in the education of mentally retarded children in the last one hundred years." By using Feuerstein's methods "we may finally be able to realize the dream of J.M.G. Itard . . . that the intellect actually can be trained. . . . [and] we will in a real sense have cured learning disabilities accompanying mental retardation" (p. 115).

An early progress report presented data from three sites: Nashville, Louisville, and Phoenix (Haywood & Arbitman-Smith, 1981). As part of the project, separate classrooms were provided for students classified as educable mentally retarded, learning disabled, behavior disordered, culturally and linguistically different, and varying exceptionalities. The experimental groups received IE 3 to 4 hours a week, while during those periods the control groups continued to receive their regular academic curriculum. The students ranged from 11 to 18 years of age, with educational achievement levels that were 2 to 7 years below expectations. In Nashville and Louisville, black children made up 60% of the samples, but in Phoenix most of the families of the children were Mexican-American migrant farm workers who spoke Spanish at home. In this respect, they resembled more closely the immigrants taught by Feuerstein and his colleagues than did the students at the other sites.

An assessment was made after an average of 58 hours of intervention for the first or "pilot" year, 1977–1978. For the Nashville and Louisville groups, 16 EMR students rose from a mean IQ of 69 (rounded) to 76 on the Lorge-Thorndike Nonverbal Intelligence Test. For all experimental students combined, the mean IQ rose from 83 to 90, while the control group's mean rose from 84 to 87. On the Letter Series of the PMA, the EMR treatment group was the only group to show no improvement; in fact their scores declined slightly.

In the fall of 1978, new groups of students in the three cities began the program and completed an average of 93 hours of intervention. The results were less encouraging than results for the pilot groups, except for the "varying exceptionality" students (students who were undiagnosed but were in resource rooms because they learned poorly), the only group to show a reliable increase in IQ relative to its comparison group. Most interesting, however, was the finding that the Phoenix group's mean Lorge-Thorndike Nonverbal IQ went from 95 on pretest to 104 on posttest, compared to the control group's gain from 105 to 108. These students were obviously not retarded, and the 6-point gain relative to the control group is the same as in the Israeli study. However, regression toward the mean appears to have played a role here; the control group started at a much higher level and consequently the amount it could gain was limited. On Raven's Progressive Matrices Test, the performance of the 29 combined students in the IE groups rose much higher than did the 41 control students, but again they started at an appreciably lower level. On a self-concept scale, the mean score of the EMR intervention group remained the same, whereas it declined in the control group.

These gains in psychometric intelligence were quite modest, and even though the duration of intervention was not great, there was not even a glimmer of evidence to support Itard's dream that intellect can be trained.

In a later paper the project personnel minimized the importance of showing IQ gains (as had the administrators of Project Head Start), and turned their attention to positive changes that intelligence tests are not designed to measure (Arbitman-Smith, Haywood, & Bransford, 1984). On an interview technique, for example, the IE students were said to respond in a more sophisticated manner than control students to questions concerning real life problems. They were rated as concentrating more and as being more involved than comparison students when answering test questions. However, when the EMR group showed no improvement on a multiple choice vocabulary test composed of terms usually introduced during the IE exercises, it was concluded that the test was inadequate. Indeed, classroom observation and specific questioning were said to reveal that EMR students spontaneously used many of these sophisticated terms appropriately.

Based on published reports available at this time, the North American Project has had difficulty in objectively evaluating the proposal that the intelligence of retarded persons can be trained by mediated learning. Attrition of subjects has been high and consequently the number of subjects in some groups is very small. There are large pretest mismatches between control and experimental groups, but regression toward the mean is never mentioned. In some publications, standardized tests are disparaged in favor of unstandardized instruments, anecdotal observations, and general impressions. Complete data are not given, and frequently the results of all four special education groups are combined, making it impossible to gauge the performance of the EMR groups. We can only hope that subsequent published reports will be more complete so that a fuller assessment of the effects of IE on the intellectual functioning of mentally retarded persons can be made.

Although Feuerstein and his colleagues prescribe a general regimen of mediation that will reverse the ill effects of inadequate mediated learning, the MLE concept was stretched to the breaking point when applied to the claims of Skeels and Dye (1939) that retarded women raised the intelligence of retarded orphanage pre-schoolers (see our Chapter 5). Conceding that these women could not have engaged in a very sophisticated form of mediation, Feuerstein et al. (1979) suggested that: "What was significant was not the quality of mediation, but that it existed at all" (p. 73). Active affection, they went on, activated the entire mediational process, which then was responsible for changing the children's cognitive structure. But in this example mediated learning is so loosely applied that it loses all its force. A concept applied so generously cannot have any useful defining properties.

Moreover, Feuerstein and his followers claim that IE and the teaching methods that accompany it are special pedagogical techniques that provide retarded students with thinking skills and attitudes not routinely provided by special educators. But although the mediation provided in countless special classes is a more informed mediation than that provided by the retarded nursemaids in the Skeels and Dye study, there is no evidence that special education has ever produced the kind of cognitive gains reported by Skeels and Dye, or even come close to the gains predicted for the IE program by Feuerstein and Haywood and their colleagues.

The IE program is designed to alter total cognitive functioning. "One of the major ways to produce insight in the FIE learner is to continuously demonstrate that the goals of FIE and the functions it teaches are prerequisites for the mastery of specific tasks with which he is confronted and for his successful adaptation to life at large" (Feuerstein et al., 1980, p. 279). Training on the *Organization of Dots,* for example, is not designed simply to make students competent at finding and tracing figures in an array of dots, but more importantly to establish certain principles of thought, such as the principle that organization can be imposed on the environment in an active way (Arbitman-Smith et al., 1984). IE is nothing less than an attempt to teach students to think, and its success depends entirely on the ability of the students to generalize to novel life situations. But there's the rub. Even when teachers intervene to generate and communicate the principles illustrated by these exercises, do retarded individuals who learn, for example, to connect dots to form figures also learn that they can now organize a complex environment? The hope that such transfer can be induced is as old as faculty psychology, as pervasive as the hope that training "perception" somehow will improve thinking (Mann, 1979). I know of no good, objective evidence that retarded persons have ever accomplished this kind of magical transfer.

In the end, Feuerstein's major contribution may be the LPAD, which he had developed with Rand and which is now being honed into a more formal instrument by the Feuerstein group. Other workers have tried, and many continue to try to develop a reliable measure of intellectual potential that would supplement the assessment of present intellectual performance, but this group is pursuing that commendable goal most assiduously. In instances where poor performance results from the cultural differences of immigrants, as so frequently is the case in Israel, such an instrument is invaluable. Whether it is equally useful in other circumstances remains to be seen.

10 A Potpourri of Claims and Issues

PATTERNING

Mental handicap attracts not only the dedicated and the caring, but also the self-deluded and the unscrupulous who are quick to make outrageous claims and who profit from the gullibility that is fostered by wishful thinking.

There is, for example, a very clever propaganda tract for the Philadelphia-based Institutes for the Achievement of Human Potential (IAHP), presented in the form of a book titled *A Boy Called Hopeless, by M.J.* (Melton, 1977). It is a fictionalized account of one family's experience with their youngest member, a brain-damaged boy named Jeremiah, as seen through the eyes of his sister, the M.J. of the title. This slick little tear-jerker is filled with pathos and joy, determination, hope, and disappointment. Fatherly Mr. Doman, the director of the Institutes, and his friendly, capable staff will take only brain-injured children, not children who are psychotic or have "deficient brains." But this family is lucky. "Congratulations, Mr. and Mrs. Rodgers. You have a brain-injured child" (Melton, 1977, p. 101), says Mr. Doman. The child is accepted, but the family is warned that there is much work ahead and that the outcome is never a certainty.

The Rodgers' house is practically turned into a physical therapy clinic, and for 10 hours every day, including weekends and holidays, little Jeremiah is provided with therapy. Forty-two neighbors, friends, and volunteers take turns working with Jeremiah. He is "patterned," which consists of moving his head, arms, and legs in a specified sequence. He must crawl on his stomach, creep on his hands and knees, roll and somersault, swing from one rung to another across a horizontally suspended ladder, and be held upside down. He is given eye exercises, a reading program, and a tactile program. Progress is slow and there is the temptation to quit, but this gritty family perseveres and after 2 years of sacrifice they are rewarded when Jeremiah is placed in a regular class and described by his teacher as a bright little boy.

The book's message is clear: Ignore what you have been told by others and have your retarded child checked out by the Institutes; the child may be brain injured and may be able to benefit from their program. This book feeds on parents' anguish and guilt, for it is well known that most parents have difficulty accepting a diagnosis that their child is retarded, and continue to search for alternative diagnoses and possible cures.

The raising of false hope is a cruel deception and a very costly one; training of the parents (who pattern their child and in turn train others to help) can cost up to $4 thousand, but in this book money is never mentioned by the stern but compassionate Mr. Doman, who sees himself as the luckiest man alive because he is privileged to meet such parents and work with children like Jeremiah. "As we left the office, I glanced back at Mr. Doman standing in the doorway. I thought for a moment there were tears in his eyes. I liked him" (Melton, 1977, p. 229).

Since 1962, many popular magazines have published articles extolling the work of the Institutes (see critique by Robbins & Glass, 1969), including an article by Melton (1971) in *Coronet,* entitled "Body Exercises That Make Children Smarter, Too." *Reader's Digest* printed "Hope for Brain-Injured Children" (Maisel, 1970), along with another laudatory article the same year (Blank, 1970). Blank's article, however, carried a disclaimer stating that patterning is a controversial technique and that *Reader's Digest* was not taking a position on one side of the controversy but rather was presenting the heartwarming story of how a family's plea for help rallied a community.

Periodically the public has been cautioned about the claims made by the Institutes. In 1968, a number of medical and health organizations, including the National Association for Retarded Children, the American Academy for Cerebral Palsy, and the American Academy of Pediatrics, issued a joint statement questioning the efficacy of patterning therapy and charging the Institutes with making undocumented claims of cures (American Academy of Pediatrics, 1968). But periodic statements (The American Academy of Pediatrics issued another warning as recently as 1982) have had little effect on the growth of the Institutes, which has a huge waiting list and publishes numerous books and pamphlets. In addition to providing home training, the Philadelphia campus of the Institutes has a school for a selected few brain-injured young adults who have successfully completed the home program. Satelite programs have developed in this country and in many other countries.

The IAHP was established in 1962 by Glenn Doman, a physical therapist, and Carl Delacato, an educator who is no longer on the staff. Also instrumental in the Institutes' development were Glenn Doman's brother, physician Robert Doman, neurologist Eugene Spitz (no relation), and the late Temple Fay, a neurosurgeon. The basis for patterning is a theory of neurological organization that Delacato (1959) had applied to the understanding and amelioration of reading deficiencies, and that he and Doman subsequently amplified and applied to the treatment of brain-injured children (Doman, Spitz, Zucman, Delacato, & Doman, 1960; LeWinn, Doman, Doman, Delacato, Spitz, & Thomas, 1966).

Essentially, patterning and related therapies were said to reproduce in brain-injured children the developmental sequence of normal children, thereby enhancing neurological organization. The pattern of correctly coordinated head, arm, hand, and leg movement was imposed on the passive child so that, presumably, the functional activity was adopted by undamaged brain cells. Where possible, the child actively engaged in a number of exercises. The form of the patterning was geared to the child's level of development, going from simple movement of arms and legs without forward progress, to crawling, creeping, and finally walking. Developing hemispheric dominance and functional laterality was an important goal of the exercise program, representing the level of development required for talking, reading, and writing.

Subsequently, brachiation (i.e., swinging by each arm from one hold to another) supplied a link between creeping and walking. During the course of evolution, the theory goes, our ancestors held onto overhead tree branches for support. Their ability to swing through the trees straightened their bodies into an erect position until eventually they walked upright. Because the Doman-Delacato position incorporates the view that ontogeny recapitulates phylogeny, brachiation exercises supplied a necessary link with the other exercises in replicating normal development from infancy to childhood, as well as replicating the development of the species. Brachiation had the additional benefit of increasing lung capacity and the amount of oxygen delivered to the brain.

Carbon dioxide treatment (breathing in a bag for a brief period to improve blood circulation to the brain) along with visual-motor and sensory training were included in the therapeutic procedure. Reading disability was also ascribed to poor neurological organization. Consequently, children with reading (and other) disabilities followed a similar program, including crawling and creeping (even though they could walk), in order to properly induce the correct neurological organization.

A study by Robbins (1966a) precipitated an exchange with Delacato (1966) in which Robbins (1966b) suggested that they join in a major research project to test the efficacy of the Doman–Delacato system, a proposal that had the support of respected leaders in special and general education. According to the joint statement questioning the efficacy of the Doman-Delacato treatment, a carefully designed study supported by federal and private agencies was in fact in the final planning stage when the Institutes withdrew their original agreement to participate (American Academy of Pediatrics, 1968). The IAHP no longer appears to be interested in a scientific evaluation of their techniques; they have grown large, wealthy, and independent, and their staff is satisfied to provide case histories and propaganda tracts in support of their claims.

Robbins and Glass (1969) carefully examined the Doman-Delacato position and found its underlying theoretical rationale to be internally inconsistent and unsupported by empirical data. In evaluating 11 studies that Delacato had cited as experimental evidence for the beneficial effects of the exercise program on reading ability, they uncovered numerous sources of error. These included failure to include a control group, or—where there was a control group—nonrandom assignment of subjects, failure to properly control for statistical regression effects or for the effects of maturation, inappropriate statistical analyses, and uncontrolled practice effects. Statistical regression artifacts were particularly blatant because in many studies the experimenters selected for their treatment group the subjects who scored lowest on reading tests. It is well known that students who are chosen because of extremely low scores will score higher on subsequent testing even without therapeutic intervention, which is why a randomly selected control group is required.

Based on their own clinical experience with disabled children, Cohen, Birch, and Taft (1970) suggested that the changes in behavior reported by the IAHP were a result primarily of the children's maturation rather than the patterning technique. Unfortunately, they cited the Skeels (1966) study to support another of their contentions, that a favorable atmosphere can raise IQ. Aside from the questionable validity of the Iowa studies, the orphanage children in those studies had little in common with the children treated by the IAHP group.

In 1965, Doman and Delacato published an article in *McCall's* titled "Train Your Baby to be a Genius," and in 1978 the Better Baby Institute of the IAHP offered its first course on "How to Multiply Your Baby's Intelligence." What was required to raise intelligence was the induction of correct neural organization. Not surprisingly, then, the Doman-Delacato method has been tried with mentally retarded individuals regardless of whether or not they were brain damaged.

Results of an early experimental study with retarded subjects were promising. Kershner (1968) reported that following participation in a 74-day Doman-Delacato treatment program, the mean IQ of 14 trainable retarded children and adolescents rose 12 points, compared with a 3-point loss for

16 control subjects. Unfortunately, despite a randomization procedure, the pre-program mean IQ of the experimental group was much lower than that of the control group (40 compared with 62).[1] Consequently, their rise in IQ might have been due largely to regression toward the mean, as Hallahan and Cruickshank (1973) pointed out.

Neman, Roos, McCann, Menolascino, and Heal (1975; see also Neman, 1975; Zigler & Seitz, 1975) provided almost 7 months of sensorimotor patterning and related exercises to a retarded sample (mean age, 15 years; mean IQ, 40) and found no dramatic cases of individual improvement and no changes in global intelligence. Sparrow and Zigler (1978) applied the IAHP method for about 2 hours a day, 5 days a week, for a full year to 15 brain damaged, seriously retarded children (mean IQ, 18). The therapy had no effect on intelligence.

In 1981, Edward Zigler pointed out how callous it appears "to try to counter, with cold scientific data, the moving accounts of individual families' courageous efforts to help their profoundly disabled children" (p. 388). But he rightly raised questions about the feelings of parents whose high hopes are dashed when the treatment is unsuccessful, or whose burden of guilt is enlarged because they blame themselves for not producing an effective patterning program. The wasted money and shattered marriages are undocumented in the information provided to its potential customers by the Institutes for The Achievement of Human Potential, which must take its place in the long list of pseudoscientific, impressive sounding remedies sold by self-righteous advocates who feed on human anguish.

OTHER SENSORY AND MOTOR THERAPIES

Despite the fact that the theory behind patterning stresses the natural unfolding of developmental stages, it clearly embodies the empiricist bias. "At the root of all learning are stimulation of the senses and organization of the nervous system, because the brain learns how to be brainy by building its experience on a foundation of early sensations and certain very basic body movements," wrote Doman and Delacato (1965, p. 65). Proper stimulation of the senses is deemed crucial, and is said to be a prerequisite for motor development. In claiming that sensorimotor therapy is a cure for many maladies, including deficient intelligence, the IAHP has much historical company, as should be obvious to anyone who has read this far. A small sampling of some relatively recent sensory and/or motor therapies is

[1]A selection procedure that avoids this infrequent randomization failure is to match pairs of subjects on as many traits as possible, then randomly assign one member of each pair to the experimental group and the other member to the control group.

briefly reviewed in this section (see Hallahan & Cruickshank, 1973, for a fuller treatment and for a fine description of the historical development of the perceptual-motor approach).

At the outset it should be stated that other workers who take this approach have not made the exaggerated claims of the Doman-Delacato group; to my knowledge they do not claim that they can cure children who are brain-damaged or retarded. They are included here only because they recommend perceptual and/or motor training as a means of improving cognitive function, and thus are the modern torchbearers of Séguin's "physiological method." They are empiricists to the extent that they emphasize the role of perceptual and motor processes in the development of intelligence.

Carrying forward the environmentalist tradition and drawing particularly on the work of Hebb, Newell C. Kephart perpetuated the belief that form perception is learned. "What a young child sees when he looks out on the world is probably nothing more than a series of ill-defined blobs having no qualities in and of themselves except their extension and intensity" (Kephart, 1971, p. 124). Therefore, the ability to distinguish objects representing relative positions in space requires "a very long and very complicated process of learning" (p. 123), beginning in the first few days of life. Some detail of a blob must become associated with some predictable characteristic, which then allows the infant to control, to some extent, the accompanying blob. However, "the child initially obtains most of his or her information about objects and space through motor activity" (Kephart, 1975, p. 63). Through exploring objects by hand, the child establishes the qualities of the objects.

Even shape and size constancy are learned through touch, according to Kephart (1975). The apparent increase in size of an object approaching the young child's eyes is gradually corrected by using kinesthesis as a standard for comparison. All the senses are tuned to the master sense of kinesthesis, the way various orchestral instruments are tuned to the piano, and kinesthesis continues to play this role throughout life, insuring that perceptual data remain related to the response.

This view of the origins of visual form perception, which descended from Berkeley and Condillac, is refuted by persuasive evidence that newborn infants have, to the contrary, remarkably good vision and can see relatively fine patterns even during the first few weeks of life (Fantz, 1958, 1963). Kephart was repeating the error of transferring to the sense of touch the ability to recognize form, which then somehow relays this information to the visual sense. It was a viewpoint that placed Kephart in Séguin's footsteps for it was Séguin, remember, who emphasized that after the development of motor control, the sense of touch should be the first sense trained (Ball, 1971). The legacy of using touch to teach deaf-mutes has, in this manner, continued to influence the training of retarded and learning disabled children.

The entire rationale for Kephart's perceptual-motor therapy rested on this flawed base. But developmental disabilities cannot result from early difficulties in differentiating elements out of a globular mass if there was no globular mass to begin with. Similarly flawed was Kephart's belief that "Many more children break down at the higher levels where the details, having been differentiated [out of the globular mass], must be integrated into a constructive form" (Kephart, 1971, pp. 132–133), which also assumes that the infant sees a globular mass from which details must gradually be extracted and then somehow reintegrated, an entirely unlikely sequence of events.

The Kephart training procedure requires first an evaluation of the earliest developmental level at which there was a breakdown in learning, the nature of the breakdown, and the resulting compensations and distortions of learning. Numerous training activities are detailed by Kephart (1971) and include (for gross motor training) a walking board, a balance board, and a trampoline to aid in developing dynamic balance, laterality, directionality, and body image. Training then shades into finer motor skills, and eventually into eye–hand coordination so that the visual sense can begin to take over and the child can become "perceptual," depending on vision alone. Templates are supplied to the child to aid in the transition from hand to eye control, as well as to train form perception. Just about every conceivable kind of game and activity is described, an entire curriculum of activities to choose from in order to remedy poor learning by reinstating the necessary sequence of proper perceptual-motor (actually, motor-to-perceptual) development.

According to Kephart and his followers, these activities should improve the cognitive and academic performance of participating children, but to the extent that sensory and motor abilities are distinct from central intellectual processes (as we can judge from the brilliant achievements of many persons who have motor or visual disabilities), there is no rational reason why training visual and motor functions should have any effect on general intelligence. It is not surprising, therefore, that studies assessing the effects of perceptual-motor training on retarded children have occasionally produced some improvement in motor functions, but without comparable effects on intelligence or academic performance (Bruininks, 1974; Fisher, 1971).

Nevertheless, for individuals who are severely or profoundly retarded, sensorimotor training has produced some modest benefits. Edgar, Ball, McIntyre, and Shotwell (1969) reported that their experimental group of 3- to 8-year-old children (mean IQ, 34) made greater gains on the Gesell Developmental Schedules than did their control group. Webb and Koller's

(1979) profoundly retarded young adults, who had a mean IQ of only 9, produced a reliable raw score gain of 2.5 points. One can only applaud the dedicated workers who produce any improvement in the performance and behavior of persons so markedly debilitated, but needless to say these modest increments still leave their subjects severely and profoundly retarded.

In addition to Kephart's program, there are many similar programs that train sensory, perceptual, and/or motor skills in the belief that it will improve learning and cognitive performance. Optometrist Gerald Getman collaborated with Kephart prior to developing his own approach. Like Doman, Delacato, and Kephart, Getman too found the key to intellectual excellence and published it in a book titled *How to Develop Your Child's Intelligence* (Getman, 1962). With Kephart, Getman (1965) "holds that visual perception . . . is learned and is based upon developmental sequences of physiological actions of the child" (p. 50). Visual perception (vision) is not simply "sight," but rather a complex "derivative of the entire visuomotor organization of the organism," (p. 57) and evolves from the actions of the entire organism (see also Getman, 1981). Furthermore, the child must be taught to acquire all possible body manipulative skills before being taught to read. Paraphrasing Hebb: "The ultimate in mental ability is the result of the ultimate in motor ability" (Getman, 1965, p. 50).

As noted in Chapter 4, infant tests of sensorimotor performance are not the best predictors of later intelligence, so that the belief that sensorimotor activity is a foundation for later intelligence would appear to lack support. A more promising predictor of later intelligence are tests of an infant's responsiveness to novelty and discrepancy, tests that presumably measure the ability to attend to and assimilate the information contained in a sequence of stimuli and to abstract the invariant elements—processes that are descriptive also of adult intelligence (Fagan, 1984b; Kearsley, 1981).

Infants use all the sensory modalities available to them to receive information, and if one modality is closed (by blindness, for example) they will use the remaining available modalities. There is nothing essential or crucial about exploration by touch; indeed, limbless babies develop average intelligence, as studies with infants affected by thalidomide clearly show (Décarie, 1969; Kopp & Shaperman, 1973). The best available evidence as well as careful observation indicate that whereas the senses must provide information to the central nervous system, the development of normal and superior intelligence is not a function of any particular sequence of motor or sensory dominance, but rather depends on the ability of the brain to efficiently process incoming information.

I wonder how sensory- and perceptual-motor theorists explain the accomplishments of someone like Christy Brown (1970)? Mr. Brown was crippled at birth with a severe form of cerebral palsy. He was never formally educated, speaks with difficulty, is carried and transported by others, and because of his severe motor problems can do little for himself. Nevertheless he taught himself to read, and with the little toe of his left foot he typed a beautiful novel that attests to his sensitivity, his lively intelligence, and his ability not only to read but to write far better than the theorists who believe that the development of active motor skills is a precondition for the development of reading, writing, and other cognitive competencies.

* * *

Many workers who are identified with the sensory- or perceptual-motor approach have established private institutes. There is, for example, the Center for the Study of Sensory Integrative Dysfunction in Pasadena, California, founded by A. Jean Ayres, an occupational therapist. Ayres (1978) warns us that her program of vestibular and tactile stimulation should be used only by specifically trained personnel, and should not be confused with perceptual-motor training. Nevertheless, it includes many of the features of the other programs mentioned here.

According to Ayres, learning deficits are frequently caused by disorders in the vestibular system, located in the brain stem. To rectify these disorders, sensory integration therapy places its emphasis on sensory input and on the organization of sensory input through motion. Training is individually prescribed and stresses vestibular, tactile, and proprioceptive stimulation. For children who have brain stem disorders in the vestibular, somatosensory, and related systems, improved postural and related responses are said to improve their ability to integrate intersensory information acting through these systems. This improved integrative functioning will then enhance the children's ability to overcome language disorders and to learn academic subjects, abilities that require intersensory integration and the organization of incoming information at the brain stem level (Ayres, 1972, 1977).

Sensory integration procedures were originally designed for learning disabled children, but the description of the program provided by the Western Psychological Services, which sells the assessment tests, checklists, and books for Ayres and her colleagues, describes the program as useful for developmentally disabled or delayed children ranging from trainable mentally retarded to learning disabled. For the most part, studies with retarded children have been poorly designed, but in one study in which adequate experimental controls were used, sensory integration training was no better than a program of gross motor control in improving the performance of preschool children (many of whom were retarded and all of whom exhibited motor delays) on a sensorimotor integration test (Jenkins, Fewell, & Harris, 1983). Whether or not sensory integration therapy is of any benefit in certain kinds of learning disability, there is no evidence that it can improve the cognitive or academic skills of retarded children.

* * *

Another private institute is the Marianne Frostig Center of Educational Therapy in Los Angeles. Its founder, the late psychologist Marianne Frostig, was careful to point out that in educating children generally, as well as in diagnosing learning disabilities, all abilities (and the child's emotions) must be considered. Nevertheless, she believed that perceptual capacities are the most fundamental. "Language, motor functions, and higher thought processes are all dependent on perceptual processes and are likely to be disturbed if perception is disturbed" (Frostig, 1975, p. 117). She cited the familiar support structure for her perceptual approach, including Hebb's theory of cell assemblies and Piaget's concepts of schemata and stages of development.

In contrast to Kephart, Frostig believed that visual perceptual activities *precede* goal-directed movement and that vision teaches movement and carries the major responsibility for the integrative functioning of the organism (1975, p. 122). Physical movement plays an important role, however, because "no other education method is [as] . . . well suited [as movement education] for developing and integrating the perceptual functions of the child" (p. 135).

Frostig is best known for her Developmental Test of Visual Perception, which consists of five subtests purported to measure five different perceptual abilities that form the basis of her remedial program (Frostig & Horne, 1964; Maslow, Frostig, Lefever, & Whittlesey, 1964). However, factor analytic studies provide no empirical support for her claim that the five subtests measure separate abilities (Allen, 1968; Corah & Powell, 1963; Olson, 1968; Silverstein, 1965; Ward, 1970). In general, scores on each of the subtests are best accounted for by a single general factor, and in mentally retarded individuals this common factor appears to be general intelligence (Allen, Haupt, & Jones, 1965). It is not too surprising, then, that educable retarded children trained with the Frostig program showed no greater improvement on a concept formation task than did an appropriate control group, although it is surprising that they did not improve reliably more than the control groups on sensorimotor or visual-perceptual tasks (Alley, 1968), or on the Frostig Developmental Test itself (Allen, Dickman, & Haupt, 1966, when the misplaced decimal point in their Table 2 is corrected).

* * *

Critics of Kephart, Getman, and Frostig point out that there is no important relationship between scores on perceptual tests and the reading scores of first and second grade students, and studies provide no good support for the claim that perceptual-motor training improves reading or general cognitive skills (Goodman & Hammill, 1973; Hammill, 1972; Mann, 1970). The tenor of the intense debate over the use of unproven therapies to improve cognitive function is captured in a symposium issue of the journal *Academic Therapy,* where Doman and Delacato, Ayres, and Getman, among others, respond to a very critical paper by Robert Sieben (1977). These debates will continue, for the vacuum created by the absence of sound and validated treatment for many developmental and academic disabilities will continue to fill with debris which must patiently be sorted out.

In a paper published in 1907, Norsworthy made the following statement:

> On the mental side the effect of physical training has probably been as much exaggerated and misconstrued as that of manual training or a laboratory course in science, due to the influence of faculty psychology. None of these subjects have a mystic, wide-spread influence on mental life as a whole. (p. 14)

Almost 80 years later her sentiments are right on the mark, particularly if we add perceptual to physical training.

OTHER PROGRAMS FOR INCREASING INTELLIGENCE

The Venezuelan Project

In March 1979, the President of Venezuela appointed Luis Alberto Machado the first Minister of State for the Development of Intelligence. Machado's goal was nothing less than to raise the intelligence of the entire population of Venezuela. He believes that the human brain today is fundamentally the same as it was at the beginning of human history and that education and learning, transmitted through each generation, are responsible for human progress. In order that all persons can share in this progress they must reach their intellectual potential, and methods are now available that can produce a nation of intellectually competent, creative citizens. These methods are to be taught to expectant mothers and applied to people from infancy to adulthood (Machado, 1981; Walsh, 1981).

In a pamphlet distributed by this new ministry, 14 projects are described (Minister of State, 1980). Starting with good prenatal care and infant nutrition, emphasis during the first 6 years of life is on the application of adequate stimulation, which eventually will reach the entire population through the mass media. In a pilot study, 200 children 7 to 11 years old receive a special chess curriculum to reveal how best to incorporate chess into all levels of education. Beginning in the fourth grade, children take classes in "learning to think." In the seventh grade there are courses on logic and problem solving, among other skills, derived from the work of Edward de Bono, director of the Center for the Study of Thinking Skills, Cambridge, England. Professor de Bono is a consultant to the project, as is Reuven Feuerstein, whose program is being applied initially to 3,200 ten-year-old school children, after which it will gradually be introduced throughout the entire country. All college students preparing to be teachers must study Feuerstein's Instrumental Enrichment program. In turn, Bar-Ilan University in Israel has established a Luis Alberto Machado Chair for Research into Human Modifiability and the Development of Intelligence (Walsh, 1981).

As another demonstration project, a group of 100 fourth grade students from the poor districts will be trained to perform the symphonic works of famous composers, and to "demonstrate great creative capacity in musical composition, the plastic arts, and in the use of techniques for solving problems." This demonstration will prove that "what is important is the teaching method . . . [and] that by means of well-devised and co-ordinated plans, anybody can project . . . the immense potentialities inherent in all human beings," and thereby prove that "it is not necessary to possess anything other than normal ability to obtain results which it is usually thought can only be obtained by people gifted with particular faculties" (Minister of State, 1980, pp. 7–8).,

Among a number of other projects is a program for developing the intelligence of the Venezuelan Armed Forces, and a program for achieving a higher degree of creativity in public officials.

When in 1984 a new Venezuelan president was elected, Machado's ministerial position was eliminated and he was replaced by a commissioner, Aline Lampe, who has a doctoral degree in education and psychology (Cordes, 1985). Dr. Lampe is reevaluating all the programs, and although some of the content will be modified, she intends to continue the extensive classroom training of thinking skills. Machado, meanwhile, has been traveling around the world, encouraging other countries to adopt similar programs.

One of the major influences on Machado's thinking has been B.F. Skinner, who described the project as "one of the great social experiments of this century" (quoted by Walsh, 1981, p. 641). Skinner was properly impressed, for here, come to fruition, is an experiment that Lockian empiricists could have only wistfully dreamed about.

Raising the IQ of Down's Syndrome Children

Because Down's syndrome is a chromosomal disorder, the lowered intelligence level that typically accompanies the syndrome cannot be due, in any extensive way, to inadequate early stimulation; indeed, many children with Down's syndrome come from very stimulating environments. This syndrome thus provides a test of the extent to which environmental intervention can boost IQ when the deficiency has a known physiological basis. But the test, as always, must be soundly made, with the usual scientific safeguards. Too often, case histories are exhibited to prove the efficacy of a particular training program; yet we know that the range of intelligence in Down's syndrome children is quite large. There are different forms and degrees of this disorder, and there have been reports of average intelligence in some children with the mosaic form of Down's syndrome (Fishler, 1975). Consequently, case histories are inadequate as empirical evidence for particular intervention procedures.[2]

Periodically, we are informed of rather dramatic IQ gains made by this population. On the basis of a personal communication, a highly respected and influential psychologist (Scarr-Salapatek, 1975) reported that John Rynders, of the University of Minnesota, had raised the mean IQ of 25 Down's syndrome children to 85 at 3 years of age, when the expected level is 50 and other training programs had raised it to 68. In other words, the project co-directed by Rynders and Horrobin, called Project EDGE (Expanding Developmental Growth through Education), was 17 points better than other training programs.

In Project EDGE, 3- to 9-month-old Down's syndrome infants were given daily 1-hour EDGE instruction by their mothers (who were trained by the project staff), or occasionally by another family member. When the infants reached 30 months of age they attended a preschool staffed by project personnel. The special intervention ended when the children reached 5 years of age.

Professor Rynders graciously sent me recent published reports and related papers of assessments made when the children were 5 years old. These results present a different story. Although the Project EDGE subjects had been given the Stanford–Binet, the IQs were not reported by Rynders and Horrobin (1980). In order to "minimize IQ as a focal point for future use of our work" (Rynders, 1982), "decimal ratio scores" were used, a decision for which Rynders later expressed some misgivings.

The decimal ratio score is obtained by dividing the total raw score (number of individual items correct) by the child's age and multiplying the result by 100. As Rynders (1982) points out, this score is deceptive because experimental children could get a higher decimal ratio score but not necessarily a higher IQ than control children. For example, on a subtest where, say, five of six correct items were required to pass, children who failed the first two items would not be presented the remaining items on

[2]Nigel Hunt (1967) is one example of the range of abilities that can be found in persons with Down's syndrome, even those with trisomy 21. By himself he typed a fascinating description of his experiences, an accomplishment that attests to his remarkable language facility.

that subtest, whereas children who passed the first four items and failed the last two would have been given all six. The latter children would have had more opportunity for a higher raw score (and would have obtained a higher raw score), although this would not have unduly affected their IQ. Or an examiner might have skipped one level of a particular subtest and gone on to a higher level, and the child would have been exposed to fewer items, with less chance to raise his or her raw score.

In fact when the children were 5 years old, whereas the difference between the decimal ratio scores of the experimental and control groups was reported to be statistically reliable, the difference on the ratio IQ scores (MA/CA × 100) was not reliable until the statistical treatment was adjusted for unequal sex distribution (Dorsher, 1981). However, the use of this statistical adjustment was inappropriate because the sex distributions of the two groups (4 girls and 13 boys in the experimental group, 8 girls and 10 boys in the control group) were not reliably different. Note also that at this maturational level the ratio IQs—used because some children did not reach the basal level—are much higher than normed IQs. The mean ratio IQs (reported by Dorsher) of 63 for the experimental and 56 for the control group would actually be about 52 and 45, respectively, using the IQ table in Terman and Merrill (1973). The 52 IQ of the treatment group is a long way from the 85 originally reported by Rynders to Scarr-Salapatek, but this melting away of initial gains is typical of early intervention projects.

* * *

Many intervention programs are designed to counteract the especially slow rate of motor, mental, and language development of children with trisomy 21, the most common form of Down's syndrome (Cornwell & Birch, 1969; Dicks-Mireaux, 1972; Fishler, 1975; Melyn & White, 1973). This depressed rate of maturation creates an increasing disparity between their achievements and the achievements of the normal child. Intervention programs and stimulating environments can do much to offset this widening disparity (e.g., Bayley, Rhodes, Gooch, & Marcus, 1971; Ludlow & Allen, 1979), but it is surprising when they produce a *faster* rate of development in Down's syndrome children relative to normal children, for this would mean that they are approaching the normal children in achievement. In such instances it is particularly important to assess the maintenance at later ages of initially reported intervention effects, a procedure that is rarely followed (see Gibson & Fields, 1984, for a thorough review).

The Down's Syndrome Program at the University of Washington has reportedly been unusually effective. Down's syndrome children were assigned to one of four Model Preschool Programs—infant, early or advanced preschool, or kindergarten (Hayden & Haring, 1976). The Infant Learning

Class met once a week for 30 minutes, during which time the parents were trained to develop their children's motor and sensory skills. The other three classes met for 1.5 to 2 hours a day, four times a week. Depending on their level of development, the children were trained in fine and gross motor development, self-help, social and cognitive skills, music, language, number concepts, and reading. According to the initial project reports, the children were actually approaching the performance level of normal children, but Hayden and Dmitriev (1975) were properly cautious: "Because parents often have their hopes raised and then dashed by unrealistic expectation, it is important to avoid overstatement of what can be achieved from programs such as those we are developing" (p. 216).

This project was provided with additional funding from the Bureau of Education for the Handicapped in order to establish, in the Seattle public schools, primary level classes patterned after the Model Preschool Program. This permitted the project staff to continue to foster the development of the children from their preschool project and to compare their development with that of other Down's syndrome children. Although intelligence tests were among the assessment instruments that were used, IQ results were not presented in the published report (Hayden & Haring, 1977). Rather, results were given for the Down's Syndrome Performance Inventory. These results were quite startling. Children who had been in the Model Preschool program and who continued in the project's primary level program were, by the time they were 8 years old, developing at a normal rate! Furthermore, based on the graphic figures presented as evidence (but without any information on the number of children contributing to each of the data points, and without accompanying statistical analyses) one must assume that the project children were functioning at close to an average level of intelligence. Hayden and Haring (1977) specifically stated that "children who have been in the program for several years and fall between the ages of 60 and 72 months are typically performing 95% of the tasks expected of normal children" (p. 129).

Before accepting these results, however, it would be prudent to consider the criterion measure of normal developmental level, the Down's Syndrome Performance Inventory. It was described as a "criterion-referenced objective checklist developed by the Model Preschool staff . . . to monitor each child's quarterly progress. . . . Items are age-referenced according to when a normal child might be expected to master them" (Hayden & Haring, 1977, p. 132). But no results for normal children were given and the inventory was never standardized. Apparently, no one knows how normal children perform on this inventory. Consequently there is no evidence that it is a true measure of normal development, and there is no valid basis for the statement that the project children were performing 95% of the tasks expected of normal children. Presenting data from the intelligence tests and other standardized measuring instruments would have been more convincing.

The caution expressed by Hayden and Dmitriev in their 1975 report began to dissipate 2 years later. After warning that the results were still very tentative, Hayden and Haring (1977) wrote that "there is now reason to believe that the conclusions drawn from *previous* studies were in themselves quite pessimistic" (p. 141).

Based on a follow-up study, however, they should have remained suitably cautious. Eleven Down's syndrome children who had attended both the University of Washington's Model Preschool Program and the special grade school program were tested some 8 years later, in 1983, when their mean age was 13.6 years (du Verglas, 1984). Their mean Stanford–Binet IQ at that time was 49. Though reliably higher than the mean IQ of 41 obtained by a control group, this level of intellectual functioning would appear to justify reinstating the initially cautious attitude about prematurely raising the hopes of parents. Note too that for seven control and seven experimental children who had Stanford–Binet scores taken in both 1975 and 1983, the mean IQ of the control subgroup rose from 34 to 42, whereas for the experimental subgroup it dropped from 52 to 50. Assuming that these children are representative of the two groups, they are closing the gap between them, reenacting the script of other intervention studies.

Early environmental stimulation appears to have a favorable effect on the social and cognitive development of some Down's syndrome children, although more long-term studies are needed. But the advocates of early stimulation damage their cause when they make exaggerated claims based on very preliminary, and often inadequate, evidence. A quotation from LaVeck and Brehm (1978) pinpoints some of the inadvertant anxiety aroused by broad claims and raised expectations. They noted the "genuine distress [of] parents of nonreading 5- to 8-year-olds, and anger at school programs for 'holding children back.'" It is sad, they write, to hear the parents of Down's syndrome children "hold themselves responsible for the failure of their children to make gains similar to those in others' testimony" (p. 135).

Teaching Intelligence

Numerous programs are available to teach not only social and academic skills but the "conceptual and problem solving skills that constitute intelligent behavior" (Bijou, 1981, p. 40). One of these is the DISTAR System (Direct Instruction System in Arithmetic and Reading) for primary-age children. The origins of this teaching system date from the early 1960s, when Siegfried Engelmann and Carl Bereiter, at the University of Illinois, developed a preschool teaching program that featured Skinnerian reinforcement techniques. The program emphasized intensive, teacher-directed, carefully sequenced, small group, verbal instruction (Becker, Engelmann, Carnine, & Rhine, 1981).

A detailed, book-length description of the language-oriented preschool curriculum that antedated DISTAR was provided by Bereiter and Engelmann in 1966. They included only a short section on its successful use with preschool children, but 4 years later Engelmann (1970) more fully described the dramatic results they achieved with disadvantaged 4-year-olds. After 2 years of daily, 2-hour participation in a preschool Direct Instruction program, 12 experimental children—who had entered the program with a mean Stanford-Binet IQ of 97—had a mean IQ of 121. This rise in IQ was 19 points greater than the 5-point rise (from 95 to 100) of 28 control children who had received 2 years of traditional preschool education.

Some of the assumptions underlying the Direct Instruction program reveal its debt to behaviorism:

> Operant (voluntary) behavior is learned.
> The teacher can control environmental events to make learning happen.
> Intelligent behavior is operant behavior; therefore, it is learned and can be taught.
> Thinking and related covert cognitive processes can be taught first as overt (usually verbal) processes.
> If the students fail, do not blame the students; diagnose the teaching history. The teaching sequences control what can be learned. (Becker, Engelmann, Carnine, & Maggs, 1982, p. 154)

According to Engelmann (1970), any child can reach average intelligence if instruction is effective, although children differ in the amount of instruction they require. Consequently, if disadvantaged children, or any children for that matter, are taught at a faster rate, they will become smarter. However, the long range effectiveness of intervention may be adversely affected if the children are subsequently taught at a slower rate, accounting for the later drop in intelligence scores so typical of intervention programs. Intelligence is controlled by the environment, genetic influence being a minor factor, according to Engelmann.

Because of the success of the preschool program, the USOE funded a similar program for kindergarten through the third grade, and included it in Project Follow Through. Although Bereiter had by then left Illinois, the new program, based on techniques he had been so instrumental in developing, was produced by Engelmann and Wesley Becker (both of whom later moved to the University of Oregon). Under the general rubric of "Direct Instruction" they developed a number of teaching programs, the best known being the DISTAR language, reading, and arithmetic programs for kindergarten through third grade (available commercially from Science Research Associates).

A number of sites using the Direct Instruction model were included in the evaluation of Project Follow Through made by Abt Associates Inc. when the children had completed third grade (e.g., Bock et al., 1977). In general, the children in this program fared better than did the children in other Follow Through programs, particularly on measures of basic skills, which the program had stressed. The Direct Instruction model was the only exception to the general rule that Follow Through programs had more negative than positive effects on basic skills test scores when compared with a comparison group of disadvantaged children who were not in a Follow Through program.

Unfortunately, after the students left the Direct Instruction programs and progressed through the upper grades in regular school classes their academic achievement scores dropped appreciably, an outcome attributed by Becker et al., (1981) to ineffective teaching (see also Miller & Bizzell, 1983).

As noted previously, the differential performance of Follow Through children at different sites, even when the same program model was being used, had more influence on the results than did differences between programs, and this pronounced difference between sites was also found for the Direct Instruction program. Of most interest in the present context, the Direct Instruction groups rarely did better, and at a number of sites did reliably worse, than the comparison groups on the only test of general intelligence included in the Abt Associates' evaluation: Raven's Coloured Progressive Matrices Test. Becker and Carnine (1981) later wrote that their project children gained significantly on the Slosson Intelligence Test that was administered under the supervision of project personnel, but they presented no data.

Miller and Dyer (1975) reported that after a gain of 5.4 IQ points attributable to Direct Instruction pre-school intervention, these children showed a sharper decline (from 98.4 to 92.9) in Stanford-Binet IQ than did children from three other Head Start programs and a control group. Direct Instruction children still available after the eighth grade had a mean Stanford-Binet IQ of 87 (Miller & Bizzell, 1983). During this same period the mean IQ of the control group generally hovered between 90 and 92. Similar ebbing of heightened Stanford-Binet IQs was found by Karnes, Shwedel, and Williams (1983). From an initial mean IQ of 94 at age 5, children in the Direct Instruction preschool program showed a dramatic rise of 20 points at age 6, but at age 9 their mean Stanford-Binet IQ had returned about half way to the starting level, and at age 16 their mean WISC-R IQ was about 91.

The DISTAR Language I program was used with 14 institutionalized moderately and severely retarded children, 6 to 14 years of age (Maggs & Morath, 1976). Following the 2-year, 1-hour-per-school-day treatment period, the mean MA of the treatment group rose 22.5 months, whereas the control group's mean MA rose only 7.5 months over the same period. The IQ scores were not provided by Maggs and Morath, but based on the Stanford–Binet conversion tables (Terman & Merrill, 1973) it would appear that there was a mean IQ gain of about 10 points for the treatment group relative to their controls, a typical result for intervention programs.[3]

In a related study, 12 retarded children, 6 to 12 years old with a mean adjusted Stanford–Binet IQ of 45 (adjusted from 42 to compensate for regression artifacts) gained 6 IQ points following an intensive 5-year application of DISTAR reading and language programs (Gersten & Maggs, 1982).

These modest results did not prevent Lockery and Maggs (1982) from ardently extolling Direct Instruction technology, in a review of results that they considered "remarkable." Among other reported findings, a small sample of moderately and severely retarded children (who became mildly and moderately retarded after intervention with the DISTAR System), mastered the first 22 modules of a microcomputing program. "The indications are that these microcomputing skills are within the reach of such retarded people, opening up wider vocational avenues in our increasingly technological society. . . . A vast employment avenue is opened" (pp. 278, 285). Furthermore, "given suitable environmental factors, such as Direct Instruction teaching technology and reinforcement procedures, these children can increase their intellectual functioning" (p. 284).

The claims that teaching systems exist that will permanently raise the intelligence of retarded persons to a material and useful degree continue to be published, lacking only the required empirical support. The suggestion that with the use of a behavioral teaching procedure moderately and mildly retarded individuals will develop computing skills that will make them more employable in an increasingly technological society is simply irresponsible.

Before leaving this section it should be noted that Carl Bereiter has not taken the extreme empiricist stance of others who are identified with the Direct Instruction system. He did not argue with critics who pointed out that students who improved their basic skills become better "learners," not better "thinkers," but he rightly insisted that learning is in itself an important human accomplishment (Bereiter, 1970). He also pointed out that, all

[3]For a 10-year-old child to retain an IQ of 40 over a 2-year period, he or she would have to gain only 4 months of mental age (Terman & Merrill, 1973). Because in this study the control group gained 7.5 months over the 2-year period, the statement made by Gersten & Maggs (1982) that the Maggs and Morath control sample demonstrated a significant loss in IQ is inaccurate. (The mean IQ was not reported in the paper, but I assume it was around 35 or 40.)

things being equal, even a heritability ratio for intelligence of 80% would allow environmental factors to change IQ by as much as 28 points, although we are a long way from knowing how to produce this kind of effect. We return to this important point in a later discussion.

* * *

There are other writers who are not only incautious in their claims, but also injudicious in titling their books. What are parents of a retarded child to make of a book titled *Intelligence Can Be Taught* (Whimbey, 1980)? Are they angry with the author or outraged that their professional consultants have been unable to raise the intelligence of their child? It is true that Whimbey exempts individuals whose low intelligence is due to neurological injury or disease, but most retarded persons in the 50 to 70 IQ range, the so-called cultural-familial retarded, show no evidence of neurological insult. They are therefore potential students for Whimbey's intelligence curriculum.

For Whimbey, intelligence is largely a learned mental skill that can be trained through demonstration and guided practice. His message is that "as it becomes clearer that intelligence is a teachable skill, the need for improved methods of training that skill should be clear to all" (Whimbey, 1980, p. 69). He writes, in italics, that *"Intelligence is paying careful skilled attention to the analysis of relations,"* and adds that, "though somewhat simplified, this appears to be the sum and substance of intelligence" (p. 119). It follows, then, that if you teach this skill—by, for example, teaching individuals to direct their attention to discerning relations—you will raise intelligence.

Whimbey's emphasis is on the ability to train specific skills, within limits that are never precisely defined but that are quite large, judging by the tenor of his book. Subjects in his own studies have been primarily college students who already have a high level of general intelligence, and therefore successfully training them to improve on analogies tests, for example, is not particularly surprising. For the application of his thesis to groups of lower intelligence he draws on a number of sources, including the results of the Bereiter-Engelmann Direct Instruction Program, the Klaus-Gray Early Training Project, and in particular Heber's Milwaukee Project, three projects that have been reviewed here with decidedly different conclusions than those arrived at by Whimbey.

The pivotal question in the present context is not whether the kind of mental skills training advocated by Whimbey improved performance on particular isolated skills, but whether it so changes the trainees that they move perceptibly to a higher level of general intelligence. Whimbey himself has not applied his cognitive therapy program to mentally retarded populations. Although he believes it is best to train children when they are young, he asserts throughout his book that cognitive training can be employed profitably with older children and even with adults. If intelligence can be taught, ethical and moral considerations alone would point Whimbey and his cognitive therapy in the direction of retarded persons who show no evidence of neurological damage.

* * *

Over a period of 25 years, Arthur Staats has been a prolific and influential spokesman for the empiricist belief that intelligence can be taught. According to Staats (1971), "the child's intellectual qualities, his intelligence, is acquired through learning" (p. 287). Intelligence consists of various repertoires of learned skills. "How well the child will learn ordinarily is determined not by the child's internal organic-mental quality but by the basic behavioral repertoires that he brings to the task. There is no evidence that there are organic-mental differences that determine the child's learning rate" (p. 287). Not only do children learn a repertoire of useful skills, but they can also learn a repertoire of anti-learning behaviors, and it is these that are frequently acquired by children labeled mentally retarded. Moreover, "if such children were provided with appropriate reinforcers, they would learn as well as other children" (p. 227), and this applies to the vast majority of retarded persons (p. 317).

Because the deficiency in behavioral repertoires is cumulative, extraordinary conditions of training would be required to compensate for their absence. Staats believes, therefore, that placement of retarded children in special classes merely compounds the problem because such classes cannot provide for the enriched training experiences that are required.[4]

Staats and his coworkers published a series of experiments purporting to illustrate that intelligence can be raised. Staats and Burns (1981, p. 244) claimed that a previous study had produced preliminary evidence that the mean IQ of educationally disadvantaged 4-year-olds had been raised 12 points (rounded). In what way these 4-year-olds were "educationally disadvantaged" was not detailed, but Staats, Brewer, and Gross (1970, p. 11) described the children as being primarily from families with below average incomes.

In one experiment, Staats et al. (1970) used the principles of operant conditioning to teach two 3-year-olds and nine 4-year-olds to read the letters of the alphabet. The mean IQ of the group was 105, and all but one of the children had an IQ of over 90; three had IQs of 119, 121, and 123. However, the child who had an IQ of 84 was one of three who failed to

[4]Staats apparently forgot about the Skeels and Dye (1939) study in which retarded children were cured after only 9.5 months in a ward for retarded women (see Chapter 5).

learn. One other child, who had an IQ of 119, was excluded from this part of the study because his mother had already taught him the alphabet, apparently without benefit of the instrumental discrimination learning technique that was used by the experimenters. Four of the children who had excelled in learning the alphabet were also taught to read a number of words. In addition, almost all of the children—most of whom had rudimentary counting skills—improved their counting ability by some three to seven numbers over an average of 37 sessions. Mean post-training IQ for the entire group rose to 112, a gain that was not statistically reliable.

In the same monograph, Staats et al. (1970) reported once again a study previously reported by Staats (1968). This was the study that, according to Staats and Burns (above), had provided "preliminary evidence" that IQ could be raised. In this study, a group of "culturally deprived" 4-year-olds with IQs ranging from 88 to 130 were taught to *write* the letters of the alphabet. Although two of the children made little progress and were therefore excluded from the analysis (!), many of the other children made modest gains. Mean IQ scores over the course of the experiment were 101, 106, 104, and 113, but the authors warned that repeated testing on the same instrument may have made the children "test-wise." Yet this is the increase of 12 IQ points that is repeatedly referred to in subsequent publications. No control group was used.

As part of another series of experiments (Staats & Burns, 1981), 16 children enrolled in a Head Start program were placed either in an experimental or a control group and pre- and posttested on 27 items dealing with number concepts taken from various intelligence tests. Although the training given to the experimental group was said not to be on the actual intelligence test items, it was very close. For example, children were taught to count up to 16 randomly arrayed objects, whereas one of the intelligence test items requires them to count a row of 12 pictured trees. As another example, when presented with a number of objects the children were trained to remove or cover all but 1, 2, 5, 8, 11, and 12 of them, whereas on the intelligence test items they were presented with a picture of 12 trees and asked to cover all but 4, and then 8, of them. Note that the actual numbers differed, but the concept was the same. Not surprisingly, after 48 training sessions the experimental children performed better on the intelligence test items than the control children, who received no special training. However, only four of the eight experimental children learned to do the more difficult items, which included the "cover all except" items mentioned above. In fact, they were still working on the basic counting skills when the experiment ended.

Still another group of preschoolers was trained in tracing, copying, reading, and writing the alphabet, and then tested on three subtests used in

Intelligence tests: Geometric Designs, Mazes, and Comprehension. Compared with a control group the experimental children were, after training, superior on the two tests that require drawing, but not on the unrelated Comprehension subtest, thereby illustrating that specific intellectual skills are related to learning, according to the author.

A final experiment with preschool, kindergarten, and first grade students was designed to increase performance on Similarities subtests (e.g., In what way are a cat and a mouse alike?). Children were trained to describe 70 pictures in terms of the concepts that are used in the Similarities items. For example, when shown a picture of a wheel the children were asked, "What type of round object is this?" and then taught to say that a wheel is a round object. Ditto for a ball, and so on. Thirty-nine of 70 pictures were of the words actually used in the Similarities subtests. After all five pictures of round objects were presented, the child was asked to recall the names of all the round objects. Similar training was given on the other categories. As expected, the experimental children, when compared with the control children, excelled on Similarities items (e.g., In what way are a wheel and a ball alike?), as well as on sorting and category identification tasks, but not on an unrelated Mazes subtest.

What all this proves escapes me. Had Staats waited a year or two the children would have learned all these skills with much less effort, but apparently he was intent on demonstrating that there is no inborn timetable of maturation that sets limits on what can be learned at different ages. According to the behaviorist approach, cognitive development is not a result of maturation, but "comes about largely or entirely through learning" (Staats et al., 1970, p. 80), and according to Staats there is a cumulative effect, so that the earlier you learn something the easier it is to learn related but more complex skills and the brighter and brighter you'll become.

Taken as a group, though, these experiments are not persuasive, and the time spent by the participating children might better have been spent in other pursuits.

THEORETICAL AND ACTUAL RANGE OF ENVIRONMENTAL EFFECTS

As a number of workers have pointed out, even if broad heritability (defined as the genetic proportion of the variation of a given trait in a population) is as high as 80%, the 20% attributable to environmental factors would be substantial in terms of IQ effects. Ignoring, for illustrative purposes, gene-environment interactions and interrelations, environmental variance could be responsible for IQ differences of 35 points, by one estimate

(Jensen, 1981).[5] This is sufficient to bring children with IQs of 60 to well within the normal range if the malignant effects of a poor environment were compensated for.

However, these theoretical speculations always flounder when there are extreme circumstances, as when a child is brought up in an isolated room, an environmental manipulation that has a far greater impact than a mere 35 IQ points. But these extreme effects seem to be confined only to *reducing* intelligence—which can then be raised when the children are freed from their inhuman bondage—whereas empiricists claim that extremely felicitous environments can raise intelligence to the same extent that abominable environments can lower it.

Some light on the extent to which intelligence is influenced by less radical differences in environment is provided by a recent French adoption study in which researchers followed the development of children who, born of unskilled workers, had been abandoned at birth and adopted by the age of 6 months (mean adoption age of 4 months) by upper-middle-class parents (Schiff, Duyme, Dumaret, & Tomkiewicz, 1982). At the time of testing, the adopted children ranged from 6 years to 13 years of age. The control group consisted of half-siblings who shared the adopted children's biological mothers, but in most cases not their biological fathers, and who remained in the lower-class environment. On the French version of the WISC, 32 adopted children had a mean IQ of 110.6 (SD = 2.0) compared to a mean of 94.2 (SD = 2.5) for 20 control children. The adopted children were also much more successful in school. The mean difference of about 16 IQ points is well within the theoretical limits attributable to environmental variance if broad heritability were considered to be 80%.

The mystery, then, is why intensive training has failed to cure mental retardation in instances where there is no evidence of central nervous system pathology. If the empiricists are correct and intelligence is largely learned, it should be possible to unlearn bad habits and replace them with good ones. That this hope remains unrealized suggests that the effects of the environment during development become so ingrained that it is impossible to change them by any known pedagogical or psychological techniques, and/or that there are undiscovered pathologies in the central nervous systems of most mentally retarded persons. It is possible also that individ-

---

[5]The environmental variability (SD) equals the SD of the intelligence test times the square root of the number produced by subtracting the broad heritability from the reliability of the test. Thus, assuming a test reliability of .95 and a test SD of 15, the SD of environmental effects is $15(\sqrt{.95 - .80})$, or 5.8. Assuming environmental influences over a range of 6 SDs (± 3 SD), we arrive at the figure of 35 points (6×5.8). If heritability is assumed to be .70, the range of environmental influences could be 45 points, and so on. If it is assumed that the range of environmental influences can encompass ± 4 SD, then the size of the IQ change could be appreciably larger.

ual variations in the inherited structure of the central nervous system are related to the potential for change; that there is, in other words, a biological basis for an inverse relationship between intelligence and intellectual malleability.

THE FREQUENTLY REPORTED INCREASE OF 10 ± 2 IQ POINTS

In the course of this review, reports of raising low intelligence by about 10 IQ points have been frequent enough that the term 10 ± 2 can serve to encompass a fair proportion of intervention studies. For instance, Kephart (1939) reported that his training procedure raised retarded IQs by an average of 10 points. Kirk (1958) reported an average gain of 11 to 12 points as a result of preschool experience. Woolman (1971, Vol. II) reported a 10-point IQ rise in his experimental group. Based on reported changes in MA, the mean IQ of retarded children given Direct Instruction training rose about 12 points (Maggs & Morath, 1976). Over a 1-year period, Gray et al.'s (1982) combined experimental group of Head Start children rose 10 IQ points. Token reinforcements given to mildly retarded children during testing produced a mean IQ that was 9 points higher than that of a control group (Johnson et al., 1984).

This phenomenon did not escape the notice of Edward Zigler and his colleagues, who, in a series of studies, searched for its source. In one study, an "optimizing" procedure intended to heighten test-taking motivation raised the Stanford–Binet IQ of culturally deprived children by 10 points over standard testing given three weeks previously (Zigler & Butterfield, 1968). In a related study the Peabody Picture Vocabulary Test (PPVT) was given twice within 1 week to a group of disadvantaged children who, on the average, scored 10 points higher on the second administration given by the same examiner (Zigler, Abelson, & Seitz, 1973). Both administrations of the test were preceded by a play period to acclimate the children, yet in a second study reported in the same paper, disadvantaged children who had no preliminary play period and different examiners in the second than in the first test, nevertheless rose 12 IQ points on retest. Over all conditions, the average increase was about 8 points. Nondisadvantaged children showed a 5-point retest increase. Note that in the above studies the examiners were familiar with the purposes of the experiments and aware of each child's group membership.

The IQ scores of Head Start and non-Head Start children who were retested on the PPVT after a 1-week interval rose an average of 11 points, and whether they were tested in their homes or in an office or school room had no significant effect on the size of the increase, although non-Head

Start Children who were tested in their homes performed more poorly overall than those tested elsewhere (Seitz, Abelson, Levine, & Zigler, 1975). In a later study the mean IQ of both Head Start and non-Head Start children rose 6 points on the short form of the Stanford–Binet when they were retested after a 2-month period. Six months later, the Head Start children rose another 4 points, making their overall increase 10 points, while the comparison group dropped 3 points (Zigler, Abelson, Trickett, & Seitz, 1982).

These studies, and others like them, indicate that a substantial portion of the frequently reported increase in IQ following intervention does not reflect true changes in cognitive functioning because initial (baseline) tests often underestimate the true score. Practice, familiarity, and changes in motivation of the children (as well as bias in the examiner and the various other sources of error reported throughout this book) will, to varying degrees, contribute to the increase.

OLD HOPES IN NEW GUISES

Periodically there arise, phoenix-like, new and zealous groups, ranging from mental health workers to experimental psychologists, who are convinced that the art and/or science of psychology has reached the stage where it can raise retarded intelligence. We have met some of these ardent groups, usually led by particularly charismatic leaders, but have not yet discussed those who are engaged in more basic, or fundamental, research. Experimental psychologists, trained to be cautious and wary of the many variables that can affect their data, would be the last group one would suspect of allowing their theories and experiments to be tainted. But scientists are human, and, as illustrated in the Introduction, even in the "hard" sciences there is an alarming history of traveling down dubious paths and dead end streets.

In experimental psychology, cognitive theories, including particularly information-processing theory, have become increasingly popular, and they now dominate the field. This "new" psychology was in part a reaction against an oversimplified view of humans, as exemplified in the stimulus-response psychology of the behaviorists. Information-processing theory considers the individual to be a symbol-manipulating organism, a processor of information. As its name implies, it is a theory of processes, and in this sense it is reminiscent of the venerable philosophical and psychological quest for faculties of the mind, faculties (processes) that not only can be measured but also trained (Mann, 1979).

Because the processing of information occurs linearly over time (and because the theory is so intimately intertwined with computer science), elemental information processes are represented in flow diagrams as nodes (boxes) with, for example, separate nodes for *attend, select, apply, store, evaluate, choose, retrieve, test, respond,* and so on, depending on the task at hand. Newell and Simon (1972) sum up their description of the application of information-processing theory to an understanding of problem solving as follows: "Our theory posits internal mechanisms of great extent and complexity, and endeavors to make contact between them and the visible evidence of problem solving. That is all there is to it" (p. 10).

The Executive Function

With all of these processes operating within the organism there is a need for an organizing agent, some process that can control all the other processes, that can prod the selector to select something from memory, or order the search process to search for more information, and so on. To simply say that the *individual* controls these processes will never do, for the individual could not be a box like any other box. All the processes represented by the boxes are inside the individual, after all, and if the individual were represented by a box it would have to encompass the entire flow diagram! Consequently, theorists created a supreme commander, which came to be called the executive, an internal agent or homunculus that (although there is no evidence that it exists) plays a major role in current attempts to train retarded individuals.

It is difficult to find the exact origin of the idea of an executive function because it has masquaraded in so many different costumes. Guilford (1967, 1972) applied the term *executive function* to two factors that, he said, appeared serendipitously in one of his factor analytic studies and that "seem to be concerned with intentions and with initiation and management of motor responses" (p. 279). Note that the performance represented by these factors was nevertheless under the control of the individual, not some independent internal agent. The modern homunculus was borrowed from the computer programmer's "executive routine" function. Neisser (1967) found unpalatable but unavoidable the notion of using an executive system that selects and uses stored information, but his executive had nowhere near the power it came to assume in later theories. The "control processes" described by Atkinson and Shiffrin (1968), initially described as being under the individual's control, were quickly emancipated to assume independent duties, such as selecting particular portions of incoming information for transfer to short-term store.

In the 1970s the executive played an important role in theories of memory. Bower (1972) rejected criticisms that it is a "shadowy homunculus" and declared that in simulation programs it is "a well specified piece of program that makes a series of elementary decisions (e.g., does symbol A match symbol B?).... When tens of thousands of small decisions are cascaded in a large hierarchially organized program, the operation of the entire system appears complex and intelligent" (p. 108).

In the view of Baddeley & Hitch (1974), the executive is a system "responsible for setting up the appropriate phonemic 'rehearsal' routines, i.e., of loading up the phonemic buffer and of retrieving information from the buffer when necessary.... When the capacity of the phonemic buffer is exceeded, then the executive component of working memory must devote more of its time to the problem of storage" (p. 77).

But despite this initially limited use of the term, tied as it was to specific computer programs, the little homunculus—a veritable Sorcerer's Apprentice—grew so rapidly it became a multifaceted dictator. According to Sternberg (1984), the executive is made up of subprocesses, called "metacomponents," or "higher order control processes that are used for executive planning and decision making in problem solving" (p. 99). He lists six metacomponents in intellectual functioning: (1) Decision as to just what the problem is that needs to be solved, (2) selection of lower-order components, (3) selection of one or more representations of organizations for information, (4) selection of a strategy for combining lower order components, (5) decision regarding tradeoffs in the speed and accuracies with which various components are executed, and (6) solution monitoring. As the reader can see, the executive function is a powerful agent that makes decisions of utmost importance for the individual's very survival. Freed from its specific role in a computer program, it became a hypothetical construct that mediates intellectual performance.

The executive was introduced to the experimental psychology of mental retardation in an influential paper by Butterfield, Wambold, and Belmont (1973). They reported that retarded persons do not spontaneously adopt efficient mnemonic strategies, although they can make short-lived use of specific strategies on which they are trained. In concluding their paper, the authors express dismay at the prospect of trying to train retarded persons in each separate cognitive domain, and mention, almost in passing, that it would be more efficient "to train executive function instead of the particular skills for whose success it [the executive] must be ultimately responsible" (p. 668). Executive function—the "selecting, sequencing, and coordinating processes that are in the cognitive repertoire" (p. 668)—had become an "it," something within the person that can be trained. Based on a description of individual behavior during short-term memory experiments, the authors proposed to train, not the individual, but a process or faculty. This is not an inconsequential transformation; all the past failures to improve the intelligent performance of retarded *individuals* could be forgotten, for here was an opportunity to improve intellectual performance by training a *process,* the executive function, and it carried with it an aura of scientific respectability. If, in the past, immense efforts had been expended in training sensory processes, an equally dedicated effort could now be expended on the training of a higher level process assumed to exist as a separate entity in the brain.

That any description of the executive function can serve as a workable description of intelligence—and that, therefore, in attempting to train this process one is, in truth, attempting to train intelligence (Blackman & Lin, 1984)—was no deterrence. Butterfield and Belmont (1977) argued that their efforts to train the executive to deal with a variety of problems are more promising than the efforts of others to train "control" processes for specific tasks. Derived from the work of Atkinson and Shiffrin (1968), control processes are conceived as those features of a person's memory system that can be changed by training and experience, and that are contrasted with the unchanging (hard-wired) features referred to as "structural" aspects of the memory system. Although originally proposed as a theoretical concept useful for the study of memory, the control-structural dichotomy has taken on wider implications. If the *executive* is another term for intelligence, and if there is disagreement about whether it is a control or structural feature of the human brain, then one can readily see how the current debate in the experimental psychology of mental retardation reflects the age-old debate not only about whether retarded intelligence can be appreciably raised, but also about where to search for knowledge about the nature of intelligence.

For Fisher and Zeaman (1973), intelligence is a stable trait and consequently one should attempt to derive descriptive parameters reflecting structural features rather than control processes. But for Butterfield and his colleagues, neither the control processes nor the structural features are of much interest because that ever more powerful homunculus, the executive, had taken command of the control processes, those "goal directed tactics of cognition, . . . [whose] deployment is the objective outcome of executive planning and revision" (Butterfield & Belmont, 1977, p. 281). Furthermore, although "executive functions are close to what is meant by intelligence," there is no irremediable limitation on the retarded child's "capacity to make an active, planful approach to information-processing problems" (p. 280). Once we understand the executive function we need to "arrange special educational procedures that will improve the child's executive functioning, thereby avoiding the overwhelming undertaking of outfitting him with many cognitive strategies, which he would then have to generalize for himself" (p. 280). "The final step of our approach, yet to be implemented, will be to design instructional techniques to instill normal adult executive functions in mentally retarded children" (p. 314), a declaration that can be interpreted in no other way than as an intention to cure mental retardation.

By 1983, the final step had not yet been achieved, but the hope was as bright as ever. "This chapter presents an optimistic case for the heady possibility that behavioral science is on the threshold of delivering ways to improve thinking to the extent that we will be able to claim cures for the cognitive deficits that lead to mental retardation" (Butterfield, 1983, p. 203).

In their review of the literature on retarded persons' maintenance and generalization of skills and strategies, Borkowski and Cavanaugh (1979) were also optimistic, primarily because of evidence that in some instances retarded groups had been able to transfer a trained strategy. Because it was said to reflect the operation of executive functioning, strategy transfer provided them with evidence of how fully and permanently the executive had been changed. Presumably, if retarded children generalize a strategy to rather different problems than those on which they were originally trained, the executive function has somehow been upgraded. However, the concept of generalization is a murky one, as Zeaman and House (1984) have skillfully demonstrated. That retarded persons, after having their executive functions trained in the laboratory or classroom, will be changed in any noticeable way, or will be better able to face life's myriad problems, has yet to be demonstrated.

The executive control process became a central concept for Brown and Campione and their co-workers. In one paper, they described the hallmark of intelligence as the ability to generalize information, which in turn is dependent upon effective control processes, defined as "the rules and strategies available to the thinker for memorizing, understanding, solving problems, etc." (Campione & Brown, 1978, p. 284). Furthermore, "training attempts should be aimed at the executive functions. . . . rather than at training specific routines" (p. 293), a prescription in tune with that of Butterfield et al. (1973); yet the pervasive problem of limited generalization in retarded persons may limit the effectiveness of such training (Campione & Brown, 1977).

Executive function was joined by the apparently synonymous "metacognition,"—the indices of which were described as "*checking, planning, monitoring, testing, revising,* and *evaluation*" (Brown & Campione, 1979, p. 521)—and had taken on a good deal of independent functioning: "The executive competes for workspace with the subroutines it controls" (pp. 521–522). An alternative (additional?) hallmark of intelligence is the capacity for "multiple and reflective access to knowledge" (p. 522), still another arm of the ubiquitous executive control processes. It was these metacognitive skills that must be trained in order to improve retarded persons' memory, because inadequate metacognitive skills are responsible for an inability to transfer strategies. Metacognitive skills, in fact, were defined by the function they perform; that is, very general skills that can be applied in a wide variety of situations (Campione, Nitsch, Bray, & Brown, 1982, p. 225).

In a paper that contains the most complete statement yet from this group of prolific and respected researchers, they state that "metacognitive and executive decision-making functions [are implicated] as central to any conception of intelligence" (Campione, Brown, & Ferrara, 1982, p. 432), while the latest hallmark of intelligence consists of "the components that emerge without instruction in the intellectually average and above average but that required explicit instruction for those of below-average ability" (p. 433). (In subsequent pages, however, e.g., pp. 436, 452, and 456, intelligence is defined in terms of numerous other capacities.) Metacognition is finally separated from executive control: henceforth, they will use "*metacognition* to refer to knowledge about cognition and *executive control* to denote the overseeing, management functions," and it is "the latter [that] appears more central to notions of intelligence" (p. 434).

The authors "emphatically disavow a position of radical environmentalism or antistructuralism, . . . [for] there is little evidence to suggest that individual differences will be easy to 'train away,' except in the simplistic sense of mastery learning" (p. 453). In fact, they point out that brighter people benefit more from training than do duller persons, with the result that individual differences widen. Furthermore, if training is concerned with the modification of specific cognitive skills, the issue of modifying general intelligence need not be raised (Brown & Campione, 1982). (One might wonder how broadly these "cognitive skills" are defined, for if they resemble metacognitive or executive skills then the issue of modifying intelligence cannot be brushed aside.)

According to Allen Newell (1980), a leader in the application of information processing theory to the understanding of intelligent behavior, the executive homunculus should be banished.

> A major item on the agenda of cognitive psychology is to banish the homunculus [i.e., the assumption of an intelligent agent (little man) residing elsewhere in the system, usually off stage, who does all the marvelous things that need to be done actually to generate the total behavior of the subject]. It is the homunculus that actually performs the control processes in Atkinson & Shiffrin's (1968) famous memory model, . . . who is renamed the "executive" in many models (clearly a promotion), and who decides on and builds all those flow diagrams. (p. 715)

But if we succeed in exorcising the executive, what will we train? We will have to do, alas, what we have always done: We will have to train the person. We will have to train retarded persons to try to plan things better, to look more carefully, to monitor their thoughts better, and so on. Not as glamorous as training their executive processes, and not very different from the training strategies of thousands of dedicated workers over the past century or more, but what else is there to do?

The question of the modifiability of intelligence, particularly as it relates to mental retardation, is alive and well and roaming through books and journals. In an edited book titled: *How and How Much Can Intelligence Be Increased?* (Detterman & Sternberg, 1982), we meet again the Abecedarian and Milwaukee Projects, stressing the prevention of mental retardation by early intervention. Other contributions advocate the modification of intelligence and intelligent performance by the training of strategies, self-management skills, and "superordinate processing." There are also less sanguine, more cautionary statements (particularly in the chapters by Caruso, Taylor, and Detterman, and by Brown and Campione, previously cited), as well as sober discussions of the possibilities, complexities, and hazards of attempting to train cognitive performance.

A national conference on "Mental Retardation: The Search For Cures," produced a book titled *Curative Aspects of Intelligence: Biomedical and Behavioral Advances* (Menolascino, Neman, & Stark, 1983). Although in his introductory remarks Stark attributes 75% of mental retardation to sociocultural causes, less than one-fourth of the book is allocated to behavioral advances. The larger part of the book is devoted to biomedical research and covers the gamut from genetic screening and the prevention of genetic and metabolic disorders, to chromosomal and genetic engineering and the possibility of producing chemical memory enhancers, regenerating the central nervous system, and even brain grafting. Since biomedical research has already produced preventive and curative measures for a small percentage of the syndromes associated with mental retardation, one can only hope that at least some proportion of these projections are realized.

The contributions in the behavioral section continue the empiricist theme in modern guise, offering assurances that new teaching and training techniques have been discovered, and optimistically concluding that with the development of these techniques we will be able to raise intelligence; that, indeed, success has already been achieved. In one chapter it is suggested that by training parents and teachers to teach children more effectively, and by providing preschool instruction, we can prevent the development of mental retardation in children who, without this intervention, would have become mildly retarded. In other words, some 75% to 85% of all mental retardation can now be prevented! The major current roadblock, according to some of the participants, is integrating behavioral intervention into the educational mainstream. Familiar programs reappear as support for these claims, including the Direct Instruction Model (DISTAR), the Portage Project, and Project EDGE. Feuerstein's program is mentioned to suggest that even if an educationally and socially deprived child has not had the benefits of early intervention, compensatory programs during adolescence provide an opportunity for change.

But skepticism was expressed during the conference's question and answer period; in particular, questions were raised about the generalizations these behavioral scientists made without presenting supporting data. The questioners were assured that reliable data exist and that these behavioral techniques really work. Our own extensive review of the cited programs and related research suggests that skepticism is wholly justified, for now at least, while the search for prevention and cures continues.

Much of the evidence from basic psychological research suggests that mild and moderate mental retardation is not primarily a deficiency in learning and memory except to the extent that thinking enters into learning and memory. Mental retardation is, rather, a *thinking* disability, and intelligence is synonymous with thinking. Although it is possible to educate mentally retarded persons and to train them to perform many tasks, up to a point, we do not yet have a means of raising their general level of intelligence. We have no prescription that will change their capacity to think and to reason at the level of persons of average intelligence, to solve novel problems and real-life challenges of some complexity, and to respond effectively to an infinite variety of circumstances, not just to those used in training.

It is important, therefore, to teach retarded persons to adapt and to learn the skills that will allow them to find not only personal fulfillment but also a useful place in society. This humanistic goal of effective adaptation should not be confused with the scientific interest in whether retarded intelligence can be raised. For the present, at least, raising the capacity of retarded persons to adapt seems to be a reasonable objective, whereas raising their general level of intelligence remains an elusive goal that, unfortunately, lends itself to exaggerated claims and distortions.

11 Summing Up

A major impetus for this book was a meeting I attended, sponsored by the National Institute of Child Health and Human Development, in which many well-known psychologists doing mental retardation research, along with their students, were brought together to discuss the progress being made toward understanding the learning and thinking processes of mentally retarded individuals. The conference members soon split into two groups, one consisting of those who believed that mild mental retardation is largely the result of poor environment, the other group made up of those who believed that mild mental retardation results primarily from genetic deficiencies (including the natural consequences of the normal distribution of whatever genes are responsible for intelligence) and from known and unknown physiological pathologies. What surprised me most, however, was the pervasive lack of knowledge—shown particularly but not only by the students—about the history of attempts to raise intelligence. They appeared to believe sincerely, with no element of skepticism, that intelligence (however you define it) can now be raised appreciably by training and education so that retarded persons will behave intellectually in a manner appropriate for their chronological age, which is another way of saying that mental retardation can be cured by pedagogical methods.

If they believe this possible with the present body of knowledge, which doesn't appear to me to be very different from that available to previous workers, it is incomprehensible that there is so little curiosity about why dedicated workers in the past had not accomplished this remarkable feat. When I mentioned names from the past, names that conjured up the most extraordinary claims of raising intelligence, I drew only blank stares.

How can a field advance without an understanding of its history? We are told that the evidence that the poorer performance of retarded persons is related to immutable differences in cognitive structures "is tenuous at best. . . . The appropriate message at the present time seems to be one of optimism and hope" (Sternberg, 1981, pp. 179–180). The result of 180 years of effort is considered "tenuous evidence."

Three fallacies born in the past are thriving today. (1) In the middle of the nineteenth century it became common practice to teach deaf-mutes to communicate and thereby demonstrate intelligent behavior. This was taken as proof of the empiricist doctrine that intelligence is learned, and that therefore retardation can be cured by teaching and training techniques.

(2) Deaf-mutes learned to communicate and express their intelligent behavior after they were reached through the alternative sense organs of vision and touch. Consequently, "education of the senses," the system used by Itard and Séguin, became a slogan, a magic key for the education of the mentally retarded, despite the fact that Perèire had rehabilitated not mentally retarded individuals but deaf-mutes, and Itard's feral child never learned to speak. Itard's and Séguin's work held out the hope that retardation could be reversed. The reported improvement of Guggenbühl's patients was believed to result from the sensory training and education given in concentrated doses in an isolated institution. Throughout the world, institutions were established to cure the retarded. When disillusionment set in, institutions designed for training became primarily custodial (although education and training continued in many of them). The cycle of hope and disillusionment continued in smaller eddies, in periodic claims that certain products or certain training techniques would raise intelligence.

(3) Because extreme isolation during early development produces retarded behavior that is often reversible, it is believed that most mental retardation must be due to early isolation or, by extension, to cultural deprivation, and is therefore reversible.

There will never be a single cure for mental retardation because there are so many different known causes, 350 according to one estimate (Stark, 1983), but progress has been made. Mental retardation has been prevented through the use of iodized salt, rubella vaccination, and maternal desensitization in Rh-factor blood incompatibility (Menolascino et al., 1983). Medical cures for certain types of mental retardation have been discovered, as in the treatment during infancy of such inborn errors of metabolism as phenylketonuria and galactosemia, and the surgical intervention for hydrocephalus. Milunsky (1983) lists numerous disorders that cause mental retardation and can now be prevented.

But the largest group of mentally retarded individuals are mildly retarded, most of whom manifest no particular physical or brain pathology. It is this group that is the focus of early intervention programs because many researchers attribute this type of retardation primarily to social environmental factors, rather than to the normal distribution of whatever genes are responsible for intelligence. As the present state of affairs indicates, there is, strangely, a greater chance of discovering specific, identifiable medical causes—and consequently of finding preventive measures and cures—for severe and profound retardation than for mild retardation. For this reason it is of the utmost importance that basic psychological research in mental retardation (and into the nature of intelligence) be expanded, for it has much to contribute to a better understanding of retarded intelligence and to the improved training of mildly retarded children and adults.

It is when some psychologists (along with some workers in other disciplines) leap beyond their data to make exorbitant claims, that the entire field of psychology is embarrassed. Psychology is not a hard science, although some areas of psychological research are "harder" than others. Certain domains of psychology, interested in preventing and improving retarded intelligence, have received substantial funding, commensurate with the human importance and difficulty of their mission. But their publications indicate that, in this area at least, we are still in the dark ages, and dark ages are ruled by witches and gurus who prove their beliefs by suggestion and persuasion.

The human species is restless, curious, and unsatisfied with limits. We yearned to escape the restricting bonds of gravity and walk on the moon, and we did. We have an overriding need to control our destiny, and it is galling and frustrating to think that we cannot control intelligence. The yearning to raise the thinking capacity of retarded people is as grand and noble a yearning as any we have ever had, and perhaps some day this too will bend to our will. Unfortunately the noble in our species has always been counterbalanced by the lowly and despicable. The unsubstantiated claims that there are ways to raise intelligence and thereby cure retarded people come from earnest and dedicated workers on the one hand, as well as from scoundrels and psychopaths on the other, with all gradations in between.

A final word should be said to anyone who would try to use this book to reduce our efforts to educate and train retarded persons, or to prevent the development of better educational and training methods. No one, least of all retarded persons, is working up to his or her potential. Basic psychological research has produced a number of techniques that may prove helpful in teaching mildly and moderately retarded persons (e.g., Mercer & Snell, 1977). For the more severely retarded, behavior modification may prove useful in training self-care. There is ample opportunity for anyone interested in increasing our understanding of this syndrome and in improving special educational techniques. There is much to be done.

Inevitably there will be those who warn that this book should not have been written, that it will contribute to the movement to abandon early education and the special help provided to our retarded citizens. But surely the accumulation of evidence that intelligence cannot be substantially and permanently raised by special training is unrelated to the humanistic concern to educate and assist mentally retarded persons to the best of our ability. *All retarded persons must be given the best education and the best environment possible to allow them to grow to their fullest potential, and training for academic, social and vocational adjustment must be vigorously pursued.*

The diagnosis of mental retardation requires both low intelligence and inadequate adaptive behavior (Grossman, 1983). It has been shown that even when IQ remains the same over a 40-year period, most persons in the mildly retarded and borderline range of intelligence are no longer labeled mentally retarded when they leave school and enter the work force (Ross, Begab, Dondis, Giampiccolo, & Meyers, 1985). They are better able to adjust to the lesser intellectual demands of unskilled and semi-skilled jobs than to the academic demands of the classroom; consequently their adaptive behavior, in terms of social and job-related measures, is perfectly adequate. For many, families and spouses provide indispensable support. Low intelligence, then, is no bar to becoming happy, productive, law-abiding, and self-fulfilled members of society, which is, after all, what really matters.

This book was written to show how mentally retarded persons and their families and friends have been and are being victimized by unscrupulous, and even well meaning, professionals. It is a history, not a prophecy; it presents the way things have been, not (we hope) the way they will be.

References

Abt, C. C. (Ed.). *The evaluation of social programs.* Beverly Hills, CA: Sage, 1976.

Ainsworth, M. D. Reversible and irreversible effects of maternal deprivation on intellectual development. In O.J. Harvey (Ed.), *Experience, structure & adaptability.* New York: Springer, 1966.

Albert, K., Hoch, P., & Waelsch, H. Preliminary report on the effect of glutamic acid administration in mentally retarded subjects. *Journal of Nervous and Mental Disease 1946, 104,* 263-274.

Albert, K., Hoch, P., & Waelsch, H. Glutamic acid and mental deficiency. *Journal of Nervous and Mental Disease,* 1951, *114,* 471-491.

Albert, K. E., & Warden, C. J. The level of performance in the white rat. *Science,* 1944, *100,* 476.

Allen, M. K. A comparison between test scores on the original and revised Stanford-Binet Intelligence Scales administered to a group of retarded and mentally deficient subjects. *American Journal of Mental Deficiency,* 1942, *46,* 501-507.

Allen, R. M. Factor analysis of the Developmental Test of Visual Perception performance of educable mental retardates. *Perceptual and Motor Skills,* 1968, *26,* 257-258.

Allen, R. M., Dickman, I., & Haupt, T. D. A pilot study of the immediate effectiveness of the Frostig-Horne training program with educable retardates. *Exceptional Children,* 1966, *33,* 41-42.

Allen, R. M., Haupt, T. D., & Jones, R. W. Visual perceptual abilities and intelligence in mental retardates. *Journal of Clinical Psychology,* 1965, *21,* 299-300.

Alley, G. R. Perceptual-motor performance of mentally retarded children after systematic visual-perceptual training. *American Journal of Mental Deficiency,* 1968, *73,* 247-250.

American Academy of Pediatrics. Statement on the Doman-Delacato treatment of neurologically handicapped children. *Journal of Pediatrics,* 1968, *72,* 750-752.

Anastasi, A. *Psychological testing,* (2nd ed.). New York: Macmillan, 1961.

Anastasi, A. *Psychological testing,* (4th ed.). New York: Macmillan, 1976.

Arbitman, H. D. The present status of glutamic acid therapy for mental deficiency. *Training School Bulletin,* 1952, *48,* 187-199.

Arbitman-Smith, R., Haywood, H. C., & Bransford, J. D. Assessing cognitive change. In P.H.

Brooks, R. Sperber, & C. McCauley (Eds.), *Learning and cognition in the mentally retarded.* Hillsdale, NJ: Lawrence Erlbaum Associates, 1984.

Arthur, G. The predictive value of the Kuhlmann-Binet Scales for inmates of a state school for the feebleminded. *Journal of Applied Psychology,* 1933, *17,* 188-194.

Astin, A. W., & Ross, S. Glutamic acid and human intelligence. *Psychological Bulletin,* 1960, *57,* 429-434.

Atkinson, R. C., & Shiffrin, R. M. Human memory: A proposed system and its control processes. In K. W. Spence & J. T. Spence (Eds.), *The psychology of learning and motivation* (Vol. 2). New York: Academic Press, 1968.

Ayres, A. J. *Sensory integration and learning disorders.* Los Angeles: Western Psychological Services, 1972.

Ayres, A. J. A response to defensive medicine. *Academic Therapy,* 1977, *13,* 149-152.

Ayres, A. J. Learning disabilities and the vestibular system. *Journal of Learning Disabilities,* 1978, *11,* 30-41.

Baddeley, A. D., & Hitch, G. J. Working memory. In G. A. Bower (Ed.), *The Psychology of learning and motivation* (Vol. 8). New York: Academic Press, 1974.

Bakwin, H. Glutamic acid and mental functioning. *Journal of Pediatrics,* 1947, *31,* 702-703.

Ball, T. S. *Itard, Seguin, and Kephart: Sensory education—a learning interpretation.* Columbus, OH: Charles E. Merrill, 1971.

Barr, M. W. *Mental defectives: Their history treatment, and training.* Philadelphia: Blakiston's Sons & Co., 1904.

Baumeister, A. A. More ado about operant conditioning—or nothing? *Mental Retardation,* 1969, *7,* 49-51.

Baumeister, A. A. The American residential institutuon: Its history and character. In A. A. Baumeister & E. Butterfield (Eds.), *Residential facilities for the mentally retarded.* Chicago: Aldine, 1970.

Bayley, N. Consistency and variability in the growth of intelligence from birth to eighteen years. *The Journal of Genetic Psychology,* 1949, *75,* 165-196.

Bayley, N. Development of mental abilities. In P. H. Mussen (Ed.), *Carmichael's manual of child psychology* (Vol. I; 3rd ed.), New York: Wiley, 1970.

Bayley, N., Rhodes, L., Gooch, B., & Marcus, M. Environmental factors in the development of institutionalized children. In J. Hellmuth (Ed.), *Exceptional infant* (Vol. 2): *Studies in abnormalities.* New York: Brunner/Mazel, 1971.

Beck, C. S., McKhann, C. F., & Belnap, W. D. Revascularization of the brain. *American Journal of Mental Deficiency,* 1950, *55,* 218-219.

Becker, W. C., & Carnine, D. W. Direct Instruction: A behavior theory model for comprehensive educational intervention with the disadvantaged. In S. W. Bijou & R. Ruiz (Eds.), *Behavior modification: Contributions to education.* Hillsdale, NJ: Lawrence Erlbaum Associates, 1981.

Becker, W. C., Engelmann, S., Carnine, D. W., & Maggs, A. Direct instruction technology: Making learning happen. In P. Karoly & J. J. Steffen (Eds.), *Improving children's competence: Advances in child behavioral analysis and therapy* (Vol. 1). Lexington, MA: Lexington Books, 1982.

Becker, W. C., Engelmann, S., Carnine, D. W., & Rhine, W. R. Direct instruction model. In W. R. Rhine (Ed.), *Making schools more effective: New directions from Follow Through.* New York: Academic Press, 1981.

Benda, C. E. *Down's syndrome: Mongolism and its management* (Rev. ed.). New York: Grune & Stratton, 1969.

Bennett, F. C., McClelland, S., Kriegsmann, E. A., Andrus, L. B., & Sells, C. J. Vitamin and mineral supplementation in Down's syndrome. *Pediatrics,* 1983, *72,* 707-713.

Bereiter, C. Genetics and educability: Educational implications of the Jensen debate. In J. Hellmuth (Ed.), *Disadvantaged child* (Vol. 3): *Compensatory education: A national debate.* New York: Brunner/Mazel, 1970.

Bereiter, C., & Engelmann, S. *Teaching disadvantaged children in the preschool.* Englewood Cliffs, NJ: Prentice-Hall, 1966.

Berrueta-Clement, J. R., Schweinhart, L. J., Barnett, W. S., Epstein, A. S., & Weikart, D. P. Changed Lives: The effects of the Perry Preschool Program on youths through age 19. *Monographs of the High/Scope Educational Research Foundation,* 1984, No. 8.

Berry, C. S. The intelligence quotient of mentally retarded school children. *School and Society,* 1923, *17,* 723-729.

Bicknell, E. P. Custodial care of the adult feeble-minded. *Journal of Psycho-Asthenics,* 1896, *2,* 51-63. (This is a reprint from *Charities Review,* no date or volume supplied.)

Bijou, S. W. Theory and research in mental (developmental) retardation. *Psychological Record,* 1963, *13,* 95-110.

Bijou, S. W. A functional analysis of retarded development. In N. R. Ellis (Ed.), *International review of research in mental retardation* (Vol. 1). New York: Academic Press, 1966.

Bijou, S. W. Environment and intelligence: A behavioral analysis. In R. Cancro (Ed.), *Intelligence: Genetic and environmental influences.* New York: Grune & Stratton, 1971.

Bijou, S. W. The prevention of retarded development in disadvantaged children. In M. J. Begab, H. C. Haywood, & H. L. Garber (Eds.), *Psychosocial influences in retarded performance* (Vol. 1): *Issues and theories in development.* Baltimore, MD: University Park Press, 1981.

Bijou, S. W., & Dunitz-Johnson, E. Interbehavioral analysis of developmental retardation. *Psychological Record,* 1981, *31,* 305-329.

Binet, A., & Simon, Th. [The intelligence of the feeble-minded] (H. H. Goddard, Ed., E. S. Kite, Trans.). Baltimore, MD: Williams & Wilkins, 1916. Original papers published in 1908 and 1909.

Binet, A., & Simon, Th. [The development of intelligence in children (the Binet-Simon Scale)] (H. H. Goddard, Ed., E. S. Kite, Trans.). New York: Arno Press, 1975. (Originally published in 1916 from papers published in 1905, 1908, and 1911.)

Birch, J. W. The utility of short forms of the Stanford-Binet tests of intelligence with mentally retarded children. *American Journal of Mental Deficiency,* 1955, *59,* 462-484.

Blackman, L. S., & Lin, A. Generalization training in the educable mentally retarded: Intelligence and educability revisited. In P. H. Brooks, R. Sperber, & C. McCauley (Eds.), *Learning and cognition in the mentally retarded.* Hillsdale, NJ: Lawrence Erlbaum Associates, 1984.

Blank, J. P. Tom Morgan's two-way gift. *A Reader's Digest Reprint,* April, 1970.

Blatt, B., & Garfunkel, F. *The educability of intelligence: Preschool intervention with disadvantaged children.* Washington, DC: Council for Exceptional Children, 1969.

Bliven, B. Can brains be stepped up? *New Republic,* 1947, *116,* 20-24.

Block, N. J., & Dworkin, G. IQ, heritability, and inequality. In N. J. Block & G. Dworkin (Eds.), *The IQ controversy: Critical readings.* New York: Pantheon Books, 1976.

Bloom, B. S. *Stability and change in human characteristics.* New York: Wiley, 1964.

Bock, G., Stebbins, L. B., & Proper, E. C. *Education as experimentation: A planned variation model* (Vol. IV-B), *Effects of Follow Through models.* Cambridge, MA: Abt Associates, 1977.

Boring, E. G. *A history of experimental psychology* (2nd ed.). New York: Appleton-Century-Crofts, 1950.

Borkowski, J. G., & Cavanaugh, J. C. Maintenance of generalization skills and strategies by the retarded. In N. R. Ellis (Ed.), *Handbook of Mental Deficiency* (2nd ed.). Hillsdale, NJ: Lawrence Erlbaum Associates, 1979.

Bower, G. H. Organizational factors in memory. In E. Tulving & W. Donaldson (Eds.), *Organization of memory.* New York: Academic Press, 1972.

Bower, T. G. R., Broughton, J. M., & Moore, M. K. The coordination of visual and tactual input in infants. *Perception & Psychophysics,* 1970, *8,* 51-53.

Boyd, W. *From Locke to Montessori: A critical account of the Montessori point of view.* New York: Henry Holt, 1914.

Bradley, T. B. Remediation of cognitive deficits: A critical appraisal of the Feuerstein model.

Journal of Mental Deficiency Research, 1983, *27,* 79-92.

Bradway, K. P., Thompson, C. W., & Cravens, R. B. Preschool IQs after twenty-five years. *Journal of Educational Psychology,* 1958, *49,* 278-281.

Brebner, A., Hallworth, H. J., & Brown, R. I. Computer-assisted instruction programs and terminals for the mentally retarded. In P. Mittler (Ed.), *Research to practice in mental retardation* (Vol. 2): *Education and training.* Baltimore, MD: University Park Press, 1977

Bringuier, J. *Conversations with Jean Piaget* (B. M. Gulati, Trans.). Chicago: University of Chicago Press, 1980.

Brown, A. L., & Campione, J. C. Inducing flexible thinking: The problem of access. In M. P. Friedman, J. P. Das, & N. O'Connor (Eds.), *Intelligence and Learning.* New York: Plenum Press, 1979.

Brown, A. L., & Campione, J. C. Modifying intelligence or modifying cognitive skills: More than a semantic quibble? In D. K. Detterman & R. J. Sternberg (Eds.), *How and how much can intelligence be increased.* Norwood, NJ: Ablex, 1982.

Brown, B. The treatment and cure of cretins and idiots, with an account of a visit to the Institution on the Abendberg in Switzerland. *American Journal of Mental Science,* 1847, *14,* 109-117.

Brown, C. *Down all the days.* Greenwich, CT: Fawcett, 1970. Paperbook reprint by arrangement with Stein & Day.

Bruininks, R. H. Physical motor development of retarded persons. In N. R. Ellis (Ed.), *International review of research in mental retardation* (Vol. 6). New York: Academic Press, 1974.

Bumbalo, T. S., Morelewicz, H. V., & Berens, D. L. Treatment of Down's syndrome with the "U" series of drugs. *Journal of the American Medical Association,* 1964, *187,* 361.

Burks, B. S. Book review of Marie Skodak: Children in foster homes; a study of mental development. *Journal of Educational Psychology,* 1939, *30,* 548-555.

Butterfield, E. C. To cure cognitive deficits of mentally retarded persons. In F. J. Menolascino, R. Neman, & J. A. Stark (Eds.), *Curative aspects of mental retardation: Biomedical and behavioral advances.* Baltimore, MD: Brookes Publishing, 1983.

Butterfield, E. C., & Belmont, J. M. Assessing and improving the executive cognitive functions of mentally retarded people. In I. Bialer & M. Sternlicht (Eds.), *The psychology of mental retardation: Issues and approaches.* New York: Psychological Dimensions, 1977.

Butterfield, E. C., Wambold, C., & Belmont, J. M. On the theory and practice of improving short-term memory. *American Journal of Mental Deficiency,* 1973, *77,* 654-669.

Campbell, D. T., & Frey, P. W. The implications of learning theory for the fade-out of gains from compensatory education. In J. Hellmuth (Ed.), *Disadvantaged child* (Vol. 3): *Compensatory education: A national debate.* New York: Brunner/Mazel, 1970.

Campione, J. C., & Brown, A. L. Memory and metamemory development in educable retarded children. In R. F. Kail, Jr. & J. W. Hagen (Eds.), *Perspectives on the development of memory and cognition.* Hillsdale, NJ: Lawrence Erlbaum Associates, 1977.

Campione, J. C., & Brown, A. L. Toward a theory of intelligence: Contributions from research with retarded children. *Intelligence,* 1978, *2,* 279-304.

Campione, J. C., Brown, A. L., & Ferrara, R. A. Mental retardation and intelligence. In R. J. Sternberg (Ed.), *Handbook of human intelligence.* New York: Cambridge University Press, 1982.

Campione, J. C., Nitsch, K., Bray, N., & Brown, A. L. Improving memory skills in mentally retarded children: Empirical research and strategies for intervention. In P. Karoly & J. J. Steffen (Eds.), *Improving children's competence.* Lexington, MA: D. C. Heath, 1982.

Carson, J. C. President's address. *Proceedings of the Association of Medical Officers of American Institutes for Idiotic and Feeble-Minded Persons.* 1891, 12-17.

Caruso, D. R., & Detterman, D. K. Intelligence research and social policy. *Phi Delta Kappan,* 1981, *63,* 183-186.

Chambers, G. S., & Zabarenko, R. N. Effects of glutamic acid and social stimulation in mental deficiency. *Journal of Abnormal and Social Psychology,* 1956, *53,* 315-320.

Chance, P. The remedial thinker. *Psychology Today,* October 1981, pp. 62-73.

Channing, W. Special classes for mentally defective school children. *Journal of Psycho-Asthenics,* 1900, *5,* 40-45.

Chipman, C. E. The constancy of the intelligence quotient of mental defectives. *Psychological Clinic,* 1929, *18,* 103-111.

Clarke, A. D. B., & Clark, A. M. Prospects for prevention and amelioration of mental retardation: A guest editorial. *American Journal of Mental Deficiency,* 1977, 81, 523-533.

Clarke, A. D. B., Clarke, A. M., & Brown, R. I. Regression to the mean—A confused concept. *British Journal of Psychology,* 1959, *51,* 105-117.

Clarke, A. M., & Clarke, A. D. B. (Eds.), *Early experience: Myth and evidence.* New York: Free Press, 1976.

Clingman, J., & Fowler, R. L. The effects of primary reward on the I.Q. performance of grade-school children as a function of initial I.Q. level. *Journal of Applied Behavior Analysis,* 1976, *9,* 19-23.

Cochran, D. C., & Shearer, D. E. The Portage model for home teaching. In C. S. Paine, G. T. Bellamy, & B. Wilcox (Eds.), *Human services that work.* Baltimore, MD: Brookes, 1984.

Cohen, H. J., Birch, H. G., & Taft, L. T. Some considerations for evaluating the Doman-Delacato "patterning" method. *Pediatrics,* 1970, *45,* 302-314.

Cole, M., & Bruner, J. S. Cultural differences and inferences about psychological processes. *American Psychologist,* 1971, *26,* 867-876.

Collmann, R. D., & Newlyn, D. Changes in Terman-Merrill IQs of mentally retarded children. *American Journal of Mental Deficiency,* 1958, *63,* 307-311.

Condry, S. History and background of preschool intervention programs and the Consortium for Longitudinal Studies. In Consortium for Longitudinal Studies, *As the twig is bent. . . Lasting effects of preschool programs.* Hillsdale, NJ: Lawrence Erlbaum Associates, 1983.

Consortium for Longitudinal Studies. *As the twig is bent. . .Lasting effects of preschool programs.* Hillsdale, NJ: Lawrence Erlbaum Associates, 1983.

Corah, N. L., & Powell, B. J. A factor analytic study of the Frostig Developmental Test of Visual Perception. *Perceptual and Motor Skills,* 1963, *16,* 59-63.

Cordes, C. Reuven Feuerstein makes every child count. *APA Monitor,* May 1984, pp. 18, 20.

Cordes, C. Venezuela tests 6-year emphasis on thinking skills. *APA Monitor,* March 1985, pp. 26, 28.

Cornwell, A. C., & Birch, H. G. Psychological and social development in home-reared children with Down's syndrome (mongolism). *American Journal of Mental Deficiency,* 1969, *74,* 341-350.

Cotton, H. A. *The defective delinquent and insane.* New York: Arno Press, 1980. (Originally published in 1921.)

Cottrell, A. W., Montague, J. C., Farb, J., & Throne, J. M. An operant procedure for improving vocabulary definition performances in developmentally delayed children. *Journal of Speech and Hearing Disorders,* 1980, *45,* 90-102.

Cronbach, L. J. *Essentials of psychological testing* (3rd ed.). New York: Harper & Row, 1970.

Darlington, R. B., Royce, J. M., Snipper, A. S., Murray, H. W., & Lazar, I. Preschool programs and later school competence of children from low-income families. *Science,* 1980, *208,* 202-204.

Datta, L. The impact of the Westinghouse/Ohio evaluation on the development of Project Head Start. In C. C. Abt (Ed.), *The evaluation of social programs.* Beverly Hills, CA: Sage, 1976.

Davis, K. Final note on a case of extreme isolation. *American Journal of Sociology,* 1947, *52,* 432-437.

Dawson, W. J. G. Results obtained from the removal of tonsils and adenoids in the feeble-minded. *Journal of Psycho-Asthenics,* 1918, *22,* 173-174.

Décarie, T. G. A study of the mental and emotional development of the thalidomide child. In B. M. Foss (Ed.), *Determinants of infant behavior* (Vol. 4). London: Methuen, 1969.

Delacato, C. H. *The treatment and prevention of reading problems.* Springfield, IL: Charles C.

Thomas, 1959.

Delacato, C. H. Delacato revisited. *Exceptional Children*, 1966, *33*, 199-200.

Detterman, D. K., & Sternberg, R. J. (Eds.), *How and how much can intelligence be increased.* Norwood, NJ: Ablex, 1982.

Diaconis, P. Statistical problems in ESP research. *Science*, 1978, *201*, 131-136.

Dicks-Mireaux, M. J. Mental development of infants with Down's syndrome. *American Journal of Mental Deficiency*, 1972, *77*, 26-32.

Dingman, H. F., & Tarjan, G. Mental retardation and the normal distribution curve. *American Journal of Mental Deficiency*, 1960, *64*, 991-994.

Doll, E. E. A historical survey of research and management of mental retardation in the United States. In E. P. Trapp & P. Himelstein (Eds.), *Readings on the exceptional child.* New York: Appleton-Century-Crofts, 1962.

Doll, E. E. Deborah Kallikak: 1889-1978, a memorial. *Mental Retardation*, 1983, *21*, 30-33.

Doman, G., & Delacato, C. H. Train your baby to be a genius. *McCall's*, March, 1965, pp. 65, 169, 170, 172.

Doman, R. J., Spitz, E. B., Zucman, E., Delacato, C. H., & Doman, G. Children with severe brain injuries: Neurological organization in terms of mobility. *Journal of the American Medical Association*, 1960, *174*, 257-262.

Dorsher, J. *Performance of young Down's syndrome children on the Stanford-Binet according to the verbal demands of the items.* Unpublished Masters thesis, University of Minnesota, 1981.

Drillien, C. M. A longitudinal study of the growth and development of prematurely and maturely born children. Part VII: Mental development 2-5 years. *Archives of Disease in Childhood*, 1961, *36*, 233-240.

Dugdale, R. L. Hereditary pauperism as illustrated in the "Juke" family. In M. Rosen, G. R. Clark, & M. S. Kivitz (Eds.), *The history of mental retardation: Collected papers (Vol. I).* Baltimore, MD: University Park Press, 1976. (Reprinted from *Proceedings of the Conference of Charities*, 1877, 81-95.)

du Verglas, G. Comparative follow-up study of Down's syndrome children who attended the Model Preschool Program. (Doctoral dissertation, University of Washington, 1984). *Dissertation Abstracts International*, 1985, *46*, 389A. (University Microfilms No. 85-08, 046)

Earhart, R. H., & Warren, S. A. Long term constancy of Binet IQ in retardation. *Training School Bulletin*, 1964, *61*, 109-115.

Edgar, C. L., Ball, T. S., McIntyre, R. B., & Shotwell, A. M. Effects of sensory-motor training on adaptive behavior. *American Journal of Mental Deficiency*, 1969, *73*, 713-720.

Elkind, D. Piagetian and psychometric conceptions of intelligence. In *Environment, heredity, and intelligence.* Cambridge, MA: Harvard Educational Review Reprint Series No. 2, 1969.

Elkind, D. Early education: Are young children exploited? A commentary on Feitelson, Tehori, & Levinberg-Green. *Merrill-Palmer Quarterly*, 1982, *28*, 495-497.

Ellis, N. R., & Tomporowski, P. D. Vitamin/mineral supplements and intelligence of institutionalized mentally retarded adults. *American Journal of Mental Deficiency*, 1983, *88*, 211-214.

Ellman, G., Silverstein, C. I., Zingarelli, G., Schafer, E. W. P., & Silverstein, L. Vitamin-mineral supplement fails to improve IQ of mentally retarded young adults. *American Journal of Mental Deficiency*, 1984, *88*, 688-691.

Ellson, D. G., Fuller, P. R., & Urmston, R. The influence of glutamic acid on test performance. *Science*, 1950, *112*, 248-250.

Elwood, M. I. Changes in Stanford-Binet IQ of retarded six-year-olds. *Journal of Consulting Psychology*, 1952, *16*, 217-219.

Engel, A. M. Constancy of IQ. *Nation's Schools*, 1937, *19*, 19-21.

Engelmann, S. The effectiveness of direct instruction on IQ performance and achievement in reading and arithmetic. In J. Hellmuth (Ed.), *Disadvantaged child* (Vol. 3): *Compensatory education.* New York: Brunner/Mazel, 1970.

Erikson, M. T. The predictive validity of the Cattell Infant Intelligence Scale for young mentally retarded children. *American Journal of Mental Deficiency*, 1968, *72*, 728-733.

Esten, R. A. Backward children in the public schools. *Journal of Psycho-Asthenics,* 1900, *5,* 10-16.

Fagan, J. F. The intelligent infant: Theoretical implications. *Intelligence,* 1984, *8,* 1-9. (a)

Fagan, J. F., III. The relationship of novelty preferences during infancy to later intelligence and later recognition memory. *Intelligence,* 1984, *8,* 339-346. (b)

Fagan, J. F. III, & McGrath, S. K. Infant recognition memory and later intelligence. *Intelligence,* 1981, *5,* 121-130.

Fantz, R. L. Pattern vision in young infants. *Psychological Record,* 1958, *8,* 43-47.

Fantz, R. L. Pattern vision in newborn infants. *Science,* 1963, *140,* 296-297.

Fantz, R. L., & Nevis, S. The predictive value of changes in visual preferences in early infancy. In J. Hellmuth (Ed.), *Exceptional infant* (Vol. 1): *The normal infant.* Seattle, WA: Special Child Publications, 1967.

Farb, J., Cottrell, A. W., Montague, J. C., & Throne, J. M. Update on research into increasing intelligence levels of mentally retarded children. In P. Mittler (Ed.), *Research to practice in mental retardation* (Vol. II): *Education and training.* Baltimore, MD: University Park Press, 1977.

Farb, J., & Throne, J. M. Improving the generalized mnemonic performance of a Down's syndrome child. *Journal of Applied Behavior Analysis,* 1978, *11,* 413-419. (a)

Farb, J., & Throne, J. M. *Generative intelligence: Improving generalized Block-Design performance of mentally retarded children.* Paper presented at the meeting of the Midwestern Association of Behavior Analysis, Chicago, May, 1978. (b)

Farb, J., Throne, J. M., Sailor, W., & Baer, D. M. *Operant investigative training of mnemonic performances of mentally retarded children.* Paper presented at the meeting of Region V of the American Association on Mental Deficiency, New Orleans, October, 1974.

Fernald, W. E. The history of the treatment of the feeble-minded. *Proceedings of the National Conference of Charities and Corrections,* 1893, 203-221.

Fernald, W. E. The burden of feeble-mindedness. *Journal of Psycho-Asthenics,* 1913, *17,* 87-99. (a)

Fernald, W. E. Discussion. *Journal of Psycho-Asthenics,* 1913, *17,* 127. (b)

Fernald, W. E. Thirty years progress in the care of the feeble-minded. *Journal of Psycho-Asthenics,* 1924, *29,* 206-219.

Feuerstein, R. Mediated learning experience: A theoretical basis for cognitive human modifiability during adolescence. In P. Mittler (Ed.), *Research to practice in mental retardation* (Vol. 2). *Education and training.* Baltimore, MD: University Park Press, 1977.

Feuerstein, R., Rand, Y., & Hoffman, M. B. *The dynamic assessment of retarded performers: The learning potential assessment device, theory, instruments, and techniques.* Baltimore, MD: University Park Press, 1979.

Feuerstein, R., Rand, Y., Hoffman, M. B., & Miller, R. *Instrumental enrichment: An intervention program for cognitive modifiability.* Baltimore, MD: University Park Press, 1980.

Field, L. Letter to E. B. Page, May 31, 1972.

Fish, W. B. President's address, Lakeville meeting, 1887. *Proceedings of the Association of Medical Officers of American Institutions for Idiotic and Feeble-Minded Persons, 1889,* 14-16.

Fish, W. B. Custodial care of adult idiots. *Proceedings of the Association of Medical Officers of American Institutions for Idiotic and Feeble-Minded Persons,* 1892, 203-221.

Fisher, G. M. A note on the validity of the Wechsler Adult Intelligence Scale for mental retardates. *Journal of Consulting Psychology,* 1962, *26,* 391.

Fisher, K. L. Effects of perceptual-motor training on the educable mentally retarded. *Exceptional Children,* 1971, *38,* 264-266.

Fisher, M. A., & Zeaman, D. Growth and decline of retardate intelligence. In N. R. Ellis (Ed.), *International review of research in mental retardation* (Vol. 4). New York: Academic Press, 1970.

Fisher, M. A., & Zeaman, D. An attention-retention theory of retardate discrimination learning. In N. R. Ellis (Ed.), *International review of research in mental retardation* (Vol. 6). New

York: Academic Press, 1973.

Fisher, R. A. The elimination of mental defect. *Eugenics Review,* 1924, *16,* 114-116.

Fishler, K. Mental development in mosaic Down's syndrome as compared with trisomy 21. In R. Koch & F. de la Cruz (Eds.), *Down's syndrome (mongolism): Research, prevention and management.* New York: Brunner/Mazel, 1975.

Fishler, K., Graliker, B. V., & Koch, R. The predictability of intelligence with Gesell Developmental Scales in mentally retarded infants and young children. *American Journal of Mental Deficiency,* 1965, *69,* 515-525.

Flynn, J. R. The mean IQ of Americans: Massive gains 1932 to 1978. *Psychological Bulletin,* 1984, *95,* 29-51.

Flynn, J. R. Wechsler intelligence tests: Do we really have a criterion of metal retardation? *American Journal of Mental Deficiency,* 1985, *90,* 236-244.

Foale, M. The treatment of mental defectives with glutamic acid. *Journal of Mental Science,* 1952, *98,* 483-487.

Fort, S. J. Special schools for special children. *Journal of Psycho-Asthenics,* 1900, *5,* 28-38.

Franks, F. *Polywater.* Cambridge, MA: MIT Press, 1981.

Frostig, M. The role of perception in the integration of psychological functions. In W. M. Cruickshank & D. P. Hallahan (Eds.), *Disabilities in children: Psychoeducational practices.* Syracuse, NY: Syracuse University Press, 1975.

Frostig, M., & Horne, D. *The Frostig program for the development of visual perception.* Chicago: Follett, 1964.

Furby, L. Interpreting regression toward the mean in developmental research. *Developmental Psychology,* 1973, *8,* 172-179.

Furth, H. *Thinking without language: Psychological implications of deafness.* New York: The Free Press, 1966.

Gadson, E. J. Glutamic acid and mental deficiency—a review. *American Journal of Mental Deficiency,* 1951, *55,* 521-528.

Garber, H. L. Intervention in infancy: A developmental approach. In M. Begab & S. Richardson (Eds.), *The mentally retarded and society.* Baltimore, MD: University Park Press, 1975.

Garber, H. L. *The Milwaukee Project: Preventing mental retardation in children of families at risk.* Paper presented at the CIBA-GEIGY Conference on Mental Retardation from a Neurological and Sociocultural Point of View, Lund, Sweden, May, 1982.

Garber, H. L. On Sommer and Sommer. Comment, *American Psychologist,* 1984, *39,* 1315.

Garber, H., & Heber, R. *The Milwaukee Project: Early intervention as a technique to prevent mental retardation* (National Leadership Institute Teacher Education/ Early Childhood Technical Paper). Storrs, CT: University of Connecticut, 1973.

Garber, H., & Heber, F. R. The Milwaukee Project: Indications of the effectiveness of early intervention in preventing mental retardation. In P. Mittler (Ed.), *Research to practice in mental retardation* (Vol. 1): *Care and intervention.* Baltimore, MD: University Park Press, 1977.

Garber, H. L., & Heber, R. The efficacy of early intervention with family rehabilitation. In M. J. Begab, H. C. Haywood, & H. L. Garber (Eds.), *Psychosocial influences in retarded performance* (Vol. II): *Strategies for improving competence.* Baltimore, MD: University Park Press, 1981.

Gardner, M. *Science: Good, bad, and bogus.* Buffalo, NY: Prometheus, 1981.

Gersten, R. M., & Maggs, A. Teaching the general case to moderately retarded children: Evaluation of a five year project. *Analysis & Intervention in Developmental Disabilities,* 1982, *2,* 329-343.

Getman, G. N. *How to develop your child's intelligence.* Luverne, MN: The Reseach Press, 1962.

Getman, G. N. The visuomotor complex in the acquisition of learning skills. In J. Hellmuth (Ed.), *Learning disorders* (Vol. 1). Seattle, WA: Special Child Publications, 1965.

Getman, G. N. Vision: Its role and integrations in learning processes. *Journal of Learning Disabilities,* 1981, *14,* 577-580.

Gibson, D., & Fields, D. L. Early infant stimulation programs for children with Down syndrome: A review of effectiveness. In M. Wolraich & D. K. Routh (Eds.), *Advances in developmental and behavioral pediatrics* (Vol. 5). Greenwich, CT: JAI Press, 1984.

Ginsburg, H. *The myth of the deprived child: Poor children's intellect and education.* Englewood Cliffs, NJ: Prentice-Hall, 1972.

Gitter, L. L. *The Montessori way.* Seattle, WA: Special Child Publications, 1970.

Goddard, H. H. The Binet and Simon tests of intellectual capacity. *The Training School,* 1908, *5,* 3-9.

Goddard, H. H. Discussion. *Journal of Psycho-Asthenics,* 1909, *14,* 37-38. (a)

Goddard, H. H. Suggestions for a prognostical classification of mental defectives. *Journal of Psycho-Asthenics,* 1909, *14,* 48-54. (b)

Goddard, H. H. A measuring scale for intelligence. *The Training School,* 1910, *6,* 146-155. (a)

Goddard, H. H. Four hundred feeble-minded children classified by the Binet method. *Journal of Psycho-Asthenics,* 1910, *15,* 17-30. (b)

Goddard, H. H. Two thousand normal children measured by the Binet measuring scale of intelligence. *Pedagogical Seminary,* 1911, *18,* 232-259.

Goddard, H. H. *The Kallikak family: A study in the heredity of feeble-mindedness.* New York: Arno Press, 1973. (Originally published, 1912.)

Goddard, H. H. The improvability of feeble-minded children. *Journal of Psycho-Asthenics,* 1913, *17,* 121-126.

Goddard, H. H. *Feeble-mindedness: Its causes and consequences.* New York: Macmillan, 1914.

Goddard, H. H. Feeblemindedness: A question of definition. *Journal of Psycho-Asthenics,* 1928, *33,* 219-227.

Goddard, H. H. In defense of the Kallikak study. *Science,* 1942, *95,* 574-576.

Goddard, H. H. In the beginning. *Training School Bulletin,* 1943, *40,* 154-161.

Goldstein, H. Treatment of mongolism and nonmongoloid mental retardation in children. *Archives of Pediatrics,* 1954, *71,* 77-98.

Goldstein, H. Sicca-cell therapy in children. *Archives of Pediatrics,* 1956, *73,* 234-249.

Goodenough, F. L. Look to the evidence! A critique of recent experiments on raising the IQ. *Educational Methods,* 1939, *19,* 73-79.

Goodenough, F. L. *Mental testing.* New York: Rinehart, 1949. (a)

Goodenough, F. L. Review of: B. G. Schmidt, Changes in personal, social and intellectual behavior of children originally classified as feeble-minded. *Journal of Abnormal and Social Psychology,* 1949, *44,* 135-140. (b)

Goodenough, F. L., & Maurer, K. M. The relative potency of the nursery school and the statistical laboratory in boosting the IQ. *Journal of Educational Psychology,* 1940, *31,* 541-549.

Goodman, L. Montessori education for the handicapped: The methods—the research. In L. Mann & D. A. Sabatino (Eds.), *The second review of special education.* Philadelphia: JSE Press, 1974.

Goodman, L., & Hammill, D. The effectiveness of the Kephart-Getman activities in developing perceptual-motor and cognitive skills. *Focus on Exceptional Children,* 1973, *4,* 1-9.

Gottesman, I. I. An introduction to the behavioral genetics of mental retardation. In R. M. Allen, A. D. Cortazzo, & R. P. Toister, (Eds.), *The role of genetics in mental retardation.* Coral Gables, FL: University of Miami Press, 1971.

Gould, S. J. *The mismeasure of man.* New York Norton, 1981.

Gray, S. W., & Klaus, R. A. The early training project and its general rationale. In R. D. Hess & R. M. Bear (Eds.), *Early education: Current theory, research, and action.* Chicago: Aldine, 1968.

Gray, S. W., & Klaus, R. A. The Early Training Project: A seventh-year report. *Child Development,* 1970, *41,* 909-924.

Gray, S. W., & Ramsey, B. K. The Early Training Project: A life-span view. *Human Development,* 1982, *25,* 48-57.

Gray, S. W., Ramsey, B. K., & Klaus, R. A. *From 3 to 20: The Early Training Project.*

Baltimore, MD: University Park Press, 1982.

Gray, S. W., Ramsey, B. K., & Klaus, R. A. The Early Training Project 1962-1980. In Consortium for Longitudinal Studies, *As the twig is bent . . . Lasting effects of preschool programs.* Hillsdale, NJ: Lawrence Erlbaum Associates, 1983.

Greene, F. M. Programmed instruction techniques for the mentally retarded. In N. R. Ellis (Ed.), *International review of research in mental retardation* (Vol. 2). New York: Academic Press, 1966.

Grossman, H. J. (Ed.). *Manual on terminology and classification in mental retardation* (Rev. ed.). Washington, DC: American Association on Mental Deficiency, 1977.

Grossman, H. J. (Ed.). *Classification in mental retardation.* Washington, DC: American Association on Mental Deficiency, 1983.

Guilford, J. P. *The nature of human intelligence.* New York: McGraw-Hill, 1967.

Guilford, J. P. Executive functions and a model of behavior. *Journal of General Psychology,* 1972, *86,* 279-287.

Hagerman, R. J., & McBogg, P. M. (Eds.). *The fragile X syndrome: Diagnosis, biochemistry, and intervention.* Colorado: Spectra Publishing Co., 1983.

Hallahan, D. P., & Cruickshank, W. M. *Psychoeducational foundations of learning disabilities.* Englewood Cliffs, NJ: Prentice-Hall, 1973.

Hamilton, H. C., & Maher, E. B. The effects of glutamic acid on the behavior of the white rat. *Journal of Comparative and Physiological Psychology,* 1947, *40,* 463-488.

Hammill, D. Training visual perceptual processes. *Journal of Learning Disabilities,* 1972, *5,* 552-559.

Harney, M. Some psychological and physical characteristics of retarded girls before and following treatment with glutamic acid. *Studies in Psychology and Psychiatry From The Catholic University of America,* 1950, 8(Series No. 1). Washington, DC, Catholic University of America Press.

Harrell, R. F., Capp, R. H., Davis, D. R., Peerless, J., & Ravitz, L. R. Can nutritional supplements help mentally retarded children? An exploratory study. *Proceedings of the National Academy of Science,* 1981, *78,* 574-578.

Hayden, A. H., & Dmitriev, V. The multidisciplinary preschool program for Down's syndrome children at the University of Washington Model Preschool Center. In B. Z. Friedlander, G. M. Sterritt, & G. E. Kirk (Eds.), *Exceptional infant* (Vol. 3): *Assessment and intervention.* New York: Brunner/Mazel, 1975.

Hayden, A. H., & Haring, N. G. Early intervention for high risk infants and young children: Programs for Down's syndrome children. In T. D. Tjossem (Ed.), *Intervention strategies for high risk infants and young children.* Baltimore, MD: University Park Press, 1976.

Hayden, A. H., & Haring, N. G. The acceleration and maintenance of developmental gains in Down's syndrome school-age children. In P. Mittler (Ed.), *Research to practice in mental retardation* (Vol. 1): *Care and intervention.* Baltimore, MD: University Park Press, 1977.

Haywood, H. C. A cognitive approach to the education of retarded children. *Peabody Journal of Education,* 1977, *54,* 110-116.

Haywood, H. C., & Arbitman-Smith, R. Modification of cognitive functions in slow-learning adolescents. In P. Mittler (Ed.), *Frontiers of knowledge in mental retardation* (Vol. 1): *Social, educational, and behavioral aspects.* Baltimore, MD: University Park Press, 1981.

Head, M. L. Some metabolic correlates of amentia and dementia. (Doctoral dissertation, New York University, 1955). *Dissertation Abstracts,* 1956, *16,* 6, 1177. (University Microfilms No. 00-13617).

Hebb, D. O. *The organization of behavior.* New York: Wiley, 1949.

Heber, R. *Rehabilitation of families at risk for mental retardation: A progress report* (for the Social Rehabilitation Service, Dept. of Health, Education and Welfare, Washington, D.C.) Madison, WI: University of Wisconsin, October, 1971.

Heber, R. Letter to E. B. Page, July 17, 1972.

Heber, R. F., & Dever, R. B. Research on education and habilitation of the mentally retarded. In

H. C. Haywood (Ed.), *Social-cultural aspects of mental retardation.* New York: Appleton-Century-Crofts, 1970.

Heber, R., Dever, R., & Conry, J. The influence of environmental and genetic variables on intellectual development. In H. J. Prehm, L. A. Hamerlynck, & J. E. Crosson (Eds.), *Behavioral research in mental retardation.* Eugene, OR: University of Oregon, 1968.

Heber, R., & Garber, H. An experiment in prevention of cultural-familial retardation. In D.A.A. Primrose (Ed.), *Proceedings of the Second Congress of the International Association for the Scientific Study of Mental Deficiency,* Warsaw: Polish Medical Publishers, 1972.

Heber, R., & Garber, H. Progress report II: An experiment in the prevention of cultural-familial retardation. In D. A. A. Primrose (Ed.), *Proceedings of the Third Congress of the International Association for the Scientific Study of Mental Deficiency* (Vol. 1). Warsaw: Polish Medical Publishers, 1975.

Heber, R., Garber, H., Harrington, S., Hoffman, C., & Falender, C. *Rehabilitation of families at risk for mental retardation: Progress report.* Rehabilitation Research and Training Center in Mental Retardation. Madison, WI: University of Wisconsin, December, 1972.

Hellmuth, J. (Ed.). *Disadvantaged child* (Vol. 2): *Head start and early intervention.* New York: Brunner/Mazel, 1968.

Hellmuth, J. (Ed.). *Disadvantaged child* (Vol. 3): *Compensatory education: A national debate.* New York: Brunner/Mazel, 1970.

Herrnstein, R. J. IQ testing and the media. *The Atlantic Monthly,* August, 1982, 68-74.

Hill, A. S. Does special eduation result in improved intelligence for the slow learner? *Journal of Exceptional Children,* 1948, *14,* 207-213, 224.

Hoakley, Z. P. The variability of intelligence quotients. *Proceedings of the American Association for the Study of the Feeble- minded,* 1932, *37,* 119-146.

Hobbs, N. Feuerstein's instrumental enrichment: Teaching intelligence to adolescents. *Educational Leadership,* 1980, *37,* 566-568.

Honzik, M. P. Developmental studies of parent-child resemblance in intelligence. *Child Development,* 1957, *28,* 215-228.

Honzik, M. P. Value and limitations of infant tests: An overview. In M. Lewis (Ed.), *Origins of intelligence: Infancy and early childhood.* New York: Plenum, 1976.

House, E. R., Glass, G. V., McLean, L. D., & Walker, D. F. No simple answer: Critique of the Follow Through evaluation. *Harvard Educational Review,* 1978, *48,* 128-160.

Hubel, D. H., & Wiesel, T. N. Brain mechanisms of vision. *Scientific American,* 1979, *241,* 150-162.

Hughes, K. R., Cooper, R. M., & Zubek, J. P. Effect of glutamic acid on the learning ability of bright and dull rats: III. Effect of varying dosages. *Canadian Journal of Psychology,* 1957, *11,* 253-255.

Hughes, K. R., & Zubek, J. P. Effect of glutamic acid on the learning ability of bright and dull rats: I. Administration during infancy. *Canadian Journal of Psychology,* 1956, *10,* 132-138.

Hughes, K. R., & Zubek, J. P. Effect of glutamic acid on the learning ability of bright and dull rats: II. Duration of the effect. *Canadian Journal of Psychology,* 1957, *11, 182-184.*

Hunt, J. McV. *Intelligence and experience.* New York: Ronald Press, 1961.

Hunt, J. McV. The psychological basis for using pre-school enrichment as an antidote for cultural deprivation. *Merrill-Palmer Quarterly,* 1964, *10,* 209-248.

Hunt, N. *The world of Nigel Hunt.* New York: Garrett, 1967.

Itard, J.-M.-G. *The wild boy of Aveyron.* (G. & M. Humphrey, Trans.). New York: Appleton-Century-Crofts, 1962. (Originally published in two parts, the first in 1801, the second in 1806).

Jaeger-Lee, D. S., Gilbert, E., Washington, J. A., & Williams, J. M. Effect of L(+) glutamic acid on mental growth. *Diseases of the Nervous System,* 1953, *14,* 368-375.

Jenkins, J. R., Fewell, R., & Harris, S. R. Comparison of sensory integrative therapy and motor programming. *American Journal of Mental Deficiency,* 1983, *88,* 221-224.

Jensen, A. R. How much can we boost IQ and scholastic achievement? In *Environment, heredity, and intelligence*. Cambridge, MA: Harvard Educational Review Reprint Series No. 2, 1969.

Jensen, A. R. *Bias in mental testing*. New York: Free Press, 1980.

Jensen, A. R. Raising the IQ: The Ramey and Haskins study. *Intelligence*, 1981, *5*, 29-40.

Johnson, C. M., Bradley-Johnson, S., McCarthy, R., & Jamie, M. Token reinforcement during WISC-R administration. II. Effects on mildly retarded, black students. *Applied Research in Mental Retardation*, 1984, *5*, 43-52.

Jones, R. L. Potpourri: Innovations in curriculum and methods of teaching; technology in special education; federal programs. In R. L. Jones (Ed.), *New directions in special education*. Boston: Allyn & Bacon, 1970.

Kamin, L. J. *The science and politics of IQ*. Potomac, MD: Lawrence Erlbaum Associates, 1974.

Kane, E. D. Differential indications for the use of glutamic acid. *American Journal of Psychiatry*, 1953, *109*, 699-700.

Kanner, L. Johann Jakob Guggenbühl and the Abendberg. *Bulletin of the History of Medicine*, 1959, *43*, 489-502.

Kanner, L. *A history of the care and study of the mentally retarded*. Springfield, IL: Charles C. Thomas, 1964.

Karnes, M. B., Shwedel, A. M., & Williams, M. B. A comparison of five approaches for educating young children from low-income homes. In Consortium for Longitudinal Studies, *As the twig is bent. . . Lasting, effects of preschool programs*. Hillsdale, NJ: Lawrence Erlbaum Associates, 1983.

Keating, F. W. Discussion. *Journal of Psycho-Asthenics*, 1906, *10*, 216.

Kearsley, R. B. Cognitive assessment of the handicapped infant: The need for an alternative approach. *American Journal of Orthopsychiatry*, 1981, *51*, 43-54.

Kellar, C. Asexualization—Attitude of Europeans. *Journal of Psycho-Asthenics*, 1905, *9*, 128-129. (This paper was translated by B. Jensen from an article in the journal "*Tiddskrift*." The title is probably not the original one.)

Kennedy, M. M. Findings from the Follow Through Planned Variation study. *Educational Researcher*, 1978, *7*, 3-11.

Kephart, N. C. The effect of a highly specialized program upon the IQ in high-grade mentally deficient boys. *Journal of Psycho-Asthenics*, 1939, *44*, 216-221.

Kephart, N. C. *The slow learner in the classroom* (2nd ed.) Columbus, OH: Charles E. Merrill, 1971.

Kephart, N. C. The perceptual-motor match. In W. C. Cruickshank & D. P. Hallahan (Eds.), *Disabilities in children: Psychoeducational practices*. Syracuse, NY: Syracuse University Press, 1975.

Kerlin, I. N. Meeting of superintendents of institutions for idiots. *Proceedings of the Association of Medical Officers of American Institutions for Idiotic and Feeble-Minded Persons*, 1877, 3-6.

Kerlin, I. N. Moral imbecility. *Proceedings of the Association of Medical Officers of American Institutions for Idiotic and Feeble-Minded Persons*, 1889, 32-41.

Kerlin, I. N. Discussion. *Proceedings of the Association of Medical Officers of American Institutions for Idiotic and Feeble-Minded Persons*, 1892, 213-214. (a)

Kerlin, I. N. President's annual address. *Proceedings of the Association of Medical Officers of American Institutions for Idiotic and Feeble-Minded Persons*, 1892, 274-285. (b)

Kerlinger, F. N. *Foundations of behavioral research*. New York: Holt, 1973.

Kerr, W. J., Jr., & Szurek, S. A. Effect of glutamic acid on mental function. *Pediatrics*, 1950, *5*, 645-647.

Kershner, J. R. Doman-Delacato's theory of neurological organization applied with retarded children. *Exceptional Children*, 1968, *34*, 441-456.

Kershner, J. R. Questioning the "Miracle." *Educational Research*, 1973, *2*(4), 2.

Kirk, S. A. An evaluation of the study of Bernardine G. Schmidt entitled "Changes in personal, social, and intellectual behavior of children originally classified as feebleminded." *Psychological Bulletin*, 1948, *45*, 321-333. (a)

Kirk, S. A. An evaluation of the study of Bernardine G. Schmidt. *Journal of Exceptional Children*,

1948, 15, 34-40, 54. (b)

Kirk, S. A. *Early education of the mentally retarded: An experimental study.* Urbana: University of Illinois Press, 1958.

Kirk, S. A. The effects of early intervention. In H. C. Haywood (Ed.), *Social-cultural aspects of mental retardation.* New York: Appleton-Century-Crofts, 1970.

Kirk, S. A. The educability of intelligence. *The Directive Teacher,* 1982, *4,* 6, 10, 12.

Kirk, S. A., & Kirk, W. D. Uses and abuses of the ITPA. *Journal of Speech and Hearing Disorders,* 1978, *43,* 58-75.

Kirk, S. A., McCarthy, J. J., & Kirk, W. D. *The Illinois Test of Psycholinguistic Abilities.* Urbana, IL: University of Illinois Press, 1968.

Klaus, R. A., & Gray, S. W. The Early Training Project for disadvantaged children: A report after five years. *Monographs of the Society for Research in Child Development,* 1968, *33*(4, Serial No. 120).

Knobloch, H., & Pasamanick, B. Predicting intellectual potential in infancy. *American Journal of Diseases of Children,* 1963, *106,* 43-51.

Knobloch, H., & Pasamanick, B. Prediction from the assessment of neuromotor and intellectual status in infancy. In J. Zubin & G. A. Jarvis (Eds.), *Psychopathology of mental development.* New York: Grune & Stratton, 1967.

Kohs, S. C. The Binet-Simon measuring scale for intelligence: An annotated bibliography. *Journal of Educational Psychology,* 1914, 5, 215-224, 279-290, 335-346.

Kopp, C., & Shaperman, J. Cognitive development in the absence of object manipulation during infancy. *Developmental Psychology,* 1973, *9,* 430.

Kruskal, W. Letter. *Science,* 1975, *188,* 1126.

Kuhlmann, F. Binet and Simon's system for measuring the intelligence of children. *Journal of Psycho-Asthenics,* 1911, *15,* 76-92.

Kuhlmann, F. The Binet and Simon tests of intelligence in grading feeble-minded children. *Journal of Psycho-Asthenics,* 1912, *16,* 173-193. (a)

Kuhlmann, F. Revision of the Binet-Simon system for measuring the intelligence of children. *Journal of Psycho-Asthenics, Monograph Supplement,* 1912, *1,* No. 1. (b)

Kuhlmann, F. The present status of the Binet and Simon tests of the intelligence of children. *Journal of Psycho-Asthenics,* 1912, *16,* 113-139. (c)

Kuhlmann, F. Degree of mental deficiency in children as expressed by the relation of age to mental age. *Journal of Psycho-Asthenics,* 1913, *17,* 132-134.

Kuhlmann, F. Some results of examining 1000 public-school children with a revision of the Binet-Simon tests of intelligence by untrained teachers. *Journal of Psycho-Asthenics,* 1914, *18,* 150-179, 233-269. (a)

Kuhlmann, F. Review of J. E. W. Wallin, The mental health of the school child. *Journal of Psycho-Asthenics,* 1914, *19,* 41-48. (b)

Kuhlmann, F. Dr. Wallin's reply to my review of his "Mental health of the school child." *Journal of Psycho-Asthenics,* 1915, *19,* 154-170.

Kuhlmann, F. The results of repeated mental re-examinations of 639 feeble-minded over a period of ten years. *Journal of Applied Psychology,* 1921, *5,* 195-224.

Kuhlmann, F. One hundred years of special care and training. *American Journal of Mental Deficiency,* 1940, *45,* 8-24.

Kurland, A. A., & Gilgash, C. A. A study of the effect of glutamic acid on delinquent adult male mental defectives. *American Journal of Mental Deficiency,* 1953, *57,* 669-680.

Lakin, K. C., Krantz, G. C., Bruininks, R. H., Clumpner, J. L., & Hill, B. K. One hundred years of data on populations of public residential facilities for mentally retarded people. *American Journal of Mental Deficiency,* 1982, *87,* 1-8.

Lally, M. Computer-assisted teaching of sight-word recognition for mentally retarded school children. *American Journal of Mental Deficiency,* 1981, *85,* 383-388.

Lamson, M. S. *Life and education of Laura Dewey Bridgman.* New York: Arno Press, 1975. (Originally published, 1881.)

Lane, H. *The wild boy of Aveyron*. Cambridge, MA: Harvard University Press, 1976.

LaVeck, B., & Brehm, S. S. Individual variability among children with Down's syndrome. *Mental Retardation*, 1978, *16*, 135-137.

Layzer, D. The heritability of IQ: Science or numerology? *Science*, 1974, *183*, 1259-1268.

Layzer, D. Letter. *Science*, 1975, *188*, 1128-1130.

Lazar, I. Personal communication, Oct. 1, 1982.

Lazar, I., & Darlington, R. B. Lasting effects of early education: A report from the Consortium for Longitudinal Studies. *Monographs of the Society for Research in Child Development*, 1982, *47*(2-3, Serial No. 195).

Lehrke, R. G. *X-linked mental retardation and verbal disability*. New York: Intercontinental Medical Book Corp., 1974.

Levine, E. S. Can we speed up the slow child? *Volta Review*, 1949, *51*, 269-270, 316-318.

LeWinn, E B., Doman, G., Doman, R. J., Delacato, C. H., Spitz, E. B., & Thomas, E. W. Neurological organization: The basis for learning. In J. Hellmuth (Ed.), *Learning disorders* (Vol. 2). Seattle, WA: Special Child Publicatons, 1966.

Lewis, M. (Ed.). *Origins of intelligence: Infancy and early childhood*. New York: Plenum, 1976.

Lewis, M., & Brooks-Gunn, J. Visual attention at three months as a predictor of cognitive functioning at two years of age. *Intelligence*, 1981, *5*, 131-140.

Lindsley, O. R. Direct measurement and prosthesis of retarded behavior. In R. L. Jones (Ed.), *New directions in special education*. Boston: Allyn & Bacon, 1970. (Chapter originally published in 1965.)

Lindsley, O. R. An experiment with parents handling behavior at home. *Johnstone Bulletin*, 1966, *9*, 27-36.

Lockery, M., & Maggs, A. Direct instruction research in Australia: A ten-year analysis. *British Journal of Educational Psychology*, 1982, 2, 263-287.

Loeb, H. G., & Tuddenham, R. D. Does glutamic acid administration influence mental function? *Pediatrics*, 1950, *6*, 72-77.

Lombard, J. P., Gilbert, J. G., & Donofrio, A. F. The effects of glutamic acid upon the intelligence, social maturity and adjustment of a group of mentally retarded children. *American Journal of Mental Deficiency*, 1955, *60*, 122-132.

Longstreth, L. E. Revisiting Skeels' final study: A critique. *Developmental Psychology*, 1981, *17*, 620-625.

Lubs, M-L.E., & Maes, J. A. Recurrence risk in mental retardation. In P. Mittler (Ed.), *Research to practice in mental retardation* (Vol. 3): *Biomedical aspects*. Baltimore, MD: University Park Press, 1977.

Ludlow, J. R., & Allen, L. M. The effect of early intervention and pre-school stimulus on the development of the Down's syndrome child. *Journal of Mental Deficience Research*, 1979, *23*, 29-44.

Lumsdaine, A. A., & Glaser, R. (Eds.). *Teaching machines and programmed learning: A source book*. Washington, DC: National Education Assoc., 1960.

Machado, L. A. The development of intelligence—A political outlook. *Intelligence*, 1981, 5, 2-4.

Maggs, A., & Morath, P. Effects of direct verbal instruction on intellectual development of institutionalized moderately retarded children: A 2-year study. *Journal of Special Education*, 1976, *10*, 357-364.

Maisel, A. Q. Hope for brain-injured children. *A Reader's Digest Reprint*, 1970. (Month not given.)

Mann, L. Perceptual training: Misdirections and redirections. *American Journal of Orthopsychiatry*, 1970, *40*, 30-38.

Mann, L. *On the trail of process: A historical perspective on cognitive processes and their training*. New York: Grune & Stratton, 1979.

Marx, M. H. Effects of supranormal glutamic acid on maze learning. *Journal of Comparative and Physiological Psychology*, 1948, *41*, 82-92.

Marx, M. H. Relationship between supranormal glutamic acid and maze learning. *Journal of*

Comparative and Physiological Psychology, 1949, *42*, 313-319.

Maslow, P., Frostig, M., Lefever, D. W., & Whittlesey, J. R. B. The Marianne Frostig Test of Visual Perception, 1963 standardization. *Perceptual and Motor Skills*, 1964, *19*, 463-469.

Mason, M. K. Learning to speak after six and one-half years of silence. *Journal of Speech Disorders*, 1942, *7*, 295-304.

Matson, J. L., & Breuning, S. E. (Eds.). *Assessing the mentally retarded*. New York: Grune & Stratton, 1983.

McCall, R. B., Hogarty, P. S., & Hurlburt, N. Transitions in infant sensorimotor development and the prediction of childhood IQ. *American Psychologist*, 1972, *27*, 728-748.

McCulloch, T. L. The effect of glutamic acid feeding on cognitive abilities of institutionalized mental defectives. *American Journal of Mental Deficiency*, 1950, *55*, 117-122.

McNemar, Q. A critical examination of the University of Iowa studies of environmental influences upon the IQ. *Psychological Bulletin*, 1940, *37*, 63-92.

McNemar, Q. *The revision of the Stanford-Binet Scale*. Boston: Houghton Mifflin, 1942.

McRae, J. M. Retests of children given mental tests as infants. *Journal of Genetic Psychology*, 1955, *87*, 111-119.

Meier, J. The New Nursey School program. *Developmental Psychology*, 1969, *1*, 178.

Meier, J. H. Autotelic training for deprived children. *Current Psychiatric Therapies*, 1970, *10*, 30-45.

Meier, J. H., Nimnicht, G., & McAfee, O. An autotelic responsive environment nursery school for deprived children. In J. Hellmuth (Ed.), *Disadvantaged child* (Vol. 2): *Head Start and early intervention*. New York: Brunner/Mazel, 1968.

Melton, D. Body exercises that make children smarter, too. *Coronet*, February, 1971, 74-80.

Melton, D. *A boy called hopeless, by M. J.* New York: Scholastic Book Services, 1977.

Melyn, M. A., & White, D. T. Mental and developmental milestones of noninstitutionalized Down's syndrome children. *Pediatrics*, 1973, *52*, 542-545.

Menolascino, F. J., Neman, R., & Stark, J. A. (Eds.). *Curative aspects of mental retardation: Biomedical and behavioral advances*. Baltimore, MD: Brookes Publishing Co., 1983.

Mercer, C. D., & Snell, M. E. *Learning theory research in mental retardation: Implications for teaching*. Columbus, OH: Merrill Publishing Co., 1977.

Meyers, C. E. Letter to H. H. Spitz, Jan. 15, 1985.

Miller, L. B., & Bizzell, R. P. Long-term effects of four preschool programs: Sixth, seventh, and eighth grades. *Child Development*, 1983, *54*, 727-741.

Miller, L. B., & Dyer, J. L. Four preschool programs: Their dimensions and effects. *Monographs of the Society for Research in Child Development*, 1975, *40*(5-6, Serial No. 162).

Milligan, G. E. History of the American Association on Mental Deficiency. *American Journal of Mental Deficiency*, 1961, *66*, 357-369.

Milliken, J. R., & Standen, J. L. An investigation into the effects of glutamic acid on human intelligence. *Journal of Neurology, Neurosurgery, and Psychiatry*, 1951, *14*, 47-54.

Milunsky, A. Genetic aspects of mental retardation. In F. J. Menolascino, R. Neman, & J. A. Stark (Eds.), *Curative aspects of mental retardation: Biomedical and behavioral advances*. Baltimore, MD: Brookes Publishing Co., 1983.

Minister of State for the Development of Human Intelligence. *The development of intelligence: Projects in progress*. Caracas, Venezuela: Ediciones de la Republica Caracas, 1980.

Mink, L. Adaptation of the Montessori method in developing visual perception in the special child. In J. Hellmuth (Ed.), *The special child in century 21*. Seattle, WA: Special Child Publications, 1964.

Minogue, B. The constancy of the IQ in mental defectives. *Mental Hygiene*, 1926, 10, 751-758.

Mogridge, G. Discussion. *Journal of Psycho-Asthenics*. 1906, *10*, 220.

Montessori, M. *Dr. Montessori's own handbook*. Cambridge, MA: Robert Bentley, 1964. (Originally published, 1914.)

Montessori, M. [The Montessori method.] (A. E. George, Trans.). Cambridge, MA: Robert Bentley, 1965. (Originally published, 1912.)

Moore, O. K. Autotelic responsive environments and exceptional children. In O. J. Harvey (Ed.), *Experience structure and adaptability*. New York: Springer, 1966.

Moore, O. K., & Anderson, A. R. The responsive environments projet. In R. D. Hess & R. M. Baer (Eds.), *Early education*. Chicago: Aldine, 1968.

Munsinger, H. The adopted child's IQ: A critical review. *Psychological Bulletin*, 1975, *82*, 623-659.

Murdoch, J. M. Craniectomy for arrested mental development with after-history of three cases. *Journal of Psycho-Asthenics*, 1901, *5*, 111-113.

Murdoch, J. M. Discussion. *Journal of Psycho-Asthenics*, 1906, *10*, 214-215.

Myerson, A. *The inheritance of mental disease*. Baltimore, MD: Williams & Wilkins, 1925.

Myerson, A. The pathological and biological bases of mental deficiency. *Journal of Psycho-Asthenics*, 1930, *35*, 203-226.

Neisser, U. *Cognitive psychology*. New York: Appleton-Century-Crofts, 1967.

Neman, R. A reply to Zigler and Seitz. *American Journal of Mental Deficiency*, 1975, *79*, 493-505.

Neman, R., Roos, P., McCann, B. M., Menolascino, F. J., & Heal, L. W. Experimental evaluation of sensorimotor patterning used with mentally retarded children. *American Journal of Mental Deficiency*, 1975, *79*, 372-384.

Newell, A. Reasoning, problem-solving, and decision processes: The problem space as a fundamental category. In R. S. Nickerson (Ed.), *Attention and performance* (Vol. 8). Hillsdale, NJ: Lawrence Erlbaum Associates, 1980.

Newell, A., & Simon, H. A. *Human problem solving*. Englewood Cliffs, NJ: Prentice-Hall, 1972.

Nolan, W. J., Westfall, B. L., Stothers, C. E., Terman, L. M., Goodenough, F., Newland, T. E., & Yepsen, L. M. A critique of the evaluations of the study by Bernadine [sic] G. Schmidt entitled: "Changes in personal, social, and intellectual behavior of children originally classified as feeble-minded." *Journal of Exceptional Children*, 1949, *15*, 225-234.

Norsworthy, N. Suggestions concerning the psychology of mentally deficient children. *Journal of Psycho-Asthenics*, 1907, *12*, 3-17.

Nowrey, J. E. A brief synopsis of mental deficiency. *American Journal of Mental Deficiency*, 1945, *49*, 319-357.

Oldfelt, V. Experimental glutamic acid treatment in mentally retarded children. *Journal of Pediatrics*, 1952, *40*, 316-323.

Olson, A. V. Factor analytic studies of the Frostig Developmental Test of Visual Perception. *Journal of Special Education*, 1968, *2*, 429-433.

Oppenheim, R. W. Laura Bridgeman's brain: An early consideration of functional adaptation in neural development. *Developmental Psychobiology*, 1979, *12*, 533-536.

Page, E. B. How we all failed in performance contracting. *Educational Researcher*, 1972, *1*, 40-42. (a)

Page, E. B. Miracle in Milwaukee: Raising the I.Q. *Educational Researcher*, 1972, *1*, 8-15. (b)

Page, E. B. Physical miracle in Milwaukee? *Educational Researcher*, 1973, *2*, 2-4.

Page, E. B., & Grandon, G. M. Massive intervention and child intelligence: The Milwaukee Project in critical perspective. *Journal of Special Education*, 1981, *15*, 239-256.

Pasamanick, B., & Knobloch, H. Epidemiologic studies on the complications of pregnancy and the birth process. In G. Caplan (Ed.), *Prevention of mental disorders in children*. New York: Basic Books, 1961.

Peniston, E. *An evaluation of the Portage Project*. Portage, WI: Unpublished manuscript, The Portage Project, Cooperative Educational Service Agency #12, 1972.

Piaget, J. Quantification, conservation, and nativism. *Science*, 1968, *162*, 976-979.

Piattelli-Palmarini, M. (Ed.). *Language and learning*. Cambridge, MA: Harvard University Press, 1980.

Pichot, P. French pioneers in the field of mental deficiency. *American Journal of Mental Deficiency*, 1948, *53*, 128-137.

Pilgrim, F. J., Zabarenko, L. M., & Patton, R. A. The role of amino acid supplementation and dietary protein level in serial learning performance of rats. *Journal of Comparative and Physiological Psychology*, 1951, *44*, 26-36.

Pinneau, S. R. *Changes in intelligence quotient: Infancy to maturity*. Boston: Houghton Mifflin, 1961.

Portage Report: A report on the Portage Project 10 years later. Portage, WI: The Portage Project, Cooperative Educational Service Agency #12, 1980.

Porter, P. B., & Griffin, A. C. Effects of glutamic acid on maze learning and recovery from electroconvulsive shocks in albino rats. *Journal of Comparative and Physiological Psychology,* 1950, *43*, 1-15.

Porter, P. B., Griffin, A. C., & Stone, C. P. Behavioral assessment of glutamic acid metabolism with observations on pyridoxine and folic acid deficiencies. *Journal of Comparative and Physiological Psychology*, 1951, *44*, 543-550.

Porteus, S. D. *Porteus Maze Test: Fifty years' application*. Palo Alto, CA: Pacific Books, 1973.

Poull, L. E. Constancy of I.Q. in mental defectives, according to the Stanford-Revision of Binet Tests. *Journal of Educational Psychology, 1921, 12*, 323-324.

President's Committee on Mental Retardation. *MR 71: Entering the era of human ecology.* Washington, DC: The fifth annual report of The President's Committee on Mental Retardation, 1971.

Price, J. C., Waelsch, H., & Putnam, T. J. *dl*-Glutamic acid hydrochloride in treatment of petit mal and psychomotor seizures. *Journal of the American Medical Association*, 1943, *122*, 1153-1156.

Punnett, R. C. Eliminating feeble-mindedness. *Journal of Heredity*, 1917, *8*, 464-465.

Quinn, K. V., & Durling, D. Twelve month's study of glutamic acid therapy in different clinical types in an institution for the mentally deficient. *American Journal of Mental Deficiency*, 1950, *54*, 321-332. (a)

Quinn, K. V., & Durling, D. I. New experiment in glutamic acid therapy: 24 cases classified as mental deficiency, undifferentiated, treated with glutamic acid for six months. II. Further studies in glutamic acid therapy. *American Journal of Mental Deficiency*, 1950, *55*, 227-234. (b)

Ramey, C. T., & Campbell, F. A. Educational intervention for children at risk for mild retardation: A longitudinal analysis. In P. Mittler (Ed.), *Frontiers of knowledge in mental retardation* (Vol. 1): *Social, educational, and behavioral aspects.* Baltimore, MD: University Park Press, 1981.

Ramey, C. T., & Campbell, F. A. Preventive education for high-risk children: Cognitive consequences of the Carolina Abecedarian Project. *American Journal of Mental Deficiency*, 1984, *88*, 515-523.

Ramey, C. T., & Finkelstein, N. W. Psychosocial mental retardation: A biological and social coalescence. In M. J. Begab, H. C. Haywood, & H. L. Garber (Eds.), *Psychosocial influences in retarded performance* (Vol. I): *Issues and theories in development*. Baltimore, MD: University Park Press, 1981.

Ramey, C. T., & Haskins, R. The modification of intelligence through early experience. *Intelligence*, 1981, *5*, 5-19. (a)

Ramey, C. T., & Haskins, R. Early education, intellectual development, and school performamce: A reply to Arthur Jensen and J. McVicker Hunt. *Intelligence*, 1981, *5*, 41-48. (b)

Ramey, C. T., Holmberg, M. C., Sparling, J. H., & Collier, A. M. An introduction to the Carolina Abecedarian Project. In B. M. Caldwell & D. J. Stedman (Eds.), *Infant education: A guide for helping handicapped children in the first three years*. New York: Walker, 1977.

Ramey, C. T., Yeates, K. O., & Short, E. J. The plasticity of intellectual development: Insights from preventive intervention. *Child Development,* 1984, *55*, 1913-1925.

Rand, Y., Mintzker, Y., Miller, R., Hoffman, M. B., & Friedlender, Y. The instrumental enrichment program: Immediate and long-term effects. In P. Mittler (Ed.), *Frontiers of knowledge in mental retardation*. (Vol. 1): *Social, Educational, and Behavioral Aspects.* Baltimore, MD: University Park Press, 1981.

Randi, J. *Flim-flam! The truth about unicorns, parapsychology, and other delusions*. New York:

Lippincott & Crowell, 1980.

Reed, E. W., & Reed, S. C. *Mental retardation: A family study*. Philadelphia: Saunders, 1965.

Rheingold, H. L. To rear a child. *American Psychologist,* 1973, *28*, 42-46.

Rheingold, H. L., & Perce, F. C. Comparison of ratings on the original and the revised Stanford-Binet Intelligence Scales at the borderline and mental defective levels. *Proceedings of the American Association on Mental Deficiency*, 1939, *44*, 110-119.

Rhine, W. R. *Making schools more effective: New directions from Follow Through*. New York: Academic Press, 1981.

Rhine, W. R. The role of psychologists in the national Follow Through Project. *American Psychologist*, 1983, *38*, 288-297.

Rhine, W. R., Elardo, R., & Spencer, L. M. Improving educational environments: The Follow Through approach. In W. R. Rhine (Ed.), *Making schools more effective*. New York: Academic Press, 1981.

Robbins, M. P. A study of the validity of Delacato's theory of neurological organization. *Exceptional Children*, 1966, *32*, 517-523. (a)

Robbins, M. P. A reply. *Exceptional Children*, 1966, *33*, 200-201. (b)

Robbins, M. P., & Glass, G. V. The Doman-Delacato rationale: A critical analysis. In J. Hellmuth (Ed.), *Educational therapy* (Vol. 2). Seattle, WA: Special Child Publications, 1969.

Roberts, A. D. Some I.Q. changes on the Stanford-Binet, Form L. *American Journal of Mental Deficiency,* 1945, *50*, 134-136.

Roberts, J. A. F., & Mellone, M. A. On the adjustment of Terman-Merrill I.Q.s to secure comparability at different ages. *British Journal of Psychology, Statistical Section*, 1952, *5*, 65-79.

Robinson, D. N. *An intellectual history of psychology.* New York: Macmillan, 1976.

Robinson, H. B. The uncommonly bright child. In M. Lewis & L. A. Rosenblum, *The uncommon child.* New York: Plenum Press, 1981.

Robinson, N. M. Personal communication to E. B. Page, May 12, 1985.

Robinson, N. M., & Robinson, H. B. *The mentally retarded child* (2nd ed.). New York: McGraw-Hill, 1976.

Rock, I., Mack, A., Adams, L., & Hill, A. L. Adaptation to contradictory information from vision and touch. *Psychonomic Science*, 1965, *3*, 435-436.

Rogers, A. C. President's address, Fairbault meeting, 1890. *Proceedings of the Association of Medical Officers of American Institutions for Idiotic and Feeble-Minded Persons*, 1891, 28-34.

Rogers, A. C. Editorial: Futility of surgical treatment of idiocy. *Journal of Psycho-Asthenics*, 1898, *3*, 93-95.

Rogers, L. L., & Pelton, R. B. Effect of glutamine on IQ scores of mentally deficient children. *Texas Reports on Biology and Medicine*, 1957, *15*, 1, 84-91.

Romski, M. A., White, R. A., Millen, C. E., & Rumbaugh, D. M. Effects of computer-keyboard teaching on the symbolic communication of severely retarded persons: Five case studies. *Psychological Record*, 1984, *34*, 39-54.

Rosanoff, A. J. Sex-linked inheritance in mental deficiency. *American Journal of Psychiatry*, 1931, *11*, 289-297.

Rosen, M., Clark, G. R., & Kivitz, M. S. (Eds.). *The history of mental retardation* (Vol. 1). Baltimore, MD: University Park Press, 1976.

Rosenthal, R. *Experimenter effects in behavioral research*. New York: Appleton-Century-Crofts, 1966.

Ross, R. T., Begab, M. J., Dondis, E. H., Giampiccolo, J. S., Jr., & Meyers, C. E. *Lives of the mentally retarded: A forty-year follow-up study.* Stanford, CA: Stanford University Press, 1985.

RT (only author identification). Cretins and idiots: A short account of the progress of the institutions for their relief and cure. Published in London, 1853. Reprinted in M. Rosen, G. R. Clark, & M. S. Kivitz (Eds.), *The history of mental retardation: Collected papers* (Vol. 1). Baltimore, MD: University Park Press, 1976.

Rushton, C. S., & Stockwin, A. E. Changes in Terman-Merrill I.Q.s of educationally subnormal boys. *British Journal of Educational Psychology*, 1963, *33*, 132-142.

Rynders, J. E. Letter to H. H. Spitz, April 12, 1982.

Rynders, J. E., & Horrobin, J. M. Educational provisions for young children with Down's syndrome. In J. Gottlieb (Ed.), *Educating mentally retarded persons in the mainstream.* Baltimore, MD: University Park Press, 1980.

Sabagh, G., & Windle, C. Recent trends in institutionalization rates of mental defectives in the United States. *American Journal of Mental Deficiency,* 1960, *64*, 618-624.

Salisbury, A. The education of the feeble-minded. *Proceedings of the Association of Medical Officers of American Institutions for Idiotic and Feeble-Minded Persons*, 1892, 219-233.

Scarr, E. H. Changes in Terman-Merrill I.Q.s with dull children. *British Journal of Statistical Psychology*, 1953, *6*, 71-76.

Scarr-Salapatek, S. Genetics and the development of intelligence. In F. D. Horowitz (Ed.), *Review of child development research* (Vol. 4). Chicago: University of Chicago Press, 1975.

Scheerenberger, R. C. Public residential services for the mentally retarded. In N. R. Ellis (Ed.), *International review of research in mental retardation* (Vol. 9). New York: Academic Press, 1978.

Scheerenberger, R. C. *A history of mental retardation*. Baltimore, MD: Brookes, 1983.

Scheinfeld, A. *You and heredity*. New York: Frederick A. Stokes, 1939.

Schiff, M., Duyme, M., Dumaret, A., & Tomkiewicz, S. How much *could* we boost scholastic achievement and IQ scores? A direct answer from a French adoption study. *Cognition*, 1982, *12*, 165-169.

Schmidt, B. G. Changes in personal, social, and intellectual behavior of children originally classified as feebleminded. *Psychological Monographs*, 1946, *60*(5, Serial No. 281).

Schmidt, B. G. A reply. *Psychological Bulletin,* 1948, *45*, 334-343.

Schweinhart, L. J., & Weikart, D. P. Young children grow up: The effects of the Perry Preschool Program on youths through age 15. *Monographs of the High/Scope Educational Research Foundation*, 1980, No. 7.

Schweinhart, L. J., & Weikart, D. P. The effect of the Perry Preschool program on youths through age 15—A summary. In Consortium for Longitudinal Studies, *As the twig is bent. . . Lasting effects of preschool programs*. Hillsdale, NJ: Lawrence Erlbaum Associates, 1983.

Séguin, E. Origin of the treatment and training of idiots. In M. Rosen, G. R. Clark, & M. S. Kivitz (Eds.), *The history of mental retardation: Collected papers* (Vol. I). Baltimore, MD: University Park Press, 1976. (Reprinted from *American Journal of Education*, 1856, *2*, 145-152.)

Séguin, E. *Idiocy: And its treatment by the physiological method* (Rev. ed). New York: Teachers College, Columbia Univ., 1907. (Originally published, 1866.)

Séguin, E. Idiocy, as the effect of social evils, and as the creative cause of physiological education. *Journal of Psychological Medicine and Diseases of the Nervous System*, 1870, *4*, 1-27.

Séguin, E. Monograph of G.C.P. *Proceedings of the Association of Medical Officers of American Institutions for Idiotic and Feeble-Minded Persons*, 1877, 11-18.

Séguin, E. Psycho-physiological training of an idiotic hand. In M. Rosen, G. R. Clark, & M. S. Kivitz (Eds.), *The history of mental retardation* (Vol. 1). Baltimore, MD: University Park Press, 1976. (Reprinted from *Proceedings of the British Medical Association*, Cork, Ireland, 1879.)

Séguin, E. A. *Traitement moral, hygiène et éducation des idiots. . . .* Paris: Baillière, 1846.

Seitz, V., Abelson, W. D., Levine, E., & Zigler, E. Effects of place of testing on the Peabody Picture Vocabulary Test scores of disadvantaged Head Start and non-Head Start children. *Child Development*, 1975, *46*, 481-486.

Share, J., Koch, R., Webb, A., & Graliker, B. The longitudinal development of infants and young children with Downs syndrome (Mongolism). *American Journal of Mental Deficiency*, 1964, *68*, 685-692.

Sharp, H. C. Glutamic-acid feeding. *Exceptional Children*, 1952, *8*, 230-233.

Shattuck, R. *The forbidden experiment: The story of the Wild Boy of Aveyron*. New York: Farrar Straus Giroux, 1980.

Shearer, D. E., & Loftin, C. R. The Portage Project: Teaching parents to teach their preschool children in the home. In R. F. Dangel & R. A. Polster (Eds.), *Parent training*. New York: Guilford, 1984.

Shearer, M. S., & Shearer, D. E. The Portage Project: A model for early childhood education. *Exceptional Children*, 1972, *39*, 210-217.

Shearer, D. E., & Shearer, M. S. The Portage Project: A model for early childhood intervention. In T. D. Tjossem (Ed.), *Intervention strategies for high risk infants and young children*. Baltimore, MD: University Park Press, 1976.

Shuttleworth, G. E. The elementary education of defective children by "special classes" in London. *Journal of Psycho-Asthenics*, 1899, *4*, 58-64.

Sidman, M. Reading and auditory-visual equivalences. *Journal of Speech and Hearing Research*, 1971, *14*, 5-13.

Sieben, R. L. Controversial medical treatments. *Academic Therapy*, 1977, *13*, 133-148.

Silverstein, A. B. Variance components in the Developmental Test of Visual Perception. *Perceptual and Motor Skills*, 1965, *20*, 973-976.

Silverstein, A. B. Note on the construct validity of the ITPA. *Psychology in the Schools*, 1978, *15*, 371-372.

Silverstein, A. B. Note on the constancy of the IQ. *American Journal of Mental Deficiency*, 1982, *87*, 227-228.

Singer, G., & Day, R. H. Visual capture of haptically judged depth. *Perception & Psychophysics*, 1969, *5*, 315-316.

Skeels, H. Mental development of children in foster homes. *Journal of Consulting Psychology*, 1938, *2*, 33-43.

Skeels, H. A study of the effects of differential stimulation on mentally retarded children: A follow-up report. *American Journal of Mental Deficiency*, 1942, *46*, 340-350.

Skeels, H. M. Adult status of children with contrasting early life experiences. *Monographs of the Society for Research in Child Development*, 1966, *31*(3, Serial No. 105).

Skeels, H. M., & Dye, H. B. A study of the effects of differential stimulation on mentally retarded children. *Journal of Psycho-Asthenics*, 1939, *44*, 114-136.

Skeels, H. M., Updegraff, R., Wellman, B. L., & Williams, H. M. A study of environmental stimulation: An orphanage preschool project. *University of Iowa Studies in Child Welfare*, 1938, *15*, No. 4.

Skinner, B. F. *Walden two*. New York: Macmillan, paperback, 1962. (Originally published, 1948.)

Skinner, B. F. Contribution in E. G. Boring & G. Lindzey (Eds.), *A history of psychology in autobiography*. New York: Appleton-Century- Crofts, 1967.

Skodak, M. The mental development of adopted children whose true mothers are feebleminded. *Child Development*, 1938, *9*, 303-308.

Skodak, M. Children in foster homes: A study of mental development. *University of Iowa Studies in Child Welfare*, 1939, *16*, No. 1.

Skodak, M. Adult status of individuals who experienced early intervention. *Proceedings of the First Congress of the International Association for the Scientific Study of Mental Deficiency*, 1968, 11-18.

Skodak, M., & Skeels, H. A follow-up study of children in adoptive homes. *Journal of Genetic Psychology*, 1945, *66*, 21-58.

Skodak, M., & Skeels, H. M. A final follow-up study of one hundred adopted children. *Journal of Genetic Psychology*, 1949, *75*, 85-125.

Sloan, W. Four score and seven. *American Journal of Mental Deficiency*, 1963, *68*, 6-14.

Sommer, R., & Sommer, B. A. Mystery in Milwaukee: Early intervention, IQ, and psychology textbooks. *American Psychologist*, 1983, *38*, 982-985.

Sommer, R., & Sommer, B. Reply from Sommer and Sommer. Comment. *American*

Psychologist, 1984, *39*, 1318-1319.

Sontag, L. W., Baker, C. T., & Nelson, V. L. Mental growth and personality development: A longitudinal study. *Monographs of the Society for Research in Child Development,* 1958, *23*(2, Serial No. 68).

Sparrow, S., & Zigler, E. Evaluation of a patterning treatment for retarded children. *Pediatrics,* 1978, *62*, 137-150.

Spaulding, P. J. Retest results on the Stanford L with mental defectives. *American Journal of Mental Deficiency*, 1946, *51*, 35-42.

Spitz, H. H. Intratest and intertest reliability and stability of the WISC, WISC-R, and WAIS Full Scale IQs in a mentally retarded population. *Journal of Special Education,* 1983, *17*, 69-80.

Sprinthall, R. C., & Sprinthall, N. A. *Educational psychology: A developmental approach* (3rd ed.). Reading, MA: Addison-Wesley, 1981.

Staats, A. W. *Learning, language, and cognition.* New York: Holt, Rinehart & Winston, 1968.

Staats, A. W. *Child learning, intelligence, and personality.* New York: Harper & Row, 1971.

Staats, A. W., Brewer, B. A., & Gross, M. C. Learning and cognitive development: Representative samples, cumulative-hierarchical learning, and experimental-longitudinal methods. *Monographs of the Society for Research in Child Development,* 1970, *35*(8, Serial No. 141).

Staats, A. W., & Burns, G. L. Intelligence and child development: What intelligence is and how it is learned and functions. *Genetic Psychology Monographs,* 1981, *104*, 237-301.

Stark, J. A. The search for cures of mental retardation: In F. J. Menolascino, R. Neman, & J. A. Stark (Eds.), *Curative aspects of mental retardation*. Baltimore, MD: Brookes Publishing Co., 1983.

Steinbach, C. Report of the special class department, Cleveland, Ohio. *Journal of Psycho-Asthenics*, 1918, *23*, 104-109.

Steller, E., & McElroy, W. D. Does glutamic acid have any effect on learning? *Science,* 1948, *108*, 281-283.

Sterling, T. D. Publication decisions and their possible effects on inferences drawn from tests of significance—or vice versa. *Journal of the American Statistical Association*, 1959, *54*, 30-34.

Stern, W. [The psychological methods of testing intelligence] (G. M. Whipple, Trans.), *Educational Psychology Monographs,* 1914, No. 13. This translation was published in hardcover, Baltimore, MD: Warwick & York, 1914. (Originally published, 1912.)

Sternberg, R. J. Cognitive-behavioral approaches to the training of intelligence in the retarded. *Journal of Special Education,* 1981, *15*, 165-183.

Sternberg, R. J. Macrocomponents and microcomponents of intelligence: Some proposed loci of mental retardation. In P. H. Brooks, R. Sperber, & C. McCauley (Eds.), *Learning and cognition in the mentally retarded.* Hillsdale, NJ: Lawrence Erlbaum Associates, 1984.

Sternberg, R. J., Conway, B. E., Ketron, J. L., & Bernstein, M. People's conceptions of intelligence. *Journal of Personality and Social Psychology*, 1981, *41*, 37-55.

Stevens, G. D. Some questions on the Schmidt study. *Journal of Exceptional Children,* 1948, *14*, 240-241.

Stoddard, L. T. An investigation of automated methods for teaching severely retarded individuals. In N. R. Ellis (Ed.), *International review of research in mental retardation* (Vol. 11). New York: Academic Press, 1982.

Stott, D. H. Observations on retest discrepancy in mentally subnormal children. *British Journal of Educational Psychology,* 1960, *30*, 211-219.

Tarjan, G., Dingman, H. F., & Miller, C. R. Statistical expectations of selected handicaps in the mentally retarded. *American Journal of Mental Deficiency,* 1960, *65*, 335-341.

Tarjan, G., Wright, S. W., Eyman, R. K., & Keeran, C. V. Natural history of mental retardation: Some aspects of epidemiology. *American Journal of Mental Deficiency,* 1973, *77*, 369-379.

Taylor, R. L. Use of the AAMD classificaton system: A review of recent research. *American Journal of Mental Deficiency,* 1980, *85*, 116-119.

Terman, L. M. *The measurement of intelligence.* New York: Arno Press, 1975. (Originally published, 1916.)

Terman, L. M., & Merrill, M. A. *Measuring intelligence*. Boston: Houghton Mifflin, 1937.

Terman, L. M., & Merrill, M. A. *Stanford-Binet Intelligence Scale: 1972 norms edition*. Boston: Houghton Mifflin, 1973.

Thompson, T., & Grabowski, J. (Eds.), *Behavior modification of the mentally retarded* (2nd ed.). New York: Oxford University Press, 1977.

Thompson, W. R. Letter. *Science*, 1975, *188*, 1126-1127.

Throne, J. M. A radical behaviorist approach to diagnosis in mental retardation. *Mental Retardation*, 1970, *8*, 2-5.

Throne, J. M. The assessment of intelligence: Towards what end? *Mental Retardation*, 1972, *10*, 9-11.

Throne, J. M. The replicability fetish and the Milwaukee Project. *Mental Retardation*, 1975, *13*, 14-17. (a)

Throne, J. M. Normalization through the normalization principle: Right ends, wrong means. *Mental Retardation*, 1975, *13*, 23-25. (b)

Throne, J. M. Raising intelligence levels of the mentally retarded: An overlooked educo-legal implication. *Journal of Education*, 1975, *157*, 45-53. (c)

Throne, J. M., & Farb, J. Can mental retardation be reversed? *British Journal of Mental Subnormality*, 1978, *24*, 63-73.

Trotter, R. Environment and behavior: Intensive intervention program prevents retardation. *APA Monitor*, Sept/Oct, 1976, 7, pp. 4-6, 19, 46.

Turkel, H. *New hope for the mentally retarded: Stymied by the FDA*. New York: Vantage Press, 1972.

Uzgiris, I. C., & Hunt, J. McV. *Assessment in infancy: Toward ordinal scales of psychological development*. Urbana, IL: University of Illinois Press, 1975.

Vogel, W., Broverman, D. M., Draguns, J. G., & Klaiber, E. L. The role of glutamic acid in cognitive behaviors. *Psychological Bulletin*, 1966, *65*, 367-382.

Walker, K. P., & Gross, F. L. IQ stability among educable mentally retarded children. *Training School Bulletin*, 1970, 66, *181-187*.

Wallin, J. E. W. An analysis of Dr. Kuhlmann's attack on "The mental health of the school child." *Journal of Psycho-Asthenics*, 1914, *19*, 95-107.

Wallin, J. E. W. *Education of mentally handicapped children*. New York: Harper, 1955.

Walsh, H. A plenipotentiary for human intelligence. *Science*, 1981, *214*, 640-641.

Ward, J. The factor structure of the Frostig Developmental Test of Visual Perception. *British Journal of Educational Psychology*, 1970, *40*, 65-67.

Weathers, C. Effects of nutritional supplementation on IQ and certain other variables associated with Down syndrome. *American Journal of Mental Deficiency*, 1983, *88*, 214-217.

Webb, R. C., & Koller, J. R. Effects of sensorimotor training on intellectual and adpative skills of profoundly retarded adults. *American Journal of Mental Deficiency*, 1979, *83*, 490-496.

Wechsler, D. *Manual for the Wechsler Intelligence Scale for Children*. New York: Psychological Corp., 1949.

Weikart, D. P., Deloria, D. J., Lawser, S. A., & Wiegerink, R. Longitudinal results of the Ypsilanti Perry Preschool Project. *Monographs of the High/Scope Educational Research Foundation*, 1970, No. 1.

Weikart, D. P., Rogers, L., Adcock, C., & McClelland, D. *The cognitively oriented curriculum*. Urbana, IL: University of Illinois Press, 1971.

Wellman, B. L., Skeels, H. M., & Skodak, M. Review of McNemar's critical examination of Iowa studies. *Psychological Bulletin*, 1940, *37*, 93-111.

Werner, E. E., Honzik, M. P., & Smith, R. S. Prediction of intelligence and achievement at ten years from twenty months pediatric and psychologic examinations. *Child Development*, 1968, *39*, 1063-1075.

Westinghouse Learning Corporation/Ohio University. *The impact of Head Start: An evaluation of the effects of Head Start on children's cognitive and affective development* (2 Vols.). Washington, DC: Clearinghouse for Federal Scientific and Technical Information, Department of

Commerce, 1969.
Whimbey, A. *Intelligence can be taught*. New York: E.P. Dutton, 1980.
Whipple, G. M. (Ed.). *Thirty-ninth yearbook of the National Society for the study of Education. Intelligence: Its nature and nurture.* Parts I and II. Bloomington, IL: Public School Publishing Co., 1940.
White, D. IQ changes in mongoloid children during post-maturation treatment. *American Journal of Mental Deficiency*, 1969, *73*, 809-813.
White, W. D., & Wolfensberger, W. The evolution of dehumanization in our institutions. *Mental Retardation*, 1969, *7*, 5-9.
Whitman, T. L., & Scibak, J. W. Behavior modification research with the severely and profoundly retarded. In N. R. Ellis (Ed.), *Handbook of mental deficiency* (2nd ed). Hillsdale, NJ: Lawrence Erlbaum Associates, 1979.
Wilbur, C. T. Institutions for the feeble-minded. In M. Rosen, G. R. Clark, & M. S. Kivitz (Eds.), *The history of mental retardation* (Vol. 1). Baltimore, MD: Univesity Park Press, 1976. (Reprinted from *Proceedings of the Fifteenth National Conference of Charities and Correction*, Buffalo, NY, 1888.)
Wilmarth, A. W. Editorial: Sensational literature. *Journal of Psycho-Asthenics*, 1898, *2*, 121-122. (a)
Wilmarth, A. W. Editorial: Future of the imbecile. *Journal of Psycho-Asthenics*, 1898, *2*, 122-124. (b)
Wolf, T. H. *Alfred Binet*. Chicago: University of Chicago Press, 1973.
Woodall, C. S. Analysis of I.Q. variability. *Proceedings of the American Association for the Study of the Feebleminded*, 1931, *36*, 247-262.
Woolman, M. *Learning for cognition* (Vols. I and II). Trenton, NJ: Report to the New Jersey State Department of Education, 1971. (Available at the New Jersey State Library, Trenton, NJ.)
Woolman, M. The Micro-Social Learning Environment: A strategy for accelerating learning. In Consortium for Longitudinal Studies, *As the twig is bent. . . Lasting effects of preschool programs*. Hillsdale, NJ: Erlbaum, 1983.
Wortis, J. Introduction: Questionable practices. In J. Wortis (Ed.), *Mental retardation and developmental disabilities* (Vol. 12). New York: Brunner/Mazel, 1981.
Zabarenko, L. M., Pilgrim, F. J., & Patton, R. A. The effect of glutamic acid supplementation on problem solving of the instrumental conditioning type. *Journal of Comparative & Physiological Psychology,* 1951, *44*, 126-133.
Zabarenko, R. N., & Chambers, G. S. An evaluation of glutamic acid in mental deficiency. *American Journal of Psychiatry*, 1952, *108*, 881-887.
Zeaman, D., & House, B. Intelligence and the process of generalization. In P. H. Brooks, R. Sperber, & C. McCauley (Eds.), *Learning and cognition in the mentally retarded*. Hillsdale, NJ: Erlbaum, 1984.
Zigler, E. Project Head Start: Success or failure? In E. Zigler & J. Valentine (Eds.), *Project Head Start*. New York: The Free Press, 1979. (Originally published, 1973.)
Zigler, E. A plea to end the use of the patterning treatment for retarded children. *American Journal of Orthopsychiatry*, 1981, *51*, 388-390.
Zigler, E., Abelson, W. D., & Seitz, V. Motivational factors in the performance of economically disadvantaged children on the Peabody Picture Vocabulary Test. *Child Development*, 1973, *44*, 294-303.
Zigler, E., Abelson, W. D., Trickett, P. K., & Seitz, V. Is an intervention program necessary in order to improve economically disadvantaged children's IQ scores? *Child Development*, 1982, *53*, 340-348.
Zigler, E., & Berman, W. Discerning the future of childhood intervention. *American Psychologist*, 1983, *38*, 894-906.
Zigler, E., & Butterfield, E. C. Motivational aspects of changes in IQ test performance of culturally deprived nursery school children. *Child Development*, 1968, *39*, 1-14.

Zigler, E., & Seitz, V. On "an experimental evaluation of sensorimotor patterning": A critique. *American Journal of Mental Deficiency,* 1975, *79,* 483-492.

Zigler, E., & Trickett, P. K. IQ, social competence, and evaluation of early childhood intervention programs. *American Psychologist,* 1978, *33,* 789-798.

Zigler, E., & Valentine, J. (Eds.). *Project Head Start: A legacy of the war on poverty.* New York: The Free Press, 1979.

Zimmerman, F. T. The glutamic acid treatment of mental retardation. *Quarterly Review of Psychiatry and Neurology,* 1949, 4, 263-269.

Zimmerman, F. T., & Burgemeister, B. B. The techniques, dynamics, and permanency of the glutamic acid treatment of mental retardation. *Education,* 1950, *70,* 410-419. (a)

Zimmerman, F. T., & Burgemeister, B. B. The effect of glutamic acid on borderline and high-grade defective intelligence. *New York State Journal of Medicine,* 1950, *50,* 693-697. (b)

Zimmerman, F. T., & Burgemeister, B. B. Permanency of glutamic acid treatment. *Archives of Neurology and Psychiatry,* 1951, *65,* 291-298.

Zimmerman, F. T., & Burgemeister, B. B. A controlled experiment of glutamic acid therapy. *Archives of Neurology and Psychiatry,* 1959, *81,* 639-648. (a)

Zimmerman, F. T., & Burgemeister, B. B. Analysis of behavior patterns following glutamic acid therapy. *Archives of Neurology and Psychiatry,* 1959, *81,* 649-657. (b)

Zimmerman, F. T., Burgemeister, B. B., & Putnam, T. J. Effect of glutamic acid on mental functioning in children and in adolescents. *Archives of Neurology and Psychiatry,* 1946, *56,* 489-506.

Zimmerman, F. T., Burgemeister, B. B., & Putnam, T. J. A group study of the effect of glutamic acid on mental functioning in children and in adolescents. *Psychosomatic Medicine,* 1947, *9,* 175-183.

Zimmerman, F. T., Burgemeister, B. B., & Putnam, T. J. The ceiling effect of glutamic acid upon intelligence in children and in adolescents. *American Journal of Psychiatry,* 1948, *104,* 593-599.

Zimmerman, F. T., Burgemeister, B. B., & Putnam, T. J. Effects of glutamic acid on the intelligence of patients with Mongolism *Archives of Neurology and Psychiatry,* 1949, *61,* 275-287. (a)

Zimmerman, F. T., Burgemeister, B. B., & Putnam, T. J. The effect of glutamic acid upon the mental and physical growth of Mongols. *American Journal of Psychiatry,* 1949, *105,* 661-668. (b)

Zimmerman, F. T., & Ross, S. Effect of glutamic acid and other amino acids on maze learning in the white rat. *Archives of Neurology and Psychiatry,* 1944, *51,* 446-451.

Author Index

Q

R

S

Y

Z

Subject Index

A

B

J, K, L

M, N

P, R

S

T, U, V, W